GOVERNANCE OF THE ILLEGAL TRADE IN E-WASTE AND TROPICAL TIMBER

As a green criminology matures it needs to be able to draw upon excellent empirical research, revealing the breadth of transnational environmental crime, and to engage with the challenges of regulation and governance. Bisschop provides an exemplary contribution, relevant not only to criminology but also the study of international relations and trade.

Nigel South, University of Essex, UK

This book is a valuable contribution to the expanding field of green criminology. By providing rare empirical evidence to the study of e-waste and tropical timber trafficking, Lieselot Bisschop uncovers new and important insights on the nature and extent of these transnational environmental crimes that all criminologists should read.

Tanya Wyatt, Northumbria University, UK

Transnational environmental crime traverses time and space and involves multiple agencies, organizations and actors. Yet how it specifically does this, and the implications of these kinds of globalized social practices have rarely been studied empirically. In this remarkable book, Lieselot Bisschop exposes the flows and networks that are associated with the illegal trade in electronic waste and tropical timber. It thus provides a major contribution to understanding the pressures and limits of environmental governance and will be an essential guide for academics and practitioners well into the future. A major achievement.

Rob White, University of Tasmania, Australia

Bisschop has made an important contribution to our understanding of transnational environmental crime and green criminology. This book is both empirically rigorous and theoretically sophisticated. Through detailed research, it provides us with valuable insight into the criminal organization and regulatory governance of two key sectors of illegal environmental trade. Highly recommended.

Lorraine Elliott, Australian National University

GREEN CRIMINOLOGY

Series Editors:

Now two decades old, green criminology – the study of environmental harm, crime, law, regulation, victimization, and justice – has increasing relevance to contemporary problems at local, national, and international levels. This series comes at a time when societies and governments worldwide seek new ways to alleviate and deal with the consequences of various environmental harms as they relate to humans, non-human animals, plant species, and the ecosystem and its components. Green criminology offers a unique theoretical perspective on how human behavior causes and exacerbates environmental conditions that threaten the planet's viability. Volumes in the series will consider such topics and controversies as corporate environmental crime, the complicity of international financial institutions, state-sponsored environmental destruction, and the role of non-governmental organizations in addressing environmental harms. Titles will also examine the intersections between green criminology and other branches of criminology and other areas of law, such as human rights and national security. The series will be international in scope, investigating environmental crime in specific countries as well as comparatively and globally. In sum, by bringing together a diverse body of research on all aspects of this subject, the series will make a significant contribution to our understanding of the dynamics between the natural world and the quite imperfect human world, and will set the stage for the future study in this growing area of concern.

Other titles in this series:

Environmental Crime and Social Conflict
Contemporary and Emerging Issues
Edited by Avi Brisman, Nigel South and Rob White

Environmental Crime and its Victims
Perspectives within Green Criminology
Edited by Toine Spapens, Rob White and Marieke Kluin

Exploring Green Criminology
Toward a Green Criminological Revolution
Michael J. Lynch and Paul B. Stretesky

Governance of the Illegal Trade in E-Waste and Tropical Timber

Case Studies on Transnational Environmental Crime

LIESELOT BISSCHOP
John Jay College of Criminal Justice, USA
and Ghent University, Belgium

LONDON AND NEW YORK

First published 2015 by Ashgate Publishing

Published 2016 by Routledge
2 Park Square, Milton Park, Abingdon, Oxfordshire OX14 4RN
711 Third Avenue, New York, NY 10017, USA

First issued in paperback 2016

Routledge is an imprint of the Taylor & Francis Group, an informa business

British Library Cataloguing in Publication Data
A catalogue record for this book is available from the British Library

The Library of Congress has cataloged the printed edition as follows:
Bisschop, Lieselot.
Governance of the illegal trade in e-waste and tropical timber : case studies on transnational environmental crime / by Lieselot Bisschop.
pages cm.—(Green criminology)
Includes bibliographical references and index.
ISBN 978-1-4724-1540-0 (hardback)
1. Offenses against the environment. 2. Offenses against the environment—Law and legislation. 3. Electronic waste—Law and legislation. I. Title.
HV6401.B57 2015
364.1'45—dc23

2014036509

ISBN 13: 978-1-138-63711-5 (pbk)
ISBN 13: 978-1-4724-1540-0 (hbk)

Contents

List of Figures

List of Abbreviations

AEO	Authorized Economic Operator
BFR	Brominated Flame Retardants
CFC	Chlorofluorocarbon (used as refrigerants (for example R11, R12), propellants and solvents; but phased out by Montreal Convention because they contribute to ozone-depletion)
CITES	Convention on International Trade in Endangered Species of Wild Fauna and Flora
CRT	Cathode Ray Tube
DRC	Democratic Republic of the Congo
EC	European Commission
EEE	Electrical and Electronic Equipment
EPR	Extended Producer Responsibility
EU	European Union
EUTR	European Union Timber Regulation
FLEGT	Forest Law Enforcement, Governance and Trade
FLI	Federal Environmental Inspection (Belgium – *Federale Leefmilieu Inspectie*)
FSC	Forest Stewardship Council
FTE	Full-time Equivalent
GDP	Gross Domestic Product
HCFC	Hydrochlorofluorocarbon (used as refrigerants, replaced ozone-depleting CFC)
IMO	International Maritime Organization
IMPEL	European Network for the Implementation and Enforcement of Environmental Law
IMPEL-TFS	Subgroup of IMPEL that focuses on the inspection and enforcement of Transfrontier Shipments of Waste
INECE	International Network for Environmental Compliance and Enforcement
ISO	International Organization for Standardization
ITTA	International Tropical Timber Agreement
ITTO	International Tropical Timber Organization
MEA	Multilateral Environmental Agreement
MSC	Marine Stewardship Council
NCTS	New Computerized Transit System
NGO	Non-Governmental Organization
ODS	Ozone-depleting Substances

OECD	Organisation for Economic Cooperation and Development
OVAM	Public Waste Agency of Flanders (*Openbare Vlaamse Afvalstoffenmaatschappij*)
PLDA	Paperless Customs and Excise (*Paperless Douane en Accijnzen*)
RoHS	Restriction of Hazardous Substances Directive
RWE	Round Wood Equivalent (measure for timber trade)
SBC	Secretariat of the Basel Convention
StEP	Solving the E-waste Problem Initiative
TEU	Twenty Foot Equivalent Unit (standardized container measure)
UEEE	Used Electric and Electronic Equipment
UNCED	United Nations Conference on Environment and Development
UNDP	United Nations Development Programme
UNEP	United Nations Environment Programme
UNODC	United Nations Office on Drugs and Crime
USD	US Dollar
VAT	Value Added Tax
VPA	Voluntary Partnership Agreement
VROM	Ministry of Housing, Spatial Planning and the Environment (Netherlands: *Ministerie van Volkshuisvesting, Ruimtelijke Ordening en Milieubeheer*)
WEEE	Waste Electric and Electronic Equipment
WSR	Waste Shipment Regulation
WWF	World Wildlife Fund

Preface and Acknowledgements

The purpose of this book is to answer to the call for more research about transnational environmental crime and contribute to the emerging and growing field of green criminology by providing empirical findings. It empirically studies the illegal trade in electronic waste (e-waste) and the illegal trade in tropical timber. In answering the research questions about the social organization and the governance of these flows, this research intends to contribute to the international knowledge base about the prevention and control of illegal transports of e-waste and tropical timber. The study applies the theoretical frameworks of legal-illegal interfaces and environmental governance to empirical cases of transnational environmental crime. This research is based on a qualitative multi-method research design combining a document analysis of various primary and secondary sources, 81 interviews with key informants and field visits.

The research findings were previously published in five journal articles and peer-reviewed book chapters.[1] I am grateful to the publishers for granting

---

1 The five articles are:

- Bisschop, L. (2011). Transnational environmental crime: exploring (un) charted territory. In M. Cools, B. De Ruyver, M. Easton, L. Pauwels, P. Ponsaers, T. Vander Beken, F. Vander Laenen, G. Vande Walle, A. Verhage, G. Vermeulen and G. Vynckier (eds), *EU Criminal Justice, Financial & Economic Crime: New Perspectives*, Governance of Security Research Papers (Vol. 5, pp. 155–83). Antwerpen: Maklu. Reproduced with permission of Maklu.
- Bisschop, L. (2012). Is it all going to waste? Illegal transports of e-waste in a European trade hub. *Crime, Law and Social Change*, 58(3), 221–49. Reproduced with permission of Springer.
- Bisschop, L. (2013). Go with the e-waste flows. The governance reality of illegal transports of e-waste in a European trade hub. In P. Van Duyne and J. Spencer (eds), *Organised Crime by Hindsight, Corruption and Crisis in Enforcement* (pp. 393–424). Nijmegen: Wolf Legal Publishers. Reproduced with permission of Wolf Legal Publishers.
- Bisschop, L. (2012). Out of the woods: the illegal trade in tropical timber and a European trade hub. *Global Crime*, 13(3), 191–212. Reproduced with permission of Taylor & Francis.
- Bisschop, L. (2013). Governance throughout the flows. Case study research on the illegal tropical timber trade. In P. Saitta, J. Shapland and A. Verhage (eds), *Getting By or Getting Rich? The Formal, Informal and Illegal Economy in a Globalized World* (pp. 167–99). The Hague: Eleven. Reproduced with permission of Eleven International Publishing.

permission to reproduce the articles and combine them into this book. This book has used these five articles and added new material as well as a comparative chapter, including theoretical implications, avenues for future research and policy recommendations. The added value of this book is that the reader gains an overview about the transnational nature of both e-waste and tropical timber crime.

I am also grateful to the University College Ghent Research Fund for the research grant.

This research would have been impossible without the willingness of my respondents to spend time answering my questions, referring me to other experts and guiding me through their world, be it in Belgium, Ghana or elsewhere. For reasons of confidentiality I cannot name them, but I am indebted to them.

Although this research was primarily an individual endeavour, I was surrounded by colleagues who advised and inspired me. I would like to take this opportunity to thank them for providing a work environment that encouraged critical review of the content, progress and gaps of my research. At the same time, my colleagues paid attention to the human side of doing research, even when I was abroad.

I would like to take this opportunity to thank Paul Ponsaers, Gudrun Vande Walle, Tom Vander Beken and Wim Huisman. Throughout this research, they never ceased to advise, inspire and believe in me.

I also thank Michael Lynch and Paul Stretesky for providing me with insightful comments on previous versions of this manuscript. I alone bear the responsibility for any remaining errors.

Although the support and advice of colleagues and advisors was essential over the years, my support network outside of academia proved equally invaluable. My dearest family and friends, you inspired me, cared for me and helped me put things into perspective. You are the stars I navigate home by. A final thank you goes out to you, Hannes, for knowing, accepting and loving me for who I am.

Lieselot Bisschop

Chapter 1
Introduction

Today, scientists and global leaders agree that the world faces serious environmental problems. Although interpretations of and responses to the state of the ecology might differ, the international community has generally acknowledged the importance of addressing these issues.[1] These environmental problems are a result of human activity through consumption and production of which the actual harm as well as the potential endangerment is often hard to assess. Environmental harm does not stop at borders and through its global interconnections it has potential – and often unpredictable – worldwide consequences. The big issue is, then, how these ecological harms can be managed.

Given the societal importance of the environment and its association with transnational environmental crime, it is remarkable that criminology has given relatively little attention to transnational environmental issues. Both the transnational and the environmental character of them require additional attention from criminologists. The transnational dimension refers to crimes that involve a movement of perpetrators, victims or the crime itself across geographic space, inherently linked to the globalization of the world economy (White 2011). It is disconnected from the nation state frame of reference which defines what is legal or illegal (Passas 2003). The cross-nation character of transnational crime makes it difficult to track the movement and to understand its occurrence, causes, let alone responses to it (Aas 2007). The transnational nature of crimes requires additional attention from criminologists in order to grasp the complexity that is inherent to them (Sheptycki and Wardak 2005).

Criminological research on the characteristics of specific types of environmental crime is also needed. Although recent decades have witnessed an increased interest in studying environmental crime, empirical investigations remain rare (Gibbs, Gore, et al. 2010; Gibbs, McGarrell and Axelrod 2010; Lynch and Stretesky 2003; White 2013; Ruggiero and South 2013). This fits within a broader critical development in criminology which looks beyond strict definitions of crime to include legally ambiguous behaviours that cause social harm (Hillyard et al. 2004). In contrast to the traditional criminological focus on criminal law, green criminology focuses on the importance of non-criminal law and even on the idea that ecological harm is not sufficiently defined by laws or regulations. In other words, there is more to transnational environmental harm than that which has been

1 See for example: United Nations Framework Convention on Climate Change, New York, 9 May 1992 (entered into force 21 March 1994); Rio Declaration on Environment and Development, adopted at the UNCED in Rio de Janeiro, Brazil, 3–14 June 1992.

criminalized or regulated, highlighting the importance of a continued discussion on how to address ecological harm (Lynch 1990; Beirne and South 2007).

Another issue criminologists, green criminologists included, have yet to address is the effect of new forms of environmental regulation on ecological harm. In response to the ecological challenges the world faces, many multilateral environmental agreements (MEAs) and national environmental regulations have been drafted. These new regulations attribute a focal role to the state and corresponded to the so-called command and control regulatory structure (Holley, Gunningham and Shearing 2012). Over the years, corporate actors, encouraged by the reorganization of government policies on the social control of environmental crime, have also developed environmental self-regulation, which sometimes goes beyond the requirements set in legislation (Stretesky 2006; Bartley 2007; Gunningham, Kagan and Thornton 2003). Besides corporate actors, civil society actors such as non-governmental organizations (NGOs) can play a role in the management of environmental harm. Taken together, these various institutional responses to ecological harms have created a regulatory hybrid where responses to (transnational) environmental issues can be found within government institutions such as the criminal justice system, but also involve regulatory initiatives in interaction with corporate and civil society (Braithwaite 2008; Shearing and Johnston 2010). The regulatory actors[2] and initiatives are also increasingly reaching across the geographical boundaries of states and have shifted upwards to transnational levels. These new governance models have yet to be examined sufficiently in the criminological literature. There is a need to study the involvement of government, business and civil society in controlling and preventing transnational environmental crime.

In this book, the term governance is used to refer to the engagement of a variety of actors in the prevention and control of environmental harm. Exactly because it is not limited to nation state institutions, it is distinguished from the term government (Holley, Gunningham and Shearing 2012; Parker and Braithwaite 2003). 'Governance refers to the emergence and recognition of principles, norms, rules, and procedures that both provide standards of acceptable public behavior, and that are followed sufficiently to produce behavioral regularities' (Keohane and Nye 2000, p. 10). Social interactions are governed by social and political units like corporations, international organizations and NGOs. It is not a reference to the general governance of economic flows or trade.

Knowledge about the governance of transnational environmental harm is a first step in knowing whether the governance framework can contribute to

2 These actors are sometimes referred to as nodes. These can refer to individuals, groups, organizations and even states. This was used with regard to communication in society (Castells 2000) and applied to governance and security issues (Shearing and Johnston 2010).

managing ecological harm. Therefore, the objective of this research[3] is to provide insights into the empirical reality of governing transnational environmental crime. By analysing the case of illegal transports of e-waste and tropical timber in a European trade hub, this research responds to the call for more empirical knowledge about transnational environmental crime. It addresses this question: what are the governance consequences of controlling and preventing transnational environmental crime flows? In this way, this study aims to contribute to theories about transnational environmental crime and environmental governance by further grounding these theories in empirical findings. The results could also prove useful for practitioners who govern transnational environmental crime.

Due to the disparity and specificity of transnational environmental crime, this research was limited to two particular phenomena: the trade[4] in tropical timber and the trade in waste from electronic and electrical equipment (e-waste[5]). The focus is on the trade flows that pass through the research setting of the Port of Antwerp (Belgium) and especially on those trade flows between Europe and West and Central Africa. A detailed explanation for choosing these cases and this research setting can be found in the methodological chapter. Both cases have been the topic of international and national policy-making, but they differ in the extent to which they have been criminalized. Both cases are also of an opposite transnational dimension. For both the illegal trade in electronic waste (e-waste) and tropical timber, it is possible to determine what is legal and illegal because these commodities are subject to international conventions. Defining what is ecologically harmful in the trade of tropical timber and e-waste is not necessarily equal to these legal definitions. The question is how this ambiguity of trade on a thin line between the legal and illegal affects the governance framework.

Before considering the governance of transnational environmental crime, it is relevant to consider its etiology. In fact, several theories about the etiology of crime can be connected to transnational environmental crime. The involvement of corporate actors connects it with theories on white-collar crime, corporate crime and other crimes of the powerful (Croall 2009; Heine 2006; Nelken 2002). In turn, the connection with organized crime makes those theoretical assumptions apparent (Ruggiero 1996; Szasz 1986) as does the inherent transnational frame of reference (Aas 2007). This implies that the scope of the trade flows will be examined together with their impact and which actors and processes shape them. In other words, this study will examine the social organization of transnational environmental crime by means of a case study on e-waste and tropical timber. It may prove difficult to draw a line between legal and illegal actors and their practices, but nevertheless this study

3 This research was funded by the Research Fund of *University College Ghent* (OF-0902).

4 The concepts illegal *trade*, *transports* and *flows* will be used interchangeably in this book.

5 E-waste is waste from electronic and electric equipment, such as television sets, refrigerators, computers, mp3 players, batteries and so on.

aims to gain a more accurate view of the network of actors and their interrelations (Passas 2002). A wide range of possible actors are considered, beyond white-collar crime, organized crime or state crime conceptualizations. In the analysis, attention is paid to the push, pull and facilitating factors that shape these transnational environmental crime flows (Coleman 1987; Antonopoulos and Winterdyk 2006). To begin to understand the consequences of governing green crime, this study also examines how the international community treats green crime, using the example of the trade in e-waste and tropical timber. An important dimension of this effort is describing the rationale nations and transnational organizations refer to in order to regulate or ignore a green crime. The first question this research aims to answer is therefore: *What elements characterize the social organization and emergence of illegal transports of e-waste and tropical timber?*

Building on the findings about the social organization and emergence of transnational environmental crime, the second research question addresses the governance of illegal transports of e-waste and tropical timber. This part of the study aims to map the governance actors – government, corporate as well as civil society actors – in these transnational trade flows. It pays attention to their interactions, potentially different finalities and to gaps and limitations in their governance. This empirical reality is compared with theoretical models that exist on the governance and regulation of corporate and environmental crime (Braithwaite 2008; Holley, Gunningham and Shearing 2012). The second question this study aims to answer is: *What elements characterize the governance of illegal transports of e-waste and tropical timber?*

The above-mentioned research questions are answered by means of a theoretical analysis in the literature review and a comparative case study into the social organization, emergence and governance of illegal trade in e-waste and tropical timber that passes through the research setting of the Port of Antwerp (Belgium) and especially on those trade flows between Europe and West and Central Africa. The comparative case study has a qualitative multi-method research design combining a document analysis, 81 interviews with key informants and field visits.

Outline of the Book

This book continues with a methodological chapter (Chapter 2) that explains the case selection, research setting, research phases, data gathering and analysis, scope and limitations of the research.

Chapter 3 clarifies the theoretical perspectives that are at the basis of the first research question of this study on the social organization and emergence of transnational environmental crime. The first part of this chapter conceptualizes transnational environmental crime and green/environmental criminology and clarifies the sensitizing – and sometimes rather heavily debated – concepts inherent to this research field. The second part gives an overview of the etiology of transnational environmental crime, in which the 'classical' elements of motivation, opportunity and neutralization serve as a guideline. This refers to the theory of legal-illegal interfaces for the social organization of transnational environmental crime. This is illustrated by means of two cases: waste and natural resources.

Chapter 4 draws upon theory and research into different dimensions of transnational environmental crime to argue that environmental governance is multi-stakeholder, multi-sector and multilevel and that it is often unclear how different actors and approaches interact. This chapter argues that it is important to study the governance of transnational environmental crime and gain insights into its characteristics. It discusses the governance of corporate, environmental and transnational crime and also explains the theoretical framework that informed the empirical research: the theories of the responsive regulatory pyramid and networked governance for the governance of transnational environmental crime. Similar to the previous theoretical chapter, this is then illustrated by means of the two case waste and natural resources.

Chapter 5 discusses the results of the case study about the illegal trade in e-waste. The first part analyses the social organization and emergence of illegal e-waste trade. Given the complexity and global nature of transnational environmental crime, it is difficult to determine which actors are involved. In this regard, a local research setting allows identifying the actors involved in illegal transports of e-waste. It tries to determine whether these actors and their roles can be considered legal or illegal and illustrates the legal-illegal interfaces in e-waste flows. Moreover, this case study analyses the push, pull and facilitating factors. In doing so, it looks at what motivations and opportunities shape the flows of e-waste. The results show that the social organization and emergence is on a thin line between legal and illegal and needs to be contextualized within the global reality of the locations of origin, transit and destination. The second part describes and discusses the governance reality of illegal transports of e-waste. It analyses which actors are involved in this governance framework and provides insights into the facilitating and hindering factors for governance throughout the e-waste flows. Besides analysing the governance actors individually, particular attention is given to their interaction. The frame of analysis used for this is a nodal-networked analysis (Shearing and Johnston, 2010). The theoretical frameworks used are the responsive regulatory pyramid and networked governance. The findings show that the governance reality of illegal transports of e-waste answers to several characteristics of these ideal-typical models. At the same time it is faced with the complexity inherent to governing the illegal trade in e-waste.

Chapter 6 discusses the results of the case study into the illegal transport of tropical timber. The first part provides insights into the social organization of the illegal transports of tropical timber. This focuses on the local research setting of the Port of Antwerp (Belgium) but meanwhile pays attention to elements throughout the flows from locations of origin over transit to destination. It is often difficult to determine which legal and illegal actors are involved in transnational environmental crime. This part sheds light on the legal-illegal interfaces in tropical timber flows connected to this European setting. The results show that the social organization of transnational environmental crime is shaped by the global context of the places of origin, transit and destination. The flows of tropical timber are continuously on a thin line between legal and illegal. The second part discusses the governance reality of illegal transports of tropical timber. The frame of analysis used is a nodal-networked governance analysis, which pays attention to the contextual surroundings that shape the governance framework. It provides insights into the facilitating and hindering factors for governance arrangements. It does so throughout the tropical timber flows, for actors individually and in their interaction. The findings use both the responsive regulatory pyramid and networked governance as ideal-typical models. The results reveal the complexity inherent to governing the illegal trade in tropical timber.

Chapter 7 is a comparative analysis of the cases. This chapter begins with a summary of findings of the separate case studies into the illegal trade in e-waste and tropical timber for both their social organization and their governance. This core of this chapter is a comparison between the two cases, pinpointing similarities and differences in their governance and etiological characteristics. This chapter puts the results into perspective by relating them to previous findings about transnational environmental crime and environmental governance. Informed by the comparative analysis, lessons are drawn for theory and research on environmental governance and transnational environmental crime.

The conclusion, policy recommendations, avenues for future research and a brief concluding summary bring this book is to a close. After that, the references and annexes follow.

Chapter 2
Methodology

Introduction

This study answers to the call for more research about transnational environmental crime by studying the illegal trade in electronic waste (e-waste) and tropical timber. The research questions are answered by means of a theoretical analysis in the literature review and a comparative case study research into the social organization, emergence and governance of illegal transports of e-waste and tropical timber. This section provides more information on the design and strategy of this study. The qualitative case study methodology, case selection, research setting, research phases, data analysis and scope and limitations of the research are explained.

Qualitative Case Study

> Having allowed passion, fascination, or indignation to influence the choice of the topic, the researcher then faces a very different kind of task: devising a research strategy. (Geddes 2003, p. 38)

This study has a qualitative research design, namely the case-study method. It looks at phenomena which have received limited attention in previous research. For the Belgian research setting in particular, no criminological studies have focused on illegal transports of e-waste and tropical timber. This study examines the social organization and emergence of these trade flows and explores and interprets the activities and interactions of different governance actors. It aims to understand and analyse the dynamics rather than simply identifying them. This study has the explicit aim to understand the cases within their real-life context and explore, describe and interpret the complex makeup of factors which set down the social organization and governance of transnational environmental crime. The case-study methodology is particularly suited for this research, because it allows for gaining context-dependent knowledge.

Much of the research in social sciences generated knowledge based on case-study designs, but there is quite some inconsistency in interpreting what a case study is (George and Bennet 2005). A case study is a research method or strategy that focuses on one or more particular phenomena, observed at a certain period or moment in time (Gerring 2007, p. 19). Typical for case studies is that they investigate a phenomenon within and in interaction with its real-life context (Yin

2009; 2003). The unit of analysis can vary from countries over organizations to individuals, depending on the discipline and aim of the research. The number of cases is usually limited to ensure the in-depth analysis. Case studies can be analytical, comparative and policy-relevant. The purpose of a case study is to go beyond the studied case(s) and shed light on a broader population. They can therefore have theoretical implications as well. The case study of this research is descriptive and interpretative. It is descriptive because it provides a detailed account of a phenomenon about which there is little research available. It is interpretative because it intends to illustrate how prior theories about organizational crime and environmental governance fit this scenario.

A case study benefits from the prior development of propositions to guide data collection and analysis (Yin 2009). Therefore, this study builds on existing theories and research on topics such as transnational environmental crime, organizational crime, crime control and governance. A theoretical triangulation was thus applied (Maesschalck 2009)[1] and helped develop the list of topics for the data gathering and analysis. These theories were the guide for the empirical exploration but findings were interpreted as close to the empirical reality as possible. The research went back and forth between theory and qualitative data to reach the most adequate description and explanation for the phenomenon under study.

The method of this research is a qualitative comparative case study. Despite the likely richness of the gathered qualitative data, there is a possible bias when using one technique.[2] Within the case-study design, different methods of qualitative data gathering and analysis were therefore triangulated (Loosveldt, Swyngedouw and Cambre 2007). This research combines document analysis, semi-structured interviews and field visits.[3] Research on transnational environmental crime requires looking beyond the classical – and inherently limited – data of the enforcement agencies and thus requires a search for alternative perspectives. Data was collected on as many observable implications of the studied phenomenon as possible to improve the quality of the data (King, Keohane and Verba 1994). This research consists of a comparative case study, which implies the two cases were studied individually (within the case) and then compared (between the cases).

1 See Chapter 3 (Explaining Transnational Environmental Crime) and Chapter 4 (Governing Transnational Environmental Crime) for a more elaborate explanation.

2 See also the section on Research Scope and Limitations in this chapter.

3 See also the section on Research Method, Data Gathering and Analysis in this chapter.

Case Selection

Both illegal transports of waste and natural resources have been subject to international laws or multilateral agreements.[4] Waste has generally received priority in policy-making and has been criminalized.[5] Natural resource crime is less of a priority but was nevertheless subject to some, albeit less all encompassing, environmental laws.[6] On the dynamic continuum from legal to illegal these cases are thus differently positioned. Both have been the topic of international and national policy-making, but they differ in the extent to which they have been criminalized. The selected cases are two extreme cases on the continuum from legal to illegal, which show variation in regulation and in the extent to which the line between right and wrong is clear. Focusing on these phenomena allowed using comprehensive definitions – staying near the law – without getting lost in normative discussions (Passas 1999).

The transnational dimension was explicitly taken into account in choosing the cases. Both phenomena are in fact generally speaking of an opposite transnational nature. For illegal transports of waste, Belgium is mainly an export country or a transit country for waste originating in other European states. These transports mostly go to West Africa or South East Asia. For illegal transports of natural resources the transnational dimension is differently oriented, given that Belgium is mainly an import country or a transit country towards other European countries. In view of the comparative design, the cases of illegal transports of e-waste and tropical timber therefore present us with opposite transnational dimensions.

The selection of the two cases was further based on the exploratory interviews with key informants (N=7): two NGO representatives, a member of European

---

4 More information about the legislative framework can be found in Chapters 5 (e-waste) and 6 (tropical timber). For a more complete list of multilateral environmental agreements, please see the International Environmental Agreements (IEA) Database Project http://iea.uoregon.edu/page.php?file=home.htm&query=static [last consulted 6 July 2012].

5 For instance: Basel Convention on the Control of Transboundary Movements of Hazardous Wastes and their Disposal (adopted on 22 March 1989, entered into force on 5 May 1992); Montreal Protocol on Ozone-depleting Substances Montreal, 16 September 1987 (entered into force 1 January 1989); OECD Decision on Control of Cross-border Movements of Waste Destined for Recovery Operations (Decision of the Council C(2001)107/Final (as Amended By C(2004)20). European Waste Shipment Regulation (Regulation (EC) No 1013/2006 of the European Parliament and of the Council of 14 June 2006 on shipments of waste (OJ L 190, 12.7.2007, 1–98)); Bamako Convention on the Ban of the Import into Africa and the Control of Transboundary Movement and Management of Hazardous Wastes within Africa (Signed 30 January 1991, entered into force on 22 April 1998) and so on.

6 For instance: Convention on International Trade in Endangered Species of Wild Fauna and Flora (CITES – Convention of Washington 1975); European Union Wildlife Trade Regulations (338/97/EC and 865/2006/EC), Forest Law Enforcement, Governance and Trade Action Plan (FLEGT).

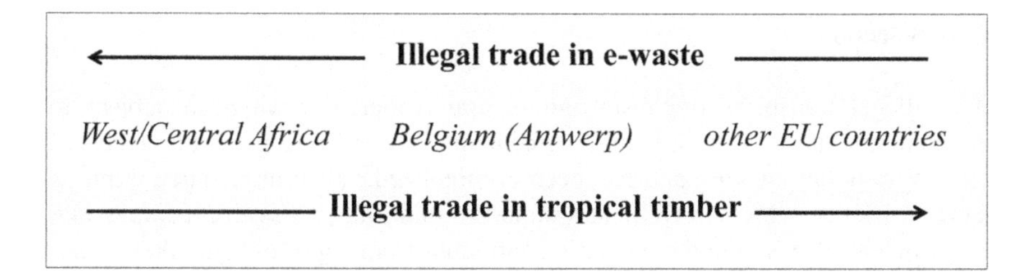

Figure 2.1 Transnational dimension

parliament, a police officer responsible for environmental issues, a customs officer, an investigative journalist and a representative from a waste sector federation were contacted. Moreover, news reports in both Belgian and international news media on transnational environmental crime were analysed. The archives were searched for the period 2000–10 for the Belgian newspapers by means of *Mediargus*.[7] Foreign newspapers were searched with *LexisNexis*.[8] Both of these sources revealed the particular relevance of illegal transports of e-waste within the chosen research setting. For natural resources, both the exploratory interviews and the media search pointed towards the importance of smuggling of endangered species (for example for Chinese medicines and ivory) and tropical timber. Given that it was theoretically interesting to look at phenomena with a link to economic sectors, the choice was made to focus on the latter.

This limitation of the research scope was necessary to allow a detailed analysis of the characteristics and dimensions of these two phenomena and their governance (George and Bennet 2005). The selection of the cases was, therefore, mostly grounded in content-wise considerations. Practical elements played a role as well, for example the accessibility of the cases (Leys 2009; Yin 2003; 2009).

Research Setting

This research focuses on transnational environmental crime and thus these processes and trends that constitute a movement between levels or geographies. This topic requires paying attention to the intertwining of both local and global elements (Aas 2007). The cases of this comparative study are examples of transnational environmental trade flows on a thin line between legal and illegal: the trade in waste and the trade in natural resources. The commodities cross national boundaries on their path from locations of departure over transit to final destinations. The cases were analysed by following the flow of goods through the various steps. However, perceiving them as a transnational environmental flow risks resulting in too relativistic approaches (Spaargaren, Mol and Bruyninckx 2006). It is important to

7 *Mediargus* is a search engine containing Dutch and Flemish news articles.

8 *LexisNexis United Kingdom* is a search engine for English language news articles.

ground the governance analysis of transnational environmental flows in empirical data. The literature review provided the inspiration to base this research in a local research setting, relevant to both phenomena (Gille 2006).

This case study focuses on a European research setting, because Europe can be considered a forerunner in environmental policy making (Vig and Faure 2004). More in particular, the research setting is the Port of Antwerp in Belgium.

This setting was chosen because Antwerp is an economically important port. Antwerp developed into an international trade market in the 15th century and despite some setbacks throughout the centuries, it developed into the well-known and flourishing international port it is today (Blondé and Deceulaer 2002). It is ranked amongst the top three ports in Europe with Rotterdam and Hamburg.[9] About 185 million tons of commodities are traded in Antwerp each year.[10] Given its inland location, the port has multiple connections to Europe's hinterland. Antwerp is a transit port, a stopover on global trade routes where cargo is unloaded and redirected within limited time frames. Of all the freight, 37 per cent is loaded back onto sea-going vessels and 35 per cent goes to neighbouring countries by inland shipping and rail. Only 12 per cent is destined for companies located in the port and 16 per cent is for Belgian distribution.

More importantly, the Port of Antwerp has been referred to in the past as a hub for both waste[11] and timber.[12] When compared with the Port of Rotterdam, Antwerp does not have the best reputation for environmental crime control (Huisman and van Erp 2013). Antwerp has been labelled a hub for environmental crime. Particularly the illegal e-waste flow from Antwerp to West-Africa has been mentioned. For transit and export of second-hand vehicles, which play an important role in e-waste transports, Antwerp is the most important port in Europe. Antwerp (and Belgium in general) is also an important destination for tropical timber originating in West Africa and the Congo Basin and these countries of origin have the biggest trade share[13] in the Port of Antwerp.

Based in the Port of Antwerp, this research pays attention to the different transnational flows influencing this local setting. The cases were studied by placing

---

9 Antwerp was the second European port after Rotterdam until February 2012, when it was passed by in terms of container volume by Hamburg. It remains the first for second-hand vehicles.

10 This equals about 8.66 million TEU (twenty foot equivalent unit) of container volume, 46 million tons of fluid bulk goods and 19 dry bulk goods were loaded or unloaded, and an additional 12.7 million tons of bulk goods and 4.2 million RoRo (*roll-on roll-off*). Available at: http://www.portofantwerp.com/nl/publications/jaarverslagen [last consulted 10 March 2014].

11 See for example Belgian news reports (Blokland 2010; Coosemans 2009; Holderbeke 2009; Anon 2009).

12 See for example Belgian news reports (Lefevere 1999; Vanacker 2010).

13 Based on the 2010 timber imports into Port of Antwerp, data received from Antwerp Port Authority, 25 August 2011. See also Chapter 6 under Emergence and Social Organization of Illegal Timber Trade.

e-waste and tropical timber within the broader dispositive of their (transnational) end-users and other involved actors (Spaargaren, Mol and Buttel 2006). In the exploratory phase of this study, both the media analysis and the expert interviews informed the decision to choose this research setting and for the connection between Antwerp and African countries of origin (timber) and destination (e-waste). This research studied the illegal tropical timber trade and e-waste between Africa and Europe, and Belgium in particular. This article makes no claims for generalization of the findings towards the other regions and trade flows.

Practical considerations also played a role in choosing this research setting of the Port of Antwerp. In order to keep this research feasible, this limitation to one particular research setting was necessary. Attention is paid, however, to transport flows that pass through this locality. The research domain is transnational environmental crime and the particular empirical reality that is analysed is the illegal trade in e-waste and tropical timber that passes through the Port of Antwerp. Throughout the transport flows, this study comes across actors in locations of origin, transit and destination that might well be located outside Belgium. The core focus of this study is on the transports, given the transnational focus, and not on the production process as such. This study does pay attention to how other actors in environmental flows can influence the illegal transports and their governance.

Many actors are at work in the port. First, multiple shipping lines have trade routes that pass through the Port of Antwerp to various parts of the world. There are numerous other businesses working in the port: terminal operators, shipping agents and storage and handling corporations. More than 200 expeditors, 300 transports corporations and numerous handlers take care of the loading and unloading of about 14,800 sea vessels and 57,000 inland waterway vessels. Besides the actors working in the port, there are multiple authorities responsible for the Port of Antwerp. Antwerp is what they call a landlord port, where the land is owned by government and managed by a port authority who gives up its control over port operations by leasing the infrastructure to private terminal operators (Talley 2009). The Antwerp port is a complex area for prevention and control. It covers 130 km², has 180 km of quay, 400 km of roads and 1000 km of railway. The port area is located on the left and right banks of the Scheldt estuary which each have different judicial and municipal authorities. In fact, the territory of the Port of Antwerp is governed by two jurisdictions (Dendermonde and Antwerp) and three municipalities (Antwerp, Beveren and Zwijndrecht) and falls under the responsibility of two provincial governments (East-Flanders and Antwerp). Authorities on both side of the Scheldt thus govern the port. Depending on the *locus operandi*, the judicial authority is either in the district of Antwerp or Dendermonde. The Antwerp Port Authority determines strategic options and long-term policy guidelines for the port and is responsible for the coordinating and management.[14] The Harbourmaster's Office, which is part of the Antwerp Port Authority, has the responsibility to

14 Port Glossary, available at: http://www.portofantwerp.com/portal/page/portal/POA_EN/Havenhandboek/Havenlexicon [last consulted on 28 December 2011].

safeguard the security, peace, public order, integrity and environment of the port area. This happens through regulations of storage and handling, of port access and other policing activities. Customs play an important role as well. They are responsible for fostering international trade and for the security and safety of society.[15] Customs has a department that is responsible for risk analysis for the waste transports as well as a department that is responsible for controlling timber traffic. Both services were therefore contacted in this study. The Maritime Police guarantee an integrated and consistent police policy in Belgian ports and waterways. Besides policing ports and waterways, the maritime police are the first-line actors for a number of particular phenomena in which they aim for high-quality determinations. These phenomena are: illegal immigration and human trafficking, drugs, environmental degradation, theft, terrorism and traffic safety. Of particular interest to this study is their responsibility for environmental issues.[16] Besides the port Authority, the Maritime Police and customs, the environmental inspectorates are important actors in the research setting of this study. For all transit goods, the federal environmental inspectorate is the responsible authority. For all imported and exported goods, the Flemish environmental inspectorate, or its counterparts in the Brussels region and the Walloon region, are responsible.[17] The responsibilities of each of these actors are discussed in detail in the case studies.[18]

Research Phases

This study has five research phases which overlap to a certain extent and influenced each other. The research model is visualized in Figure 2.2 (inspired by Verschuren and Doorewaard 2010, Chapter 3). Each of the phases has particular aims and intended outcomes, which are explained below. The methods used for Phases 3 and 4 – document analysis, interviews and field visits – are explained later in this methodological chapter.[19]

---

15 Missie, available at: http://fiscus.fgov.be/interfdanl/nl/publications/missie.htm [last consulted on 29 December 2011] and European Customs Information Portal, available at: http://ec.europa.eu/ecip/ [last consulted on 21 January 2012].

16 De Scheepvaartpolitie, available at: http://www.polfed-fedpol.be/org/org_dga_spn_nl.php [last consulted 21 January 2012].

17 In 2014, after the data gathering was finished, the responsibility for waste was regionalized and now rests with the Flemish environmental inspectorates as far as the Port of Antwerp is concerned. The decision about this had been made back in 2011 but was not yet implemented. Available at: http://www.vlaamsparlement.be/Proteus5/getFile.action?id=500422

18 More information can be found in the chapters about the illegal trade in e-waste (Chapter 5) and tropical timber (Chapter 6).

19 See under the section: Research Method, Data Gathering and Analysis in this chapter.

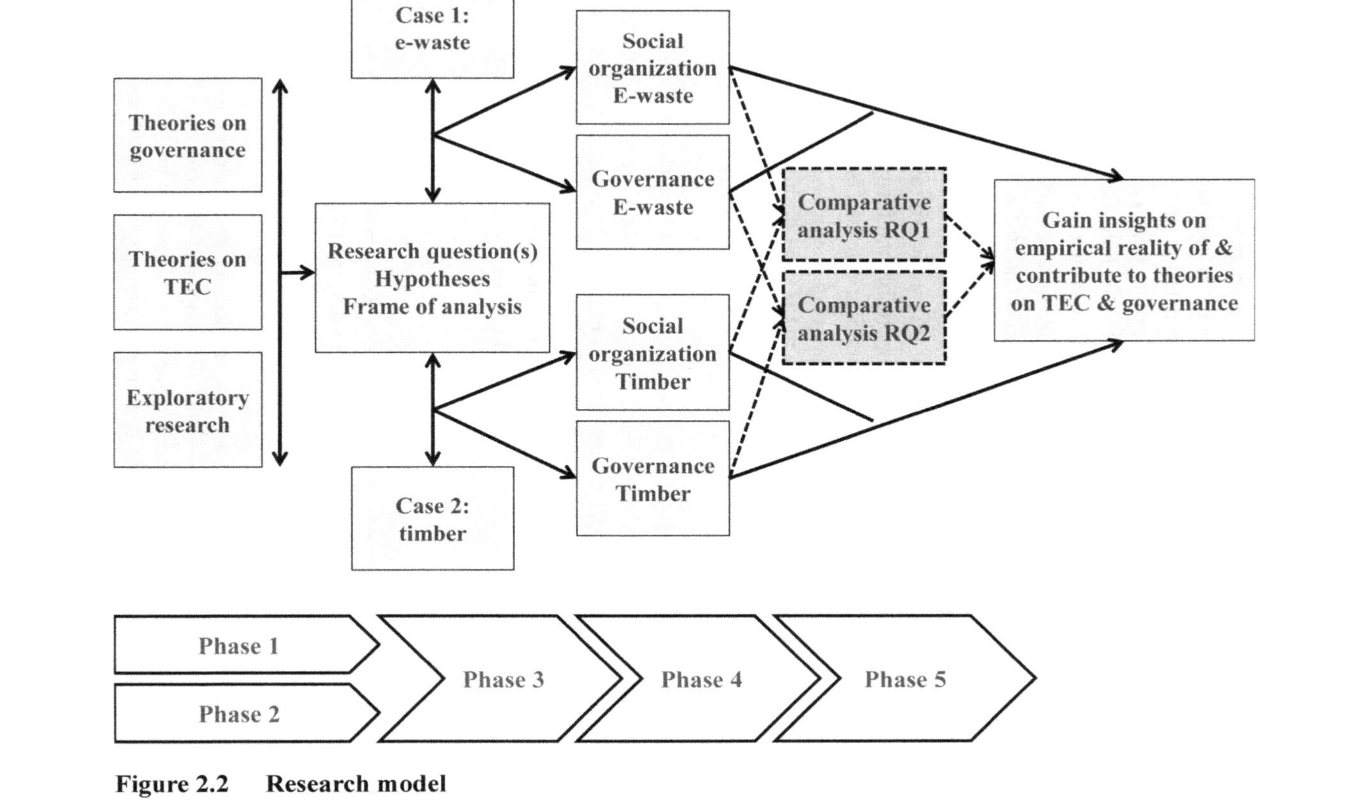

Figure 2.2 Research model

Literature Review

In this first phase, literature was reviewed on green criminology, environmental justice, corporate and organizational crime, conflict criminology, transnational crime, environmental law, responsive regulation, governance, ecology, environmental sociology and other topics related to transnational environmental crime and its governance. This provided a state of the art of theory and research on the topic. It allowed getting a grip on the knowledge base and the remaining gaps in literature. This helped frame the research questions about the social organization and emergence as well as the governance of transnational environmental crime. Besides this review of the more generic literature, theory and research on illegal transports of waste and natural resources was reviewed. Available literature on illegal transports of e-waste and tropical timber was analysed as well. This research phase partially coincided with the other phases and was thus not limited to the first months of the research. As an iterative process requires, the analysis of data and the writing up brought me back to these theoretical foundations.

Exploratory Study of Transnational Environmental Crime Phenomena

Different methods of data gathering were used for this exploratory study of transnational environmental crime phenomena. First, various open sources were studied such as reports by NGOs, environmental inspectorates and other national and international government agencies to get a first grip on the phenomena of illegal transport of waste and natural resources. Second, interviews were conducted with experts who worked for the federal police department for the environment, for two environmental NGOs, for the European Parliament, for Belgian customs, for a waste sector federation; one was an investigative journalist (N=7). These interviews were of an exploratory nature and were intended to guide the choices of the specific cases to study in the following research phases. A study of media communication on transnational environmental crime was conducted as well. This allowed identifying cases of transnational environmental crime that came into the public attention in recent years. The interviews and media analysis revealed the relevance of illegal transports of e-waste and tropical timber within the research setting and thus allowed narrowing down the case selection. The information from this exploratory phase was included in the theoretical framework and helped describe the characteristics of the studied cases. Five out of seven of the experts who were contacted for the exploratory interviews were contacted again in a later stage of the research (see Phases 3 and 4).

Social Organization and Emergence of Illegal Transports of E-waste and Tropical Timber

Phase 3 focuses on what elements characterize the social organization and emergence of illegal transports of e-waste and tropical timber (*research question 1*).

This research question about the social organization and emergence of the flows is divided into three sub-questions, in order to avoid this from staying on a general and abstract level. The precise operationalization of the questions is outlined in the checklist in annex 1.

The first objective in this third research phase is to put a finger on what the environmental problem is that is associated with illegal transports of e-waste and tropical timber, according to the different stakeholders. This entails illustrating the harmfulness (or potential harm) of the behaviours, their frequency, their market value and so on because these arguments are at the basis of the choice to make this the topic of international environmental conventions and other agreements.[20] This is reflected in sub-question (1.1) *What elements of harmfulness or scope are taken into account in the criminalization of illegal transports of e-waste and tropical timber?*

The second objective of this research phase moves beyond the descriptive. It aims to gain insights into the social organization of illegal transports of e-waste and tropical timber (Passas 2002; Szasz 1986; van der Pijl, Oude Breuil and Siegel 2011). This study considers a wide range of possible actors, beyond white-collar crime, organized crime or state crime conceptualizations (Coleman 1987; Nelken 2002; Passas 2002; Tijhuis 2006). This allows a more accurate view on legal and illegal actors and their interrelations and can advance theoretical developments as well as provide input for policy-making. This implies analysing who is involved and how they interact.

The theoretical background for these legal-illegal interfaces in transnational crime is the framework developed by Passas (2002, 2003) and further refined by Tijhuis (2006). The two broad categories are antithetical and symbiotic interfaces between legal and illegal actors. In general, antithetical interfaces are those where legal and illegal actors oppose each other, whereas symbiotic interfaces are those where they cooperate.[21] This research analyses the legal-illegal interfaces for two particular types of transnational crime: illegal trade in e-waste and tropical timber. This will allow the further analysis of the thin line between legal and illegal in transnational environmental crime. In this way, this study aims to gain insights into the social organization of the cases. This is reflected in sub-question (1.2) *How are illegal transports of e-waste and tropical timber socially organized?*

The social organization of illegal transports of e-waste needs to be understood against a broader political, social, economic and cultural background. This can provide insights into the underlying causes – the etiology of transnational environmental crime – which was long disregarded in criminology (Nelken 2002; Rock 2002). This research, therefore, pays attention to how the motivations of

20 This study will not go into the reasons why certain behaviours are criminalized and others are not. This goes beyond the scope of this research. It would be an interesting question for future research on transnational environmental crime.

21 A more detailed explanation of this theory can be found in the theoretical Chapter 3.

the different actors shape the flows of transnational environmental crime. In doing this, it pays attention to individual, organizational and societal levels of analysis as each contributes to the emergence of illegal e-waste and timber flows (Clinard and Yeager 1980; Coleman 1987; Huisman 2001; Slapper and Tombs 1999). Furthermore, the unlevel playing field in today's globalized world can play a role, because asymmetries in laws, culture and economy foster the demand for illegal goods or services, are an incentive to participate in illegal markets and hamper the ability of authorities to control (Passas 1999, p. 402). For that reason, it is important to place transnational environmental crime within the broader context of today's globalized society that facilitates crime (Ruggiero 2009). Given the inherently transnational character of these flows, contributing factors in countries of origin, transit and destination should be considered (Antonopoulos and Winterdyk 2006; van Erp and Huisman 2010). This study therefore analyses how and why the illegal trade in e-waste and tropical timber occurs. These reasons are referred to as push, pull and facilitating factors. Push, pull and facilitating factors refer back to economic dynamics of supply and demand. These have been applied to transnational crimes in previous studies (Antonopoulos and Winterdyk 2006; Morselli, Turcotte and Tenti 2011). Push factors are forces that drive illegal transports away from their origin (supply). Pull factors are forces that draw illegal transports to their destination (demand). Facilitating factors are contextual elements that make illegal transports possible. This is the topic of sub-question (1.3) *Which push, pull and facilitating factors explain the emergence of illegal transports of e-waste and tropical timber?*

This third research phase allows illustrating the criminalization, harm, social organization and emergence of illegal transports of e-waste and tropical timber and aims to further ground the above-mentioned theories in empirical findings on transnational environmental crime. This will give added relevance to the governance part of this research (Phase 4). Results of research Phase 3 are reflected in Chapter 5: Emergence and Social Organization of Illegal Transports of E-Waste and Chapter 6: Social Organization of the Illegal Timber Trade.

Governance of Illegal Transports of E-Waste and Tropical Timber

Phase 4 focuses on what elements characterize the governance of illegal transports of e-waste and tropical timber (*research question 2*). Building on the insights of Phase 3, this examines the governance reality of transnational environmental crime. This research question translates into five sub-questions which are each explained below (Adopted from: Wood 2006). The operationalization of the questions is outlined in the checklist in annex 1.

Traditionally, the government institutions in the nation states have the central responsibility for crime and security. In fact, a lot of the environmental issues have been dealt with through command and control regulation, which implies non-compliance will be met with punishment and rules are uniformly applied (Grabosky and Gant 2000). However, this provides only part of the solution to deal with the complexity of environmental problems (Gunningham 2004). Compared to other international crimes such as drugs, the law enforcement resources invested in environmental crime can be perceived as limited since criminal prosecution of environmental cases is unlikely or at least met with low penalties (Faure 2012; White 2011).

In contemporary society, behaviour is not only regulated by government actors or by command and control regulation only. There are various regulatory hybrids that respond to transnational, environmental as well as corporate crime. This research uses two hybrid models for environmental governance as ideal-typical examples: responsive regulation (Ayres and Braithwaite 1992; Braithwaite 2008) and networked governance (Holley, Gunningham and Shearing 2012; Wood 2006).[22] In both these models, the chosen regulatory approach becomes necessarily tailor-made to the particular case or situation, involving a mix of regulatory instruments by state, corporate or civil society actors (Gunningham, Grabosky and Sinclair 1998). In these hybrid arrangements non-state actors play a role, operating at different levels within the globalized context (van Koppen 2006). States are no longer the single actors but a plurality of actors in different interactions is involved (Crawford 2006). It is not always clear what governance frameworks this results in for transnational environmental crime. Governments as well as business, civil society and international organizations have a role to play in governing e-waste and tropical timber (Gibbs, McGarrel and Axelrod 2010; Green, Ward and McConnachie 2007). This study therefore examines how this governance of security framework – in the sense of preventing illegal transports of e-waste and tropical timber from occurring – is organized. By investigating this on a case-to-case basis, insights can be gained on governance processes and behaviour.

Both ideal-typical models of the responsive regulatory pyramid and networked governance informed the governance analysis of the cases. In analysing the governance reality, this study followed the empirical suggestion of Shearing and Johnston (2010) to do a nodal analysis before a networked governance analysis. This implies an analysis of the separate nodes[23] (*nodal governance analysis*) and their governance characteristics before moving to an analysis of their interactions (*networked governance analysis*). A first stage of the nodal analysis involves the 'mapping' of the governance nodes and networks (Wood 2006). This mapping exercise can be difficult since not all of the actors are necessarily true 'security' actors as such. These nodes do not necessarily need to be formally institutionalized

22 Please see Chapter 3 for a detailed explanation of these two theoretical governance models.

23 Instead of mentioning the term actor, the concept 'node' will be used as well. Nodes are actors involved in governance.

nor legally recognized. The role of civil society actors can be more important to define, censure and sanction deviant behaviour than that of the state (Green, Ward and McConnachie 2007). This is where the qualitative orientation of the research is indispensable. It allows analysing which formal and informal actors participate in the governance of illegal transports of e-waste and timber. This is reflected in sub-question (2.1) *Who are the actors that participate in the governance of illegal transports of e-waste and tropical timber?*

In studying the governance nodes, attention is paid to both structural and cultural elements. This examines how the nodes problematize the topic of illegal transports of e-waste (so-called mentalities), what they set as objectives (so-called finalities) and what strategies they use to reach that goal (Johnston and Shearing 2003). We could for instance assume criminal justice actors adhere to a punishment mentality whereas corporate organizations could be more relying on a risk mentality. Police organizations might primarily look for judicial evidence, whereas environmental inspectorates might do that as well, while at the same time advising corporations on how to comply. Customs might be primarily focused on excise duties, whereas port authorities might focus principally on fostering trade and guaranteeing safety. This could also reveal objectives that are not necessarily identical to those originally put forward by the organization (McBarnet 2006). Their finalities might even lie outside the objective of environmental protection. This is reflected in sub-question (2.2) *What knowledge, capabilities and resources do each of actors that participate in the governance of illegal transports of e-waste and tropical timber make use of for the governance of illegal transports of e-waste and tropical timber?* and sub-question (2.3) *What is the 'mentality' of actors that participate in the governance of illegal transports of e-waste and tropical timber towards illegal transports of e-waste and tropical timber in particular?*

After the nodal governance analysis, this study analyses how the different actors interact with one another and whether these relations are of a cooperative, competitive or non-existent nature (Sheptycki 2005; Crawford 2006). This relationship might even be one where one actor takes up a leading role. There might also be a lack of information exchange and overlap of functions and expertise hampering their cooperation (Sheptycki 1995). In addition, this governance analysis pays attention to possible missing links between governance actors, where new connections could be advantageous. This is reflected in sub-question (2.4) *How do actors that participate in the governance of illegal transports of e-waste and tropical timber interact?*

This study also pays attention to facilitating and hindering factors in the governance of illegal transports of tropical timber and e-waste (Wood 2006). It is particularly interesting to look at the implications of the possibly contrasting finalities and mentalities. The analysis looks at opportunities for existing nodes to focus more intensely on the illegal transport of e-waste and timber. It also pays attention to governance gaps and missing nodes, which are individuals or groups who are currently not mobilized in these governance processes and this in spite of their relevant knowledge, capacities and resources in view of desired governance outcomes. This fifth governance aspect is reflected in sub-question (2.5) *What are the strengths and weaknesses in the governance of illegal transports of e-waste and timber?*

Answering to these sub-dimensions of the governance analysis will provide empirical data on the governance reality of the illegal trade in tropical timber and e-waste. Results of research Phase 4 are reflected in Chapter 5: Governance of Illegal Transports of E-Waste in a European Trade Hub and Chapter 6: Governance of the Illegal Tropical Timber Trade.

Comparative Analysis

This fifth phase analyses the two case studies comparatively. Although case studies are very common in social sciences, the comparative merits of those are often underappreciated (Dellepiane 2009). Although there is a debate about the transferability of conclusions from case studies (Leys 2009; Swanborn 2008), the comparative and detailed analysis of these case studies will contribute to the theoretical transferability of the findings (Maesschalck 2009). The value of case studies is increased when used comparatively. It has the potential to provide more feel and understanding about the studied phenomenon and is at the nexus of empirical reality and theory (Zartman 2005).

On the one hand, this comparative analysis takes the study back to the central research question: *What are the governance consequences of controlling and preventing transnational environmental crime flows?* The case studies already provided insights on the empirical reality of the two cases, within the research setting. The comparative analysis of these cases brings it back to the level of transnational environmental crime as a phenomenon. This comparative analysis contributes to the further development of theories on transnational environmental crime and its governance. On the other hand, this comparative analysis allows pinpointing differences and similarities between the two cases. This comparison pays attention to how one case can inspire the other. This qualitative comparative case study will not reveal generalizable conclusions for all cases of transnational environmental crime. This study can however add experience to what is already known through previous research. This comparative analysis is the topic of Chapter 7.

Research Method, Data Gathering and Analysis

The third research phase focuses on the characteristics of the criminalization, social organization and emergence of the illegal transports of e-waste and tropical timber. This is based on a document analysis of various primary and secondary sources as well as on interviews with key informants. The fourth research phase is also based on a multi-method approach. It included field visits in addition to the document analysis and interviews. Each of these methods as well as the data gathering and analysis is explained below.

Document Analysis

The document analysis of Phase 3 was based on the foundations laid in Phase 2. This was continued in Phase 4, which particularly aimed to gather in-depth knowledge about the governance of the cases. The document analysis uses governmental sources such as reports and statistics of inspectorates, police and customs, waste and timber trade statistics, data-bases of waste crimes/CITES-breaches. It also included research reports by the United Nations Environment Programme (UNEP), International Network for Environmental Compliance and Enforcement (INECE), European Network for the Implementation and Enforcement of Environmental Law, focusing on Transfrontier Shipments of Waste (IMPEL-TFS), Convention on the International Trade in Endangered Species of Fauna and Flora (CITES), World Customs Organisation, Basel Convention Secretariat, Interpol, World Bank, by independent consultants and academics. The document analysis also included corporate documents such as press releases, websites, year reports, policy plans, ethical codes. I also consulted documents by civil society actors such as non-governmental organizations (NGO) and news media.

Some of those documents were publicly available. Others were provided by various key informants, after they received the permission of their authorities to use the documents. It was the intention to consult judicial files about both cases, but the prosecution service could not grant insights into (e-)waste case files. For tropical timber there were no cases currently in prosecution in Belgium. The Flemish environmental inspectorate was reluctant to provide insights into their files about waste because many of those were still on-going. They instead allowed me to ask questions about how these dossiers are handled. For the federal environmental inspectorates I was provided insight into on-going cases, upon guaranteeing to treat this data as confidential.[24] Case files on tropical timber were not consulted since no case files were available from the last five years. Each of the inspectorates allowed contacting them several times with questions about the governance of these cases.

Interviews

The selection of interviewees was based on purposive sampling and more in particular the sub-category of expert sampling (Trochim 2006). It was the

24 The cases of the federal environmental inspectorate used to be merely sent back to the country of origin. The alternative was to have the waste treated environmentally sound and send the bill to the owner. The recent change in the legislation now provides them with more opportunities for the follow-up of these cases. Their inspectors, as officers of judicial police, are now allowed to write an official (police) report.

intention to gain insights from different perspectives and areas of expertise about the cases. These relevant experts are government, corporate and civil society respondents. Within these three major groups of respondents, the study aimed for a sample of people working in different organizations and departments. Given the transnational focus, respondents in other countries involved in the flows of e-waste and tropical timber were also contacted. Based on available literature and the document analysis, a list of relevant stakeholders was drafted.

A total of 73 semi-structured interviews were conducted related to research Phase 3 with 38 government actors, 24 corporate actors and 22 civil society actors. The fourth research phase is based on the same interviews as research Phase 3, with an additional 8 extra interviews conducted. This brings the total number of semi-structured interviews to 81 with 43 government actors, 28 corporate actors and 23 civil society actors.[25] The exact number of interviews differs for each of the cases and the research questions.[26] Interviews ranged from 45 minutes to 2 hours in length.

The governmental actors are national and international government agencies such as customs, environmental inspectorates, police organizations, prosecutor service and administrations. The civil society respondents are representatives of national and international environmental NGOs, labour unions and investigative journalists. The corporate representatives are producers of (inter)national computer hardware, e-waste collectors, refurbishers and recyclers, timber importers, certification organizations and transport corporations. These respondents were guaranteed confidentiality and therefore I refer to government (G and number), corporate (C and number) and civil society respondents (S and number) for quotations. There is one list of respondents for both cases and respondents were numbered consecutively.

In order to get in touch with these different key informants, government agencies, corporations or civil society organizations were contacted. In addition, each of the respondents were asked whether they could refer me to other experts, which allowed me to 'snowball' to a broader sample (Babbie 2007; Decorte and

---

25 The number of interviews and number of respondents differs because some actors chose to address me in pairs and six actors were interviewed twice. In addition, there was one group interview with 13 government respondents, four of which had already been interviewed separately.

26 For the analysis of the first research question on the social organization of illegal flows of e-waste, a total of 50 semi-structured interviews were conducted with 29 government, 19 private sector and 14 civil society actors. For the research question on governance for the e-waste case, a total of 56 semi-structured interviews was conducted with 34 government actors, 23 corporate actors and 14 civil society actors. For the analysis of research questions on the social organization of illegal timber flows, a total of 35 semi-structured interviews was conducted with 15 government, 10 private sector and 10 civil society actors. For the analysis of the governance reality for illegal timber flows, a total of 36 semi-structured interviews was conducted with 15 government, 11 private sector and 10 civil society actors.

Zaitch 2009). After a period of about 18 months of interviewing, I noticed that the interviewees often referred to the same experts.

The semi-structured interviews were intended to gather first-hand experience about the cases. The respondents provided their perspective about the social organization, emergence and governance of illegal transports of e-waste and tropical timber. The interviewees of Phases 2, 3 and 4 each received information about the aims of the research. They were sent this information digitally before the interview and were asked whether they were willing to participate. I also guaranteed the results would be reported about confidentially. Throughout this book, I selected meaningful quotes of my respondents, whenever this did not jeopardize their anonymity. The interviews were mostly in Dutch and English, and two were in French. I translated the Dutch and French quotes to English.

From the very outset, I chose to be open about the goals of my research and revealed I was mainly interested in illegal transports of e-waste and tropical timber. Although this transparency might have scared away some potential respondents, I preferred to be open about this. Depending on whether I contacted government, corporate or civil society actors, I did highlight other aspects. For example, for corporate actors, I focused on how economic sectors are affected by illegal transports rather than directly asking about their potential involvement. For the case of e-waste, this did not pose any trouble. Many corporations were willing to participate in the research. Some even hoped their companies' names would be mentioned in the study. For tropical timber the picture was different. Many tropical timber importers simply answered that they were not involved in illegal imports and were therefore not willing to participate. It is difficult to know to what extent these corporations that were willing to participate in this research represent the 'best kids in the class'. Representatives of the sector organization were willing to talk and also got me in contact with two tropical timber importers who were willing to participate. For field visits to people and/or firms that informally make a living from e-waste and second-hand electronics, I approached this topic mostly as a matter of used goods and avoided referring to their business being involved in waste. To a certain extent, this was necessary to avoid them being offended or thinking I work for law enforcement.

I experienced it was very important to build trust with my respondents. I found different key informants to be willing to open doors to other respondents once I had gained their trust. Building up this trust required me to contact them several times. The introductory e-mail about the set-up of my study proved useful. Contacting them over the phone to allow them to ask further questions was also necessary. Once those conditions were there, the respondents were usually willing to talk. Some respondents did not want to meet at their job sites because of the sensitivity of the information. At these occasions, I met them on neutral grounds such as a coffee house or the university college. Some respondents were located in other parts of the world. These were interviewed over the phone or through video conferencing (*Skype*). At the outset of each interview, I again explained the aims of my research. I repeated that the information would be reported confidentially.

At this point I asked whether there were objections against the digital recording of the interview. Two respondents preferred that the interview would not be recorded because of bad experiences with this in the past (with journalists). In one interview, the respondent was rather hesitant and even defensive. I, therefore, chose not to ask whether the interview could be recorded since it proved already very difficult to build trust. Four Ghanaian respondents also preferred not to have their voice recorded for cultural and religious reasons. For these seven interviews, I made notes and recorded my own impressions right after the interview. The analysis was based on these notes and recordings. The interviewees could also ask to turn the recording device off temporarily in case a topic was particularly sensitive. This happened twice, once when an on-going case was discussed and once when the respondent provided critique about his own organization. A few times respondents added information once the recording was stopped and the interview ended (off-tape phenomenon Beyens and Tournel 2009, p. 224). They might have felt more liberated to talk, even though confidentiality was guaranteed. I avoided turning the recorder back on to avoid scaring them. Instead I recorded my own impressions and recollection of this information when I had left them. I also recorded my own general impressions at the end of the recording. This helped me in 'reliving' the interview while analysing. The analysis of the taped interviews was based on both the transcription of the interview and the notes. On different occasions I went back to my respondents and presented them my analysis of the cases. Sometimes they suggested a minor factual correction. The main goal, however, was to have them check the quotations I used for anonymity. Almost all respondents asked me whether they would be informed about the further developments and findings of this study. I guaranteed them I would send them publications once they were accepted. Some respondents were also interested to hear about the opinions or revelations of other stakeholders. I explained I could only report about this confidentially because I guaranteed this to all respondents. They understood this and showed appreciation for the provisional results and questions I was willing to share.

As mentioned earlier, I used a checklist for the interviews (see annex I). I, however, left ample room for flexibility. I did not have a particular order in which the questions were asked. Usually the respondent would start explaining their interest in the topic of this research or the activities of their organization after I provided them with the introductory information about my study. This flexibility allowed me to follow the reasoning of the interviewee (Beyens and Tournel 2009). In case the topic deviated too much, I used the topic list to bring the interviewee back to the topic. I also intervened in case I wanted more clarification about something. In case the respondent did not feel comfortable answering a question, I repeated that the interview was confidential and reformulated the question, but I did not persist any further after that.

At a certain point during the interviews and their analysis, I started to run into similar comments and new elements started to get less frequent. For research question 1 this occurred during the months when I was writing up the findings.

I added a few more interviews, but did not gain much new knowledge. It is at this point of theoretical saturation (Bloor and Wood 2006) that I decided to stop focusing on the first research question and focused exclusively on the second. For the second research question, I found consistent findings during the writing up of the interviews, which included additional interviews compared to Phase 3. Where elements were unclear, the respective respondents were contacted for further clarification.

Field Visits

Besides the document analysis and the interviews, the fourth research phase included field visits. These were necessary to gain contextualized real-time information about the governance of the environmental flows of e-waste and tropical timber. These field visits did not involve extensive participatory observation, but were merely meant to observe the study object in its natural setting. Downsides of this method are of course the time- and labour-intensiveness, but these observations undoubtedly allowed me to gather interesting data (Mortelmans, Decorte and Zaitch 2009). The field visits were limited to a number of crucial sites in the governance of environmental flows. This refers to observations at so-called governance 'nodes' (for example, ports) and at organizations responsible for the control of e-waste and timber. I observed the work of customs in the Port of Antwerp. This provided insights into their systems of risk analysis and scanners. Their risk analysis system determines which containers require further checks by customs officers. When particular criteria are met, containers can be selected for scanning. The container scans provide horizontal and vertical cross-sectional views of the loaded goods, similar to an MRI-scanner.[27] Besides observing customs, I accompanied the federal environmental inspectorate in their controls of second-hand vehicles which were suspected to contain e-waste. These controls happened in close cooperation with customs, harbourmaster's office and maritime police. Together, these field visits gave insights into the daily reality of the governance of illegal transports in the Port of Antwerp. Besides field visits in the Port of Antwerp, I visited one country of destination, Ghana, which is often frequented by illegal transports of e-waste that export from or transit in Belgium. In Ghana, I visited the Port of Tema and the city of Accra. In particular, the port, the informal recycling and refurbishing firms, the e-goods markets and the Agbogbloshie dumpsite were observed. I made notes during and/or after the field visits which were integrated with the interviews and document analysis in data analysis (Mortelmans, Decorte and Zaitch 2009).

The field visits allowed gaining realistic insights about the everyday reality of governing e-waste flows. It was my intention to also visit a source country of tropical timber in Africa. The first option was Cameroon. It turned out to be rather

27 Further information about the risk analysis and the container scanning can be found in Chapter 5, under the section Governance of Illegal Transports of E-Waste in a European Trade Hub.

difficult to visit this country in view of gaining qualitative insights on illegal timber trade. The concessions are very much spread out across the country and it would have taken up too much time. The second option was the Democratic Republic of Congo. For similar reasons as for Cameroon, as well as due to instabilities in the region as a consequence of the elections, I decided not to go there. In both countries, the method was changed to contacting different actors and interviewing them over the phone or over Skype. The field visit to Ghana, however, proved to be interesting as well. Ghana used to be an important exporter of timber, but less than 10 per cent of its tropical forest remains. It was also the first West African country to sign the Voluntary Partnership Agreement (VPA)[28] and several of its forests are in the process of Forest Stewardship Council (FSC)[29] certification. It was, therefore, relevant to interview people in Ghana about tropical timber and not merely e-waste. Although the methodology for the two cases is not completely equal, the case studies were made as comparable as possible.

Checklist

This research used a topic list. This list was drafted based on the literature review (Phase 1) and was further refined in the exploratory research (Phase 2). This checklist was used for data gathering in both document analysis and semi-structured interviews. It allowed for the necessary flexibility to approach respondents with different backgrounds. It also served as the backbone for the data analysis. The checklist can be found in Annex 1.

Data Analysis

There are no fixed formulas to guide case study data analysis. Data gathered in this study was coded and analysed by means of qualitative data analysis software.[30] The software allowed to triangulate findings from different types of sources (Leys 2009; Loosveldt, Swyngedouw and Cambre 2007; Yin 2009). It helped manage the massive amount of data gathered in the different research phases. I had separate files for each of my cases which formed the case study database. The files contained the interview transcripts, the case study notes from interviews and field visits and the case study documents, which included articles, reports,

---

28 The EU has tried to impose stricter controls on countries of origin of tropical timber through a licensing system based on the Voluntary Partnership Agreements (VPAs), negotiated with exporter countries under the Forest Law Enforcement, Governance and Trade (FLEGT) Action Plan (UNEP 2011).

29 Forest Stewardship Council (FSC) is a multi-stakeholder certification initiative, which integrates social, economic and environmental criteria in the certification of forests and actors in the timber chain of custody.

30 NVivo qualitative data analysis software; QSR International Pty Ltd. Version 8, 2008.

media files, statistics and so on. Publications that were digitally available were analysed with the qualitative data-analysis software. When digital files were not available, my notes about the documents were digitally stored and coded in the database. The interviews were transcribed and these transcriptions as well as the notes were coded with the software. I originally had the intention to code the audio files of the research instead of the transcription. I tested this for the exploratory interviews. This proved to be very time-consuming in coding and did not seem practical in data analysis and description. The program could neither import large audio files nor the documentaries about e-waste and tropical timber and hence failed in executing the queries. Despite these hiccups, the software undoubtedly proved useful in selecting the information and keeping it controllable. During coding of documents and interviews, it allowed making notes on what could be useful for later analysis and reporting. These notes helped to remember which elements needed further clarification by the respondents.

I analysed each case individually and did a comparative analysis of the two cases. In order to guide the data gathering and analysis, I used the checklist based on the research question and sub-questions (see Appendix 1). It soon became clear what categories were useful and which codes had to be adapted or omitted. I inevitably looked at the broader social, economic, political and legal context (*macro*). In the study of the different (governance) actors involved in illegal transport of e-waste and tropical timber, I studied the *meso* level of analysis. The micro level of analysis was also an objective for my analysis. In studying the flows, I came across particular individual motivations or characteristics which influenced the participation in the illegal transports or influenced particular actions taken in the governance of them. Both research questions take into account elements of macro, meso as well as micro level of analysis.

Research Scope and Limitations

This research does not claim to deliver representative hypothesis testing. This qualitative study cannot answer to the same criteria as quantitative studies report about. There are however other testimonies to its quality (Maesschalck 2009): I tried to be observant about the strengths as well as weaknesses of my research and the chosen methods. Case studies have the limitation of not being representative and not being able to perfectly control cases. I therefore chose to document the methodological choices and the research strategy (Maesschalck 2009; Seale 1999). By means of this transparency about the research process, I aimed to avoid random mistakes or subjectivities. By communicating transparently about the data gathering and analysis and key premises of the study, I intended to increase the transferability and dependability.[31] I hope this introductory chapter together with the discussion of the findings in Chapters 5, 6 and 7 testify to that.

---

31 In quantitative research this would be referred to as external validity and reliability.

Furthermore, this study adhered to the suggestions made by King, Keohane and Verba (1994) to improve the quality of the data. This study collected data on as many observable implications of the studied phenomenon as possible. By making sure the gathered data corresponds to the goal of the research, I tried to strengthen the credibility[32] of this study (Maesschalck 2009). By corroborating different perspectives and opinions about the cases I made sure the arguments were exposed to validation or falsification at different times. This refers to the different segments of society the respondents represent (government, corporate, civil society) and the triangulation of different methods, data and theories also contributes to this (Yin 2003). A mix of sources and methods was used. Considering the practical and methodological restrictions in studying transnational environmental crime, the most promising and available sources were used. Official data are likely to be a reflection of the priorities and means of the official agencies rather than a reflection of the real extent of the problem. These methodological limitations of official data (for example, underreporting) definitely made it necessary to look for alternative sources and strike a balance between government, corporate and civil society sources. I triangulated official data with other sources (investigative journalism reports, NGO reports and so on). In this way, I paid attention to a diversity of explanations and answers to this question (Leys 2009). Although the document analysis is a stable data source which allowed gaining insights in a broader time frame and offers detailed contents on the topic, the documents were not composed in view of this research. This required me to put them in proper perspective while interpreting them. As explained above, access to on-going cases of prosecutors and inspectorates was often restricted, proving it is not always likely to gain access to restricted information that might be useful for the study.

Not only access to documents was sometimes difficult, but access to particular groups of respondents was challenging as well. The experience in my research with contacting corporate actors is mixed. For the case of e-waste, many corporations were willing to talk about the issue of illegal transports. To a certain extent this might be explained by the fact that many of these corporations see illegal transports as competitors for their own business. However, also corporations that were involved in illegal transports or at least facilitated them were willing to talk. Gaining access to informal business working in e-waste collection and recycling was most difficult, but the Ghanaian field visit made this possible. Informal collectors in Belgium were less keen to participate. I searched for contact information (for example, through websites) and contacted five 'firms'. None of them responded. For tropical timber, the picture is a little different as well. There I did experience a reluctance to talk. I found only two out of the six contacted importers of tropical timber willing to be interviewed. The sector organization representative was willing to talk as well. The possibility exists that the corporate actors who were willing to talk represent the 'best kids in class'. This might have

32 This would be referred to as internal validity in quantitative studies.

influenced the findings, but by triangulating methods and respondents I tried to counter that as well as I could.

This research focuses on two particular flows of transnational environmental crime: illegal transports of e-waste and timber. The topic under study is in constant evolution. During the course of the research, legislation and policies for both e-waste and timber changed. These recent dynamics were taken into account as much as possible. Unavoidably there might have occurred changes over the course of this study which I could not account for. A clear example is the *European Timber Regulation* which entered into force 1st March 2013. I tried to account for this development as well as I could. I contacted several respondents after March 2013 and they explained how this is still largely a theoretical development given that a couple of months after its entry into force, not much has changed in practice.

Transnational environmental crime flows are inherently complex with global interdependencies, asymmetries, legal-illegal-informal actors and interfaces and a diversity of motivations and opportunities that shape them. It is indeed difficult to get a grip on the complete flows and I cannot claim I did. However, the method did allow me to assess an important part of it. This research is based in a local research setting: the Port of Antwerp and the trade that flows through. My analysis is thus tailored to that specific empirical reality. By putting the cases within their broader context – looking at the global trade flows – dimensions that reach beyond the local research setting of Antwerp were accounted for. The flows between Belgium and Africa were the particular focus. This case study is necessarily connected to its research setting and does not have the intention to provide generalizable results. This study, however, provides insights that help understand the social organization, emergence and governance of illegal transports of e-waste in other locations as well (Miller et al. 2012). Based on that information it was useful to try and think about the governance approach and whether and how it contributes to the prevention and control of the phenomenon.

As a researcher, I am inevitably influenced by the place where I live and work. Unavoidably this determined the starting perspective for my study. I have tried to be open to influences from other places and cultures and attempted to balance those in my research by actively listening to their stories and witnessing the effect of illegal transports first hand.

Chapter 3
Explaining Transnational Environmental Crime

Introduction

This chapter[1] is the result of a literature review that focused on theory and research that can help explain transnational environmental crime. The first part of this chapter conceptualizes transnational environmental crime and green criminology and clarifies the sensitizing – and sometimes confusing – concepts inherent to this research field. The second part gives an overview of the etiology of transnational environmental crime, in which the 'classical' elements of motivation, opportunity and neutralization serve as a guideline. This chapter illustrates these two dimensions using the cases of waste and natural resources. These case outlines are not exhaustive but serve as an illustration.[2] Particular emphasis is put on the theoretical framework used for the analysis of the case studies in Chapters 5 and 6. A final part provides a concluding analysis on the uncharted territory of transnational environmental crime and points towards avenues for further research.

Conceptualizing Green Criminology and Environmental Crime

Green criminology[3] documents environmental crime in all forms (for example, illegal logging, transportation of toxic waste, illegal dumping, poaching and so on), looks at how environmental law is developed or enforced and also focuses on topics that are more conceptual in nature. This focus fits within a broader critical development which looks beyond crime towards legally ambiguous behaviours

---

1 This chapter is an adaptation of Bisschop, L. (2011). Transnational environmental crime: exploring (un)charted territory. In M. Cools, B. De Ruyver, M. Easton, L. Pauwels, P. Ponsaers, T. Vander Beken, F. Vander Laenen, G. Vande Walle, A. Verhage, G. Vermeulen and G. Vynckier (eds), *EU Criminal Justice, Financial & Economic Crime: New Perspectives, Governance of Security Research Papers* (Vol. 5, pp. 155–83). Antwerpen: Maklu. This theoretical article was reproduced with permission of the publisher Maklu and was updated to include more recent insights from green, transnational and corporate criminology. This redrafting of the theoretical chapter was further inspired by the theoretical framework used for the case studies on the illegal trade in e-waste and tropical timber.

2 Both phenomena are studied in detail in the other chapters.

3 In addition to 'green criminology', other terms such as environmental criminology, 'conservation criminology' and 'eco-global criminology' have been used.

causing social harm (Hillyard et al. 2004). Despite its significance and harmfulness, environmental crime has not been traditionally studied in criminology. The complexity of social harms in environmental issues, especially those affecting non-humans, does not quite fit criminology's traditional focus (Lynch 2013): simply put, green or environmental crimes are crimes against the environment (McLaughlin and Muncie 2006, pp. 146–7), but green crime has been defined in various ways. The definition of environmental crime seems to depend on who is defining it and when and where the definition is used (White 2011).

Some of these definitions take a traditional legal approach and define green crime as a violation of environmental laws. When the gaze is broadened beyond law, it includes environmentally harmful actions that are not necessarily subject to the constraints of the law as a social construction affected by interests (Tombs 2008; Hillyard et al. 2004; Westra 2004). The concept of harm is then more appropriate to refer to a variety of injuries and degradations with regard to the misuse, use and poor management of the environment and natural resources (Heckenberg 2008, p. 12). A distinction between criminal and civil or administrative violations is then not a useful indicator of harm, but a mere social construction (Lynch and Stretesky 2003). It is therefore argued that major harms are not always incorporated in the law, especially when these would go against interests of capital, rendering them neither criminal nor illegal seemingly regardless of the related harms (Passas and Goodwin 2004; White 2008). For example, agro-industry and bio-technology businesses provide examples of how industrial processes contribute to the depletion of natural resources.

Environmental crimes then include abuse, exploitation or monopolization of ecosystems and natural resources (water, air, animal life and so on), industrial pollution of soil, water and air, illegal transports of (hazardous) waste, but also more recent developments such as bio-piracy.[4] The environmental harm might be apparent at some times, whereas at other times the harm is hard to define in the short term and instead emerges with the unfolding of time. An example of such a comprehensive definition of environmental crime is:

> Any intentional or negligent activity or manipulation [by an individual or a corporation] that impacts negatively on the earth's biotic [faunal/floral] or a-biotic [natural resource contamination] natural resources, resulting in immediately noticeable or indiscernible (only noticeable over time) natural resource trauma of any magnitude. (Herbig and Joubert 2006, p. 96)

Choosing a broad definition of environmental crime and keeping an open mind for other – more indirect or less visible – damages associated with environmental crimes makes it possible to pay attention to less obvious consequences, such as

4 Bio-piracy is the appropriation – usually through of the application of international property rights – of traditional knowledge, technologies and genetic resources of indigenous people (Heckenberg 2008, p. 11).

the disproportionate effects for the poor and most vulnerable (Mohai and Saha 2007; Stretesky and Lynch 2011). For that reason, it is important to take into account the social and cultural consequences beyond the more immediate effects of environmental damage. This also allows one to consider the structural effects of environmental crime that transgress regions, ecosystems and generations (Halsey 2004; White 2011). Examples are the pollution of a river by a factory located upstream across national borders hampering the growing of crops downstream (for example the 2010 toxic spill in Hungary after an aluminium plant burst its reservoirs); the pollution of oceans and the related threats to those depending on fishing or tourism near the disaster (for example the 2010 BP oil spill in the Gulf of Mexico or 2011 the nuclear disaster with the Fukushima Daiichi power plant); the damage inflicted upon livelihoods of indigenous people in search of oil (for example tar sands in Canada); or effects that are the result of long-term accumulation of smaller harms of which the future impact is hard to assess (for example the greenhouse effect or climate change). To more precisely account for the harmfulness, a definition of green crime could be grounded in ecotoxicology, environmental toxicology and green chemistry (Lynch and Stretesky 2011).

In view of legal proceedings, phrasings such as power, harm, trauma and so on are often difficult to reconcile with the legality principle. In researching environmental crime empirically, this book therefore builds upon the definition by Passas (1999, p. 17) which states that 'crime is misconduct that entails avoidable and unnecessary harm to society, is serious enough to warrant state intervention, and resembles other kinds of acts criminalized in the countries concerned or international law'. While debates about green criminology and environmental crime are important, it is not the purpose of this work to address or solve these various debates. Rather, for purposes of this work I adopt a definition of green crime that depicts its global scope and its relevance to issues that are beyond the boundaries of law. Thus, this study uses a definition of green crime inspired by those of Herbig and Joubert (2006) and Passas (1999):

> Any intentional or negligent activity or manipulation [by an individual or a corporation] that entails avoidable and unnecessary, immediately noticeable or indiscernible (only noticeable over time) environmental harm to biotic [faunal/floral] or a-biotic [natural resource contamination] natural resources, which transfers regional and national boundaries and is serious enough to warrant state intervention and resembles other kinds of acts criminalized in the countries concerned or international law.

This study uses crime as a concept (rather than harm), defining it as beyond the criminal law of nation states alone, but in respect to the boundaries of international environmental law. The basis of this view can be found in the Rio Declaration on Environment and Development of 1992, which principles were meant as a guideline for the further development of international environmental law and includes the following: the precautionary principle,[5] the principle of environmental impact assessment,[6] the polluter pays principle,[7] the no harm principle,[8] the principle of sustainable development[9] and the principle of common but differentiated responsibilities.[10] These principles have to a varying degree been incorporated into the legal frameworks of the United Nations and European Union and are part of various international conventions. There are also indications within this international environmental framework for the use of corporate liability, although the implementation – criminal, civil or administrative liability for legal persons – is left to the discretion of the signatory states.[11] In practice, such guidelines are implemented in different ways across nations, and are subject to political, social, cultural, ecological and economic forces (Alvazzi del Frate et al. 1999; South 2007). However, the above-mentioned principles could help frame this criminalization. The following section illustrates this conceptual discussion by focusing on waste and natural resources.

Waste, Natural Resources and Transnational Environmental Crime

Both waste and natural resources have been the topic of international conventions which allows this study to stay in the near of the law. For waste this refers to the Basel Convention on the Control of Transboundary Movements of Hazardous Wastes and their Disposal and the European Union Waste Shipment Regulation

5 Where there are threats of serious or irreversible damage, lack of full scientific certainty shall not be used as a reason for postponing cost-effective measures to prevent environmental degradation (Rio Declaration, principle 15).

6 Environmental impact assessment, as a national instrument, shall be undertaken for proposed activities that are likely to have a significant adverse impact on the environment and are subject to a decision of a competent national authority (Rio Declaration, principle 17).

7 National authorities should endeavour to promote the internalization of environmental costs and the use of economic instruments, taking into account the approach that the polluter should, in principle, bear the cost of pollution, with due regard to the public interest and without distorting international trade and investment (Rio Declaration, principle 16).

8 States have [...] the responsibility to ensure that activities within their jurisdiction or control do not cause damage to the environment of other States or of areas beyond the limits of national jurisdiction (Rio Declaration, principle 2). States should effectively cooperate to discourage or prevent the relocation and transfer to other States of any activities and substances that cause severe environmental degradation or are found to be harmful to human health (Rio Declaration, principle 14).

9 The right to development must be fulfilled so as to equitably meet developmental and environmental needs of present and future generations (Rio Declaration, principle 3).

10 In view of the different contributions to global environmental degradation, States have common but differentiated responsibilities (Rio Declaration, principle 4).

11 For example in the United Nations Convention against Transnational Organized Crime.

(1013/2006), Restriction of Hazardous Substances Directive (RoHS 2002/95/E) and Directive on waste electrical and electronic equipment (WEEE 2002/96/EC). For natural resources the strongest legal basis is in the Convention on International Trade in Endangered Species of Wild Fauna and Flora (CITES – Convention of Washington 1975) and in the more stringent legal framework of the European Union the Wildlife Trade Regulations (338/97/EC & 865/2006/EC), the Forest Law Enforcement, Governance and Trade Action Plan (FLEGT) and the EU Timber Regulation (995/2010). Besides these instruments there are few international agreements focused on natural resources.

The potential environmental impact of both cases is difficult to assess since many of the ecological costs are externalized, meaning they are not accounted for in production processes despite potential consequences long after the initial act (Lynch and Stretesky 2007). Inadequate recycling or dumping of waste can be a threat for both human health and the natural environment. Waste containing heavy metals[12] or radioactive material can cause organ damage and cancer, which may take decades to emerge. Hazardous waste dumping pollutes water, soil and air, irrespective of national borders. Natural resource crimes are also a biodiversity threat. Illegal clear-felling of timber reduces the habitat of local species, depletes the water, air and soil quality and causes erosion. This also hastens climate change and global warming and can lead to resource wars over food and water as well as to environmental refugees, ethnic conflict and violent protests as more indirect effects (Carrabine et al. 2009). Natural resources crimes are also a revenue loss for developing countries and when the revenue goes to rebellious groups it causes the destabilization of the state and is a source of conflict (Bannon and Collier 2003b; Le Billon 2001). For a low-income country the richness of natural resources in many cases makes poor people poorer (Bannon and Collier, 2003; Ross, 2003).

While studying these cases, it is interesting to look at the actual harm as well as the potential endangerment and the social and cultural consequences that are not necessarily accounted for in legislation. Waste and natural resources are commodities traded on the global market. These commodities are legal if they are labelled correctly, but this does not mean they are environmentally harmless. An example is the transport of 'recyclable' electronics to countries without adequate resources to process them (Gibbs, McGarrell and Axelrod 2010; Sander and Schilling 2010). Regarding timber, the logging might have been licensed, but permits are often abused or licenses are obtained through bribing of enforcement officers. The immediate and future harm is evident on both the local as well as global levels, illustrating the mobility of harm (White 2011). The local effect refers to the disappearing trees and biodiversity loss, while the global effect is climate change. Regionally, toxins can transfer through water or air, impacting

12 Cadmium, beryllium, mercury, lead, brominated flame retardants (BFRs), chlorofluorocarbon (CFCs) and so on.

soil quality, or illegal logging can cause desertification. In this way, environmental harm potentially affects other countries and even contributes to climate change.

Etiology of Transnational Environmental Crime

Theoretical and empirical underpinnings of mainstream criminological thought can be incorporated in thinking about transnational environmental issues, but the etiological picture of transnational environmental crime is complex: a complete account of the causes requires an examination of opportunities to commit the crime, of motives to take advantage of these opportunities and of control options and weaknesses (Passas 1999). This requires looking beyond the micro-level of individual perpetrators and focusing on organizational culture and structure as well as on societal levels of analysis (politics, economy) (Clinard and Yeager 1980; Huisman 2001; Punch 1996; Slapper and Tombs 1999; Lynch et al. 2013).

Causes for transnational environmental crime could refer to different elements in the corporate or organizational structure, culture and strategy and the international organizational context. Based in opportunity theory, one could scan for characteristics of sectors (for example waste management or transport sector) in view of irregularities and opportunities for informal economies to flourish (Vander Beken 2007; Vander Beken and van Daele 2008). Characteristics of the market system or society are also grounds for opportunities, motivations and rationalizations for committing environmental crime. Croall (2005, p. 241) states that '[m]any economically and socially harmful activities find space to flourish in the climate of deregulation and are morally justifiable in the context of neo-liberalism'. This implies that the global political economy with its focus on production, consumption and profit-making is a possible contributing factor – modern society creating environmental risks (Long et al. 2012; Lynch et al. 2013). Studying transnational environmental crime thus requires scholars to question the structure and systemic functioning of society as a cause of environmental crime. The following discusses the potential underlying causes and the involved actors before zooming in on waste and natural resources in particular.

Underlying Causes for the Emergence of Transnational Environmental Crime

The social organization of illegal transports of e-waste needs to be understood against a broader political, social, economic and cultural background. This can provide insights into the underlying causes of transnational environmental crime (Passas 2002; van Duyne 1993). Analysing factors that contribute to the emergence of illegal transports of e-waste and tropical timber is one of the objectives of the current study. In essence, this etiological question has occupied criminology since its emergence, but the etiology of both transnational and environmental crimes was long disregarded (Nelken 2002; Rock 2002). Different theories in criminology[13] might help understand the emergence of transnational environmental crime, but the integration of these theories results in three core elements: criminalization, motives and opportunities (van Dijk, Sagel-Grande and Toornvliet 1996). In the previous section, this chapter discussed the definition of transnational environmental crime, also relating this to the issue of criminalization. The analysis of the case studies is mainly concerned with the motives and opportunities. In doing this, it pays attention to individual, organizational and societal levels of analysis because each might contribute to the emergence of illegal e-waste and tropical timber flows (Clinard and Yeager 1980; Coleman 1987; Huisman 2001; Slapper and Tombs 1999). Characteristics of the sector or the product might be motives or opportunities for (organized) crime (van Daele, Vander Beken and Dorn 2007). The transport sector can for example be a victim of crime, but might well be a facilitator of crime (Klima 2011; Vander Beken and van Daele 2008).

Today's globalized world provides us with an unlevel playing field which is contributing to the occurrence of harms and crimes. Passas (1999, p. 402) refers to 'criminogenic asymmetries' as a cause of corporate offences: 'structural discrepancies, mismatches and inequalities in the realms of economy, law, politics and culture [...] fuelling the demand for illegal goods and services; generating incentives for people and organisations to engage in illegal practices; and reducing the ability of authorities to control crime'. These asymmetries are criminogenic because they foster the demand for illegal goods or services, are an incentive to participate in illegal markets and hamper the ability of authorities to control. Applying this to environmental matters, asymmetries in environmental regulation or ambiguities in enforcement can contribute to jurisdiction (s)hopping, in which one goes in search of the most favourable (illegal) agreement for the trade of hazardous waste or for the space between laws. Heightened environmental awareness in industrialized countries (cultural asymmetry) led to the strengthening of environmental legislation (legal asymmetry), causing prices to go up (economic asymmetry) and giving extra incentives for illegal trading of waste to countries with lower environmental awareness, lower environmental regulatory standards and lower prices (Passas 2000). Developing countries allow waste imports into their countries out of fear investors from developed countries might move out (trade/economic asymmetry). Communities affected by the environmental crimes of pollution or deforestation might be unaware of their harmfulness (knowledge asymmetry) or do not have the economic means or political rights to oppose polluters (economic/political asymmetry). Social, political and economic power asymmetries between and within nations potentially affects the occurrence of environmental crime. The etiology of transnational environmental crime is thus inherently connected to the broader context of today's globalized asymmetric society, which might facilitate crime (Ruggiero 2009).

13 Strain, social control, differential association, labelling, neutralisation and rational choice theory can each provide insights on the etiology of crime.

Given the inherently transnational character of the trade in waste and natural resources, factors in countries of origin, transit and destination should be considered (Antonopoulos and Winterdyk 2006; van Erp and Huisman 2010). The motivations and opportunities for transnational environmental crime can in fact be located in exporting and importing countries, in supply and demand chains, and are therefore impossible to explain while disregarding the economic, political, cultural and social context. This study therefore identifies push, pull and facilitating factors that will help understand how and why illegal transports of e-waste and tropical timber occur.[14]

Push factors are those forces that drive illegal transports away from their origin (supply). *Pull factors* are forces that draw illegal transports to their destination (demand). *Facilitating factors* are contextual elements that make illegal transports possible. Together, these factors provide the motives and opportunities for actors involved in illegal transports of e-waste and tropical timber. As evident from the different elements discussed above, the etiology cannot be reduced to one explanatory factor, because 'each time we subscribe to one cause of crime, we may realize that the opposite cause also possesses reasonable validity' (Ruggiero 2000, p. 6). Profit might indeed be a major etiological factor for the illegal trade in (e-)waste and (tropical) timber, but this book intends to illustrate how this key concept requires more contextualization.

To understand the nature of transnational environmental crime it is necessary to examine both the supply side *and* the demand side of our global economy (van Erp and Huisman 2010). This interplay of demand and supply not only occurs on an organizational level as illustrated above, but also at the individual level as consumers neutralize purchases of environmentally harmful goods or services (for example teak furniture, jewellery made from corals or ivory and so on). Halsey (2004, p. 844) hits the nail on the head in saying:

> Not only is it profitable to be environmentally destructive (in the sense of mining, manufacturing cars, clear felling forests), it feels good too (in the sense of purchasing a gold necklace, driving on the open road, looking at a table, chair or house constructed from redwood, mahogany, mountain ash or the like).

The low societal concern for the environment thus also contributes to occurrence of transnational environmental crime (Brack 2002) and in a global market this is reinforced by the fact that consumers are provided with commodities that were produced far away, allowing for the easy externalization of environmental harms and risks (Ruggiero and South 2013).

This study takes into account the multi-dimensional nature of the relationship between crime and economy when looking for causes of transnational

14 Push, pull and facilitating factors refer back to economic dynamics of supply and demand. These have been applied to transnational crimes in previous articles (Antonopoulos and Winterdyk, 2006; Morselli, Turcotte and Tenti, 2011).

environmental crime. However, without neglecting the significance of this rational choice or opportunity theory perspective, it is also important to gain insights on other causes of transnational environmental crime, such as insufficient knowledge of legally binding frameworks (Bhrem and Hamilton 1996) or the perception of criminal or regulatory interventions as unfair (Hatcher, Jaffry and Bennett 2000). Business ethics literature also points toward the importance of the internalization of norms for effectiveness of self-regulation (Campbell 2007). This book therefore considers multiple victims and offenders – individuals as well as businesses, small and large, legal and illegal – and acknowledges that power in politics or economy may control framing or defining transnational environmental crime (cf. criminalization processes). It is thus important to analyse how, when and why certain actions become perceived as illegal (Snider 2008) and what actors as well as systemic features play a role in the etiology of transnational environmental crime.[15]

Social Organization: Legal-Illegal Interfaces

Transnational environmental crime is complex and diversified. Given the complexity and global nature of these flows, it is in fact difficult to determine how these are organized. Transnational environmental crime involves a diversity of actors from (transnational) corporations over corrupt governments to deprived individuals. As a consequence, transnational environmental crime is not easily categorized as an organizational, state, transnational, environmental or organized crime, although some types of it fit these labels (Passas 2002; Szasz 1986; van der Pijl, Oude Breuil and Siegel 2011). Research should therefore consider a wide range of possible actors, beyond white-collar crime, organized crime or state crime conceptualizations and it might in fact be difficult to draw a line between legal and illegal actors and their activities (Nelken 2002; Passas 2002; Tijhuis 2006). Theoretical developments as well as policy on this issue can, however, be advanced by an accurate view of the actors involved and their interfaces.

Both small- and large-scale actors, both the powerful and the less affluent and both legal and illegal actors might play a role. It may prove difficult to draw a line between legal and illegal, but it is necessary to gain a more accurate view of the actors, their practices and their interrelations. This can further theoretical developments as well as provide input for policy-making. This study therefore tries to determine whether the actors involved in transports of e-waste and tropical timber and the roles they play can be considered legal or illegal. It analyses whether both legal and criminal actors are involved and whether there is an interface between the two (Huisman and Vande Walle 2010; Nelken 2002; Passas 2002).

The theoretical background for these legal-illegal interfaces in transnational crime relates back to the framework developed by Passas (2003; 2002) which was further refined by Tijhuis (2006) by applying it to the illicit antiquities and art trade.

15 This is the topic of sub-question (1.3) *Which push, pull and facilitating factors explain the emergence of illegal transports of e-waste and tropical timber?*

The two broad categories are *antithetical* and *symbiotic* interfaces. In general, antithetical interfaces are those where legal and illegal actors oppose each other, whereas symbiotic interfaces are those where they cooperate. Four antithetical and six – or eight in Passas' typology[16] – symbiotic relations can be distinguished (Passas 2002; Tijhuis 2006): in what follows, each is explained briefly.

The four antithetical interfaces are: (1) illegal actors compete with legal actors on the same market (*antagonistic*); (2) illegal actors harm legal actors (*injurious*); (3) illegal actors extort legal actors while keeping them viable (*parasitical*); or (4) illegal actors aim to destroy the legal business (*predatory*). There are six types of symbiotic interfaces: (1) legal actors hire an illegal actor to do the dirty work for them (*outsourcing*); (2) both do business independently in which they benefit from each other but one is unaware of the illegality (*synergy*); (3) legal and illegal actors have a long-lasting strong link and are both aware of the illegality (*collaboration*); (4) both experience benefits and are aware of the illegality (*reciprocity*); (5) both experience benefits but within an uneven power relation (*co-optation*); and (6) legal actors financially support illegal ones (*funding*). Passas (2003) also referred to legal actors who are committing organized crimes and legal actors who pursue legal activities, whereas Tijhuis (2006) believed those categories do not refer to illegal-legal interfaces and therefore left those out of his typology. These interfaces have not been studied often and therefore this study analyses the legal-illegal interfaces for two particular types of transnational environmental crimes: illegal transports of e-waste and tropical timber. This will make it possible to examine the thin border between legal and illegal. In this way, this study aims to gain insights into the social organization of illegal transports of tropical timber and e-waste.[17]

Waste, Natural Resources and the Etiology of Transnational Environmental Crimes

Similar to the illustration on the criminalization and definition, this chapter makes the etiology of transnational environmental crime more tangible by referring to waste and natural resources. A more detailed analysis of the social organization of the illegal trade in e-waste and tropical timber is provided in Chapters 5 and 6. In discussing these etiological characteristics of both cases, it is important to be aware of their different transnational orientation. In the case of waste, the developed countries are mainly an export country of origin or a transit country for waste and these exports mostly go to West Africa or South East Asia. In the case of natural resources the transnational dimension is differently oriented, given that developed countries are mostly import countries or transit countries and nations in development are the countries of origin.

---

16 Passas refers to eight symbiotic interfaces. Tijhuis omitted two of those from his typology.

17 This is reflected in sub-question (1.2) *How are illegal transports of e-waste and tropical timber socially organized?* and further operationalized in the following questions:

In order to account for this transnational nature, this study sees both phenomena as *flows* and studies them in this context. When researchers study flows they pay attention to departure locations, routes and final destinations of the goods. For each of these steps one could then look at what characteristics and actors play a role. In examining transnational environmental flows I follow Gille's (2006) suggestion to base a case study of environmental flows in a local context. Transnational environmental crime flows are situated within localities (for example sea- or airports) but at the same time take place within the broader international relations. By identifying the involved actors and factors, it should be possible to gain more complete insights on the social organization and emergence of transnational environmental crime.

Waste as a Transnational Environmental Crime Commodity

The waste sector operates in both legal and illegal economies (Vander Beken 2007; Passas 1999). The waste problem is significant and has increased due to a number of developments in post-World War II society. As a consequence of increased waste regulation, waste management prices have gone up in industrialized countries. The public in the industrialized world became concerned about waste landfills and this prompted many industrialized countries to ship waste abroad to avoid keeping it 'in their own backyard'.[18] This caused waste to become an article of trade that is sold and bought on the market. Due to changed production processes, our society also relies more on synthetic and chemical products, which results in considerable amounts of toxic waste (Pellow 2007). Waste management has in fact become a big and lucrative business. Moreover, there are a number of tensions inherent in waste as a commodity. Waste has an inverse incentive structure due to its negative value. It is also a product of low integrity since it can be easily mixed up or sold under-cover on the second-hand market (Gibbs, McGarrell and Axelrod 2010; Vander Beken 2007). An example are major chemical industries who contract out toxic operations to small firms who are less able to handle chemicals safely. Waste management corporations can also shop around for the lowest costs for waste disposal and offer officials in poor countries attractive prices or bribes for accepting (toxic) waste (Ruggiero 1996). Societal and environmental interests are likely to clash with the economic benefits of illegal waste treatment, since illegal profits are estimated to be three to four times higher than legal waste treatment (Bruinsma 1996; Sanax 1996). The European Union Network for the Implementation and Enforcement of Environmental Law (IMPEL) reported that illegal trade in waste is on the rise. The United Nations Office on Drugs and Crime (UNODC 2009, p. 55) estimated that the annual value of toxic waste transported to West Africa alone is 95 million US dollars.

Waste as a transnational environmental crime commodity is also closely intertwined with social and ecological inequalities. Vulnerable groups (social and economically marginal) are those most likely to suffer, because they have a bigger

18 This is often referred to as NIMBY: *not in my backyard.*

chance of working or living near the polluting factories or landfills (White 2008; Stretesky and Lynch 1998). Countries in development are especially vulnerable due to weak regulatory systems and governments, but also due to their precarious socio-economic situation. Waste often ends up in impoverished villages where people are willing to work for low wages and in which credible oversight is absent. This causes them to accept illegal but financially lucrative hazardous waste shipments. An example is the trade in e-waste: electronics are an increasingly large industry with numerous toxic substances (for example lead, mercury, hexavalent chromium). These often end up in incinerators or landfills or are gathered for 'recycling' to developing countries (Nigeria, Pakistan, India, China and so on). These countries are not, however, always equipped for its recycling, leading to inappropriate recycling practices or dumping of the materials, causing threats for human health (organ damage, cancer) and the natural environment (groundwater contamination, ozone depletion). This phenomenon is export driven, due to the high demand for recyclables in developing countries (that is, raw materials) and the high profits that can be made when transporting the waste instead of treating it properly (Gibbs, McGarrell and Axelrod 2010). A particular example of the dumping of toxic waste is the 2006 Probo Koala case in Abidjan (Ivory Coast) where 600 tons of toxic material, transported by a Dutch company (Trafigura), was dumped on waste sites near the city. According to the UN Special Rapporteur on Toxic Waste 15 people died, 69 people were hospitalized and over 100,000 needed medical attention.

Natural Resources as a Transnational Environmental Crime Commodity

Natural resource extraction can also ride the thin line between legal and illegal and cause tensions between corporate and environmental interests. There are similar economic, social and political drivers and asymmetries underlying the illegal trade in natural resources. Both legitimate and illegal corporations and individuals are involved in the commoditization of natural resources. On the supply side, various actors can be responsible for the clear-felling of a tropical forest, the extraction of minerals, raw materials (coltan, diamonds, gold, gemstones) or the poaching of elephants, such as farmers, professional loggers and armies in search of income sources. After the trees are logged, precious metals or hard rock minerals extracted or the ivory and bush meat of the elephants is harvested, the product follows a marketing chain via dealers and smugglers, who could very well be respectable businessmen. On the demand side, the product can arrive at the doorsteps of importers, manufacturers (for example furniture, paper, electronics), retailers, wholesalers and other legitimate businesses (that is, pet, jewellery or furniture stores). The demand for the products by consumers in developed countries is a major driver of natural resources crimes (Brack 2004): Friends of the Earth estimates 70 per cent of EU timber imports to be illegal (Crossin, Hayman and Taylor 2003).

Natural resource extraction and trade are also related to armed conflicts and exploitation of the poor, rendering it not necessarily illegal, but quite certainly 'dirty' (Bannon and Collier 2003a). Reference is made to the notion 'blood timber', similar to 'blood diamonds', such as in the case of Liberian hardwood exported at the time of the armed conflict under dictator Taylor's regime (Boekhout van Solinge 2008). This is an example of how political, economic and social elements coincide in the etiology of transnational environmental crime. A similar analysis is possible with respect to ivory and rhino horn (Ayling 2013; Naylor 2004). Ross (2003) illustrates how natural resource extraction affects the natural resource-rich and conflict-prone countries in Africa. For victimized communities it is often difficult to address their concerns, as they are dealing with commercially and politically powerful individuals or corporations. This is apparent in cases of *bio-piracy*, which is the commercial exploitation of third-world resources, peoples and knowledge (Walters 2010). This often happens through licit mechanisms such as patents or other judicial and institutional construction.

Natural resources crimes, however, seem to be less of a political and law enforcement priority compared to waste, although different international initiatives have been set up to counteract the trade in natural resources in general and endangered species or timber more specifically (Wijnstekers 2004).[19] Assessing the scale of the problem is difficult since information is patchy. Estimates of global illegal trade in wildlife range from 10 to 20 billion Euro annually and the World Bank estimates that illegal logging alone costs developing countries 15 billion US dollars in revenues and taxes (Schmidt 2004; Banks et al. 2008).

Conclusion

This chapter discussed how the greening and globalizing of criminology has contributed to the filling of the chart on transnational environmental crime. There is, however, room for improvement.

In first instance there is a need for theoretical and empirical criminological research which accounts for the global or *transnational nature* of (environmental) crimes (Aas 2007; Sheptycki and Wardak 2005). Society globalized and crime did as well: victims, offenders as well as the criminal behaviour can be transnational. Studying the transnational dimension is important for criminology, because this avoids methodological nationalism and pays attention to global complexities (Aas 2007). Because global dynamics also have the potential to impact diverse places differently (Gilbert and Russell 2002), analytical frameworks need to be sensitive to transnational as well as local elements influencing the criminalization and etiology of crimes. This implies the need for a broad research scope, focusing on multiple environments, disciplines, levels of analysis and actors (Sheptycki 2005; Passas 2003).

19 For example, Convention on Biological Diversity, Convention on International Trade in Endangered Species, Interpol Wildlife crime working group, International Plant Protection Convention, World Trade Organization Agreement on the Application of Sanitary and Phytosanitary Measures, EU FLEGT and so on.

A second gap refers to the *environmental dimension*. Ever since the 'greening of criminology' was first conceptualized by Lynch (1990), environmental issues have been the topic of criminological research, but there is room for improvement (Ruggiero and South 2013). Environmental crime and negligence in corporate and international contexts have been documented, but these analyses seemed to lack theoretical and methodological strength (Gibbs, Gore et al. 2010; Lynch and Stretesky 2011). This caused some scholars to say criminology risked painting a limited picture of contemporary crimes (Halsey 2004; South 1998). It is therefore important to orient the criminological focus on blind spots of nation states and green crimes are a striking example of those (Edwards, Edwards and Fields 1996; Gunningham, Norberry and McKillop 1995; White 2003). This requires thinking about both geographical and temporal dimensions to harm, evoking a more abstract and hidden victim (Croall 2009; Goodey 2005). Similarly, this implies an analysis of the causes of transnational environmental crime, even when those reside in everyday processes in our society. This can help address the knowledge gap about the nature and extent of illegal trade in waste and natural resources and the relationships of illegal traders with the legal market. A continued focus of criminology on environmental degradation allows the further re-examination of traditional roles of governments, corporations and civil society. This requires looking beyond the classical – and inherently limited – data of the enforcement agencies and reaching out for alternative perspectives to explain transnational environmental crime. Both the transnational and environmental dimension undoubtedly present challenges for future studies, but the 'greening' and 'globalizing' of criminology is necessary to continue charting the territory of transnational environmental crime.

Chapter 4
Governing Transnational Environmental Crime

Introduction

The previous chapter focused on explaining transnational environmental crime. It made clear that in studying the social organization and underlying causes, it is important to identify the involved actors while paying attention to both local and global dynamics that shape transnational flows of waste and natural resources. This chapter continues the theoretical exploration started in the previous chapter but now shifts the focus to the governance of transnational environmental crime. Environmental governance is often linked to scarce regulation, limited awareness and insufficient international cooperation especially in face of the high profits and potential involvement of organized crime (Elliott 2009). Reducing the motives and opportunities for illegal and legal but risky behaviour that harms the environment is a challenge for regulation and enforcement (Gibbs, McGarrell and Axelrod 2010).

By means of a literature review this chapter suggests how the remaining gaps in theory and research on environmental governance could be remedied and points toward implications for future research. This chapter[1] draws upon theory and research into different dimensions of transnational environmental crime to argue that environmental governance is multi-stakeholder, multi-sector and multilevel and that it is often unclear how different governance actors and approaches interact. This chapter argues that it is important to study the governance of transnational environmental crime and gain insights into its characteristics. First, the focus is on law enforcement responses to environmental harm. Second, the chapter focuses on voluntary approaches and environmental self-regulation by corporations. Third, different models of hybrid environmental regulation are discussed. Fourth, an

1 This chapter is an adaptation of Bisschop, L. (2011). Transnational environmental crime: exploring (un)charted territory. In M. Cools, B. De Ruyver, M. Easton, L. Pauwels, P. Ponsaers, T. Vander Beken, F. Vander Laenen, G. Vande Walle, A. Verhage, G. Vermeulen and G. Vynckier (eds), *EU Criminal Justice, Financial & Economic Crime: New Perspectives*, Governance of Security Research Papers (Vol. 5, pp. 155–83). Antwerpen: Maklu. This theoretical article was reproduced with permission of the publisher Maklu and was updated to include more recent insights from studies on environmental regulation and governance. This redrafting of the theoretical chapter was further inspired by the theoretical framework used for the case studies on the illegal trade in e-waste (Chapter 5) and tropical timber (Chapter 6).

illustration of environmental governance follows with a discussion of waste and natural resources as transnational environmental crime commodities. Lastly, a brief conclusion follows.

Law Enforcement Responses to Environmental Harm

In dealing with environmental issues, law enforcement options range between criminal, administrative and civil measures (Pink 2013). There are a number of difficulties in dealing with environmental issues through the criminal justice system (Alvazzi del Frate et al. 1999; White 2008; Gilbert and Russell 2002; Hall 2013; Shover and Aaron 2005). Firstly, there is the problem of liability. It is hard to hold one person responsible, let alone a company that has seen frequent management changes. Some countries also do not have a criminal liability for corporations (Heine 2006; Faure and Heine 2005). In the absence of strict liability, it is also difficult to assess the individual harmfulness of actions by different actors and to definitely prove the chain of evidence in prosecution. The potential overlap between legal and illegal actors and circumstances makes it hard to trace the chain of evidence and obscures the connections for regulators.

Secondly, the investigation of environmental crime is demanding for the criminal justice system. It requires expertise as well as sufficient resources for infrastructure and staff because environmental cases often cross jurisdictions, involve many actors and are technically complex. Environmental issues can involve police agencies as well as inspectorates and customs. In dealing with specific cases, these different authorities then need to overcome possible conflicting finalities and approaches. Trade liberalism and border control do not always go hand in hand (Brack 2002; Brack and Hayman 2002). The risk of regulatory capture is also present (Zinn 2002). Moreover, the complexity of transnational environmental crime requires sensitivity to different types of and motivations for offending.

Thirdly, even if a case leads to prosecution, it is often difficult to prove culpability or negligence beyond reasonable doubt. Trials can be lengthy and costly. When sentenced, the imposed fines are often minimal compared to the profit, rendering it easy for companies to absorb the fines or pass them to consumers. Overall, criminal trials for environmental cases are rare. Since the onus of proof in criminal cases is quite high, police or prosecutors could choose a case based on the better chance of winning a case rather than its environmentally harmful nature (Crawford 2006). The advantage of criminal responses is that is has better legal safeguards and is more authoritative, assuming to lead to more effective law enforcement (Pink 2013). Civil cases or administrative approaches might in fact allow more timely and more flexible responses and have a lesser burden of proof. Administrative cases are generally quicker because measures such as warnings or the revoking of licenses are at hand for regulatory agencies. However, these are sometimes perceived as a weak response, especially when it concerns breaches worthy of escalation or repeat offenders. Much in the same way, civil cases are seen as a weaker response, although these are often appropriate for minor breaches and have a lesser burden of proof (Pink 2013).

All of this, however, assumes the behaviour was criminalized or regulated in the first place and this is not always likely as was illustrated earlier. Different cultural traditions can also have opposing views on what is criminal or illegal. Private property rights often frame the possibilities for environmental protection (White 2008). Even when the behaviour is part of international treaties, the value of protecting the environment is often still balanced with issues of trade protection. Moreover, signing an international convention or treaty does not equal its actual implementation or enforcement by the signatory states (Alvazzi del Frate et al. 1999). Especially developing countries might lack the resources for adequate enforcement, which explains the investment of international organizations like UNDP in capacity building. Even when legislation does exist in one country, the chance of 'country shopping' remains. Given the global effect of environmental damages, there is little use in dealing with transnational environmental crime nationally when initiatives are not harmonized on an international level (Carrabine et al. 2009). An attempt to harmonize environmental legislation and law enforcement has occurred since the 1970s (for example United Nations or European Union initiatives), but there is still ample room for improvement. Limited enforcement is often seen as a great weakness of international environmental law, but the arising enforcement networks and partnerships between international organizations might be better equipped to deal with the complex topic of transnational environmental crime. Sustained socio-legal research about actual practices and outcomes of environmental prosecution could shed more light on this (Gibbs, McGarrell and Axelrod 2010; White 2010). More recently, even the possibilities of having a world environmental court or dealing with environmental cases in the international courts are being explored (Hall 2013; 2011; Vande Walle and Bisschop 2012).

Those transnational environmental crimes that have been subject to international conventions[2] often put an important governance responsibility on nation states. Traditionally, their government institutions have the central responsibility for crime and security (Shearing and Johnston 2010). In fact, many environmental issues have been dealt with through command and control regulation, assuming uniform compliance backed up by punishment (Grabosky and Gant 2000). This, however, provides only part of the solution to the complexity of environmental problems (Gunningham 2004). Faced with the globalized supply chain and transnational environmental problems, governments are challenged in drafting appropriate governance frameworks to regulate these global dimensions (Sassen 1996). Other actors, such as corporations, can then play a role in less formal, voluntary approaches.

2 For waste, this for instance refers to the Basel Convention, Montreal Convention and the European Waste Shipment Regulation (WSR) and Waste Electric and Electronic Equipment (WEEE) Directive.

Voluntary Approaches to Environmental Harm

Some claim the responsibility of a firm is the mere maximization of profit (Friedman 1970). Others see the potential of business in addressing complex problems which governments and civil society actors fail to perceive and address. Examples of these are more informal approaches to address environmental issues where corporations regulate themselves (Braithwaite and Fisse 1987) or when they cooperate with various stakeholders when establishing control institutions. Possible strategies are information, self-regulation, incentives, environmental management systems and environmental reporting[3] (Grabosky and Gant 2000; Haines 1997). These are so called 'responsabilization' strategies which relate to the 'basic sociological truth that the most important processes producing order and conformity are mainstream social processes, located within the institutions of civil society and not the uncertain threat of legal sanctions' (Garland 2001, p. 126).

Gunningham, Kagan and Thornton (2003) list several reasons for firms to set standards that go beyond the legal requirements: to increase profit; to ward off more intrusive regulation; to anticipate future tightening of rules (and avoid costs of that); and to protect the company's reputation and social legitimacy (and avoid adverse publicity). They also note that self-regulation and monitoring is a big investment which mostly big players are able to commit to. Corporations often prefer clarity in regulating their activities out of a concern for a level playing field (Delmas and Young 2009). Some are concerned with their reputation and see self-regulation as a way to distinguish themselves from the bad apples in their sector and a way to avoid these bad apples from free-riding on the image of the sector. In these cases, they sometimes choose to pre-empt state initiative for regulation (Gunningham, Kagan and Thornton 2003). Moreover, self-regulation is a way for corporations to inform consumers about their responsible business which in addition can provide them competitive advantage over firms that do not uphold these high standards.

Whether corporations behave in a socially responsible manner is mediated by a variety of institutional conditions that include: the strength of state regulation or (collective) industrial self-regulation; monitoring of corporations by NGOs or other independent organizations; pressure from consumers, investors and other firms; the presence of institutionalized norms regarding appropriate corporate behaviour; the threat of liabilities; associative behaviour between corporations; and organized dialogue amid corporations and their stakeholders (Campbell 2007; Anton, Deltas and Khanna 2004). The motivation for self-regulation lies both in market-based dynamics (win-win) and in the broader political and social context (Bartley 2007). Niche corporations in the market or those companies that are good at anticipating trends might therefore be more motivated to commit to it (Gunningham, Kagan and Thornton 2003).

---

3 For example, European Pollutant Emission Register; European Eco-label; Eco-Management and Audit Scheme.

There are a number of weaknesses related to these voluntary approaches. First, they assume a basic degree of trust in organizations and their functioning (van de Bunt and Huisman, 1999), which is a bridge too far for many critics of the capitalist system (Tombs 2008). Second, in absence of a credible threat of regulation or taxation, some companies might still be tempted to inflict harm upon the environment (van de Bunt and Huisman, 1999). These compliance strategies also tend to depict corporations as clients rather than possible perpetrators and thus holds the risk of regulatory capture (Alvazzi del Frate et al. 1999).

Several studies have tried to assess the impact of voluntary environmental programs on environmental performance. A study of S&P 500 firms showed that the adoption of environmental management systems had a negative impact on the intensity of toxic releases, especially on firms with bad environmental records (Anton, Deltas and Khanna 2004). A study of ISO 14001, one of the most widely recognized voluntary environmental programs, found that on average these firms pollute less and comply better with governmental regulations (Prakash and Potoski 2006). Other studies show very different results. An analysis of chemical emissions in the US showed that self-policing in the case of the chemical and allied products industry does not reduce emissions more than facilities that do not self-police (Stretesky and Lynch 2009). In a meta-analysis, Darnall and Sides (2008) found that collective voluntary environmental programs do not improve environmental performance. Research on these topics has increased in recent decades, but has not provided conclusive evidence on social and environmental performance of corporations (Sharp and Zaidman 2010). Despite the reliance of environmental policy on self-regulation, it is unclear whether self-regulation actually improves environmental performance. Further studies are needed to shed light on this complexity of influences and collaborations (Peloza and Falkenberg 2009).

Hybrid Environmental Governance Models

The approaches to corporate and environmental misconduct range from criminal law, to administrative law and self-regulation. These strategies involve a number of specific forms of control such as differing informal control options (for example whistle-blowing to the development of training and ethical codes). Some of these strategies aim to convince or advise companies to comply with environmental regulations, whereas others are forms of formal social control that include warnings or shaming, fines, incapacitating reactions (closure of company, withdrawal of license) and even imprisonment. These differing strategies have two different goals, those aimed at punishing bad behaviour, and those aimed at the prevention of harm or the stimulation of good behaviour (Grabosky and Gant 2000; Ponsaers anf Hoogenboom 2004; van de Bunt and Huisman 1999). As mentioned above, each of these approaches has its strengths and weaknesses. Neither mere business' self-regulation nor mere reliance on the criminal justice system is sufficient to deal with transnational environmental crime. In lack of government initiative, not only corporations but also other non-state actors have sought alternative solutions to deal with environmental issues (for example multi-stakeholder initiatives) (Bernstein and Cashore 2007). Third, actors like consumers and non-governmental organizations (NGOs) play a role in governance through labelling and certification initiatives, awareness raising and consumer boycotts.

The focus of scholarly research on these issues has often been on the evaluation of the formal approaches and in particular on those administrative or criminal reactions of police, prosecutors or special investigative services toward environmental crime (Billiet 2009; Ponsaers and De Keulenaer 2003; Struiksma, de Ridder and Winter 2007). In a society where government makes way for more informal means of governance, it is, however, also crucial to study the informal reactions and to evaluate the functioning of the entire regulatory spectrum. This includes a focus on how the different governance approaches, potentially, affect each other. When a corporation commits a crime, a spectrum of reactions arises: governmental reactions (for example withdrawing licenses, criminal prosecution), public reactions (for example shaming in the media, NGO initiatives, different consumption or investments), but also private reactions (for example changes in their structure, the introduction of management systems in corporate policy). These reactions might also interact: when NGOs are aware of a problem, they might inform the media, which might lead the criminal justice system to respond or the corporation to take actions which result in the drop of charges. This interaction of actors and levels is not easy to grasp and it has been a topic of debate amongst scholars.

The following discusses two theoretical models which combine law enforcement responses with voluntary approaches: responsive regulation and networked governance. These hybrid governance models provided inspiration for the governance analysis of the case study about e-waste (Chapter 5) and tropical timber (Chapter 6).

Responsive Regulation

A very influential theoretical model for dealing with corporate crime, and by extension with environmental crime by corporate actors, is the responsive regulatory pyramid. In responsive regulation, the approach is attuned to the motivations and characteristics of particular sectors or situations (Ayres and Braithwaite 1992) avoiding the inflexibility and inefficiency of command and control (Wright and Head 2009). The ground assumption of this model is that the choice of a regulatory strategy should be responsive to what is more appropriate for a given situation, taking into account the strengths and weaknesses of each approach (Braithwaite 2002). There is therefore no standard regulatory reaction. At the basis of the pyramid, there is ample room to act responsibly and for restorative justice.

By allowing corporate actors to self-regulate and having other actors meta-regulate,[4] the intent is to minimize regulatory burdens such as administrative burdens, an oversupply of regulation and excessive costs of compliance (Helm 2006). This requires the corporate actor to own up to responsibilities and is assumed to be the most successful in going beyond compliance (Gunningham, Grabosky and Sinclair 1998). The social context of the corporation, such as environmental organizations, suppliers, customers, neighbours and the media, also have an important role to play in this regulatory scheme (White 2008). It is difficult to know, of course, to what extent corporations actually care about their image[5] and to what extent the public actually cares about corporate images especially when the environmental damage is distant from their own 'backyard' (Carrabine et al. 2009).

The idea behind responsive regulation is to allow for flexibility. As Ayres and Braithwaite (1992, p. 6) note, this mean that 'Regulators will do their best by indicating a willingness to escalate intervention up those pyramids or to deregulate down the pyramids in response to the industry's performance in securing regulatory objectives. ... Regulatory agencies will be able to speak more softly when they are perceived as carrying big sticks'. Criminal law then equals 'wielding a big stick', as a back-up plan for the compliance model, assuming the regulatory pyramid only works when deterrence is at the top (Huisman, van Erp and van Wingerde 2009). In contrast, Baldwin and Black (2008, p. 63) state '[t]he constant threat of more punitive sanctions at the top can stand in the way of voluntary compliance at the bottom of the pyramid'. Crawford (2006) doubts whether the pyramid reflects empirical reality and sees a number of vulnerabilities: the risk of clouding accountability, regulatory capture, net-widening and regulatory overload.

In his publication *Regulatory Capitalism*, Braithwaite (2008) acknowledges the shortcomings of the pyramidal model and goes in search of a new metaphor which better envisages the governance aspect of reactions to corporate harm. The focus is then less on the vertical dimension of supervision and more on networks of organizations (van Erp 2008). In these networks various actors are involved, who could well be driven by different objectives, interpret behaviour differently and might respond in various ways. An important role in policing the environment might for example be played by environmental agencies, but they need to balance different interests (economic and environmental considerations) and act as advisories to help companies abide by the law even though they are at the same time responsible for their prosecution (South 1998; 2007). The state is then just one actor within this hybrid governance arrangement, since corporate and civil society actors also play a role. A prerequisite remains the possibility of escalation

4 Meta-regulation is regulated self-regulation which means that controls happen on a higher level either by third actors, by government or through public scrutiny, and are based on the own management system of the corporation (Gunningham, Kagan and Thornton 2003).

5 Small companies, who could very well be heavy polluters, for example, are very flexible in changing their name and location and might thus be less afraid of prosecution.

to punitive reactions when actors fail to regulate themselves and/or do not own up to their responsibility (Braithwaite 2008).

Networked Governance

Networked governance is the second model that embraces the idea of governance arrangements that go beyond the nation state paradigm and looks at the role played by non-state actors such as corporations and NGOs (Mazerolle and Ransley 2006; Wood 2006; Wood and Shearing 2007). The network governance model looks beyond the safety and security context and pays attention to other dimensions at play, such as the social problems or political and economic elements that contribute to the phenomenon. Nodal or networked governance theory looks at new developments in contemporary society, such as interdependence, globalization and transformation, and presumes these developments cause new policy arrangements to arise with new roles for different policy actors (industry, government, scientists, NGOs and so on). Particular attention is paid to the global elements at play and the focus is on networks, nodes, hybrids, spaces of flows and spaces of places (Castells 2000; Spaargaren, Mol and Buttel 2006; Urry 2003). This refers to the new institutional make-up of society, with other representations of space and place. Shearing and Wood (2003, p. 411) wrote that 'in order to gain adequate understanding of new developments in governance, and the new features of the world that these developments reflect, we must shift our focus away from state-centered lines of inquiry'. Spaargaren, Mol and Buttel (2006) further exemplified this by applying global governance theory to environmental flows. As an example of an environmental flow they discuss international shipments of waste, which cross boundaries of sovereignty, regulation and governance. They propose to take environmental flows as a case study for governance research.

Following the network governance model, researching the governance of environmental flows requires looking at various actors in the playing field across different geographical borders. Due to changes in society, economic actors, NGOs, scientists, international organizations and others are increasingly constitutive partners of governance arrangements at multiple policy levels. Nowadays, markets sometimes behave like nation states (for example transnational corporations who set high environmental standards for production) and non-state actors sometimes fill gaps left open by civil institutions (Vande Walle and Ponsaers 2006). Therefore, the basic assumption in networked governance is that different stakeholders act together towards commonly defined goals. Governance is then a complex web of international, multinational, national, regional, local, political and non-governmental institutions and private actors (Castells 2000; Oosterveer 2006, p. 268). Central to this approach is the governance role of non-state actors, which also implies a role that goes beyond a simple partnership with the state, but encompasses the true taking up of responsibilities. There could also be coalitions of non-state actors, which set regulatory standards and enforcement, independent of governments but not limited to self-regulation (Bartley 2007). Others have referred to this as plural and fragmented policing (Loader 2002), nodal and networked governance (Shearing and Johnston 2010) or polycentric or decentred governance, referring to the multiple sites of regulation (Black 2008). Holley, Gunningham and Shearing (2012) applied this idea to environmental issues, referring to the concept 'new environmental governance'.[6]

In many security matters, states are no longer the single governing actors (Wood and Dupont 2006). Third parties and governance networks can have effective ways of dealing with transnational and environmental issues (Crawford 2006). The (changing) role of the different actors in implementation and compliance and these (new) networks and governance processes in the illegal flows of environmental goods (waste and natural resources) are interesting to study (Jänicke 2006; Mol and Spaargaren 2006). The governance of environmental flows is then not limited to national policies, given the inherently transnational nature of environmental issues. Neither does this focus on flows mean that the local level can be neglected.[7] It is important to 'de-anonymize' the flows and to make the interconnections and processes within them transparent. This implies to study how the governance of environmental flows takes place in practice, who takes up the responsibility for governing those flows and what the function of the state is (Shearing and Wood 2003; Braithwaite 2008; Gille 2006; Jänicke 2006). Is the state's role a matter of setting the course, monitoring the direction and correcting deviations from the course and thus a movement away from hierarchy, command, interventionism, a rolling back of the state (Crawford 2006)? To provide an empirical underlining, this book examines how this governance of security framework – in the sense of preventing illegal transports of e-waste and tropical timber from occurring[8] – is organized. Before we move to this empirical analysis, the next section intends to illustrate some of the above concerns by exploring the governance of waste and natural resources as transnational environmental crime commodities.

Governance of Waste and Natural Resources

A look into the regulatory practice of waste and natural resources could contribute to building transnational environmental governance theory. The following illustrates some of the elements that could be taken into account when studying the governance of the illegal trade of waste and natural resources. The in-depth analysis of the cases of e-waste and tropical timber follows in Chapters 5 and 6.

---

6 They detected five basic characteristics: collaboration of different stakeholders; participation of different groups on different levels of governance; deliberation about the goals and practice of governance; learning from practice; and accountability.

7 The intertwining of these global and local elements is sometimes referred to as 'glocal'.

8 It is not a reference to the general governance of economic flows or trade.

The international political response to the risks and threats which accompany the waste problem was the adoption of preventive instruments such as the Basel Convention (1989). The Basel Convention specifies that information on the contents and destination of waste and prior permission from the importing country is needed before transport. It even foresees the ban of toxic waste shipments to industrialized nations. Some countries (for example United States) have, however, failed to ratify this amendment, which hampers the functioning of the convention. Moreover, the Basel Convention did not define the basic concepts to distinguish between one company's waste and another's recyclable material. The European Union has drafted more stringent regulations regarding waste. As a consequence of this, EU governments inspect ships and open containers in their territory to check the contents. The European Waste Shipment Regulation (WSR) for example aims to prevent illegal export of e-waste by requesting a test report and proof that the products have a market. Of course, only a small percentage of freight is checked. Estimates shows about 15 per cent of all waste transports is in violation (van Erp and Huisman 2010). Looking at the complete legislative picture, there is a lot of regulation on waste (possession) with limited blind spots (brokers being one of them, see Bruinsma 1996) but this legislative maze also causes a lot of confusion and is characterized by eminent liability problems. It is important in this respect to standardize definitions (for example of what is waste and what is recyclable) and increase the strength of governmental action through better intelligence-based enforcement and inter-agency cooperation. Even within the EU some member states fail to regularly inspect waste shipments, which increases the likeliness of 'port hopping'. A solution could be to look at the broader supply chain of e-waste (producers, recycling businesses) to prevent the externalization of risk which is the approach taken by the Dutch Inspectorate of the Environment. Eliminating or minimizing the use of harmful substances in the production of electronics is likely to be a more effective solution to environmental problems (Lazarus 1995; van Erp and Huisman 2010).

For natural resources and endangered species, the Convention on the International Trade in Endangered Species of Fauna and Flora (CITES) tried to harmonize definitions and objectives. It has for a long time been the only international framework for licensing imports and exports of natural resources focused on endangered species. Some flaws of the CITES system have been identified, such as the exemption for modified ivory and the inefficient structure for Appendix II, but it remains an initiative that is very comprehensive. CITES has been implemented more stringently in the EU legislative framework. The interpretations of this legislation between different countries (even within the EU) and also between authorities, however, still vary as does their level of commitment to tackle the problem. Once again monitoring and control are hampered due to issues of liability, as well as the difficulty of determining whether the transported goods are illegal. Transports of natural resources often have false labels to disguise their true content, such as labelling illegally caught endangered species as bred in captivity or labelling illegal timber as legally harvested. This causes considerable challenges for customs officials or other inspecting agencies. Without efficient reporting structures with a clear division of labour and effective information exchange through harmonized databases and intelligence sharing, many of these systems risk staying a mere paper tiger (Crossin, Hayman and Taylor 2003). Also other commodity tracking systems for natural resources exist, but CITES is the most comprehensive one. For timber, the International Tropical Timber Agreements[9] (ITTA) exists as well – which created the International Tropical Timber Organization (ITTO) – although these are primarily aimed to promote trade and have a focus on tropical timber as a commodity. Voluntary timber initiatives such as the Forest Stewardship Council (FSC) have been important, although still only dealing with part of the market. More recently the EU Timber Regulation has put the issue of illegal timber trade on the agenda.[10] International agreements or treaties do not exist, neither do tracking or reporting systems for timber trade.

Another difficulty is that environmental harm is extremely mobile. It is easy to imagine how this can cause tension between the transnational nature of the crimes and the national nature of jurisdictions. Due to repeated outsourcing, unscrupulous operators, circuitous routes and free-trade zones the transference of harm is facilitated (Heckenberg 2010). Polluting a river or deforestation can have consequences across the border, while air pollution easily transgresses national boundaries. Despite additional legislation and innovative enforcement, the illegal shipments of waste and natural resources will remain difficult to detect. The scope of the problem together with the number of actors and transferences is too challenging to rely on enforcement alone. Therefore, the combination of crime prevention, third-party and self-regulation and state intervention is advisable (Gibbs, McGarrell and Axelrod 2010). Preventative initiatives could involve end-of-life or product design strategies or internalizing the costs of environmental harm. Similarly self-regulation, certification programs, public awards or shaming and consumer awareness could prevent additional environmental damage. A difficult factor there is the victims' unawareness that their immediate environment was harmed as a consequence of illegal dumping of waste, deforestation or the like: harm is done to ecosystems, plants and animals as well as to future generations, who are unlikely to complain. For waste in particular, overcoming the incentive structure connected to the negative value of waste is required. For natural resource crimes such as for example illegal timber, this requires overcoming the economic dis-incentives of sustainable production. For both waste and natural resources it is a challenge to design incentive mechanisms with a minimum of criminogenic and counterproductive effects. Controlling and monitoring waste and natural resources as transnational environmental crime commodities is at the nexus of

9 The International Tropical Timber Agreement was originally adopted in 1983 under the auspices of the United National Conference on Trade and Development (UNCTAD) and was updated in 1994 and 2006. It created the International Tropical Timber Organization (ITTO).

10 The US has the Lacey Act.

law enforcement, administrative control (licensing), industrial self-regulation and surveillance by NGOs, possibly causing the boundaries between the responsibilities of these organizations to become blurred.

Conclusion

This chapter discussed theoretical developments in the governance of transnational environmental crime. This made clear that research needs to be sensitive to transnational as well as local elements influencing the governance of crimes. 'What happens to the conceptual apparatus of criminological inquiry and how salient are its taken for granted terms – crime, law, justice, state, sovereignty – at a time when global change and conflict may be eroding some elements at least of the international framework of states it has taken for granted?' (Hogg 2002, p. 195). Criminal policy was long dominated by public institutions, but in face of these worldwide complexities a shift was required from single governments to governance arrangements involving multiple actors (Loader and Sparks 2002; Sheptycki 2007). In environmental matters, new actors such as corporations and NGOs take up responsibilities formerly reserved for the nation state (Bartley 2007; Gunningham, Kagan and Thornton 2003; Holley and Gunningham 2011). This resulted in various regulatory hybrids where responses to (transnational) environmental crime may come from criminal justice system, but also from corporate self-regulation and NGOs.

Rather than merely assuming that this evolution towards multilevel and multi-actor governance took place, we need to document this and analyse what is happening in the world of environmental governance (Crawford 2006; Aas 2007; Elliott 2011). To facilitate such an analysis, this study examines the governance framework for transnational environmental crime. In particular, this refers to the framework that aims to control and prevent the illegal trade in tropical timber and e-waste. Inspired by literature on environmental and corporate regulation and governance (Braithwaite 2008; Mazerolle and Ransley 2006; Braithwaite 2002; Gunningham, Grabosky and Sinclair 1998; Wright and Head 2009; Wood 2006), the following questions support the empirical analysis:[11] Which government, corporate and third-party actors take up responsibilities in governance? Do governance actors interact within a governance network and/or pyramid, and is their interaction cooperative, competitive or non-existent? Does a government or a private actor take up a leading role? Are there individuals or groups who are currently not mobilized in these governance processes in spite of their relevant knowledge, capacities and resources (missing nodes)? This implies an analysis of the separate governance actors and their characteristics – how the nodes problematize the topic (mentalities), what they set as objectives (finalities) and

---

11 See Chapter 2: Methodology for the sub-questions that are asked in each case analysis.

what strategies they use to reach that goal – before moving to an analysis of their interactions (nodal-networked governance analysis, Shearing and Johnston 2010). The analysis also pays attention to the local and global context that shapes the governance arrangements throughout the environmental flows (Aas, 2007; Spaargaren, Mol and Bruyninckx, 2006; White, 2011).

In conclusion, various institutional responses to ecological harms have created a regulatory hybrid where responses to (transnational) environmental issues can be found within government institutions such as the criminal justice system, but also involve regulatory initiatives in interaction with corporations and NGOs (Braithwaite 2008; Shearing and Johnston 2010). The regulatory actors and initiatives are also increasingly reaching across the geographical boundaries of states and have shifted upwards to transnational levels. These new governance models have yet to be examined sufficiently in the criminological literature. By looking at the characteristics and interactions of the governance actors and processes for two types of transnational environmental crime, it should be possible to identify their strengths and weaknesses in governing environmental harm. Although empirically challenging, this assessment can help to expose the limitations and possibilities of different sites of environmental governance.

Chapter 5
The Illegal Trade in E-Waste

Introduction

This chapter[1] discusses the results of the multi-method qualitative case study[2] on the illegal trade in e-waste. The analysis focuses on the Port of Antwerp, with particular attention for the trade in e-waste between Belgium and Ghana.

The structure of this chapter is as follows. First, the scope of the illegal trade in e-waste in Europe and in the Port of Antwerp is discussed, together with an overview of the challenges this brings for data gathering. Second, attention is paid to the victimization associated with the illegal trade in e-waste (Bisschop and Vande Walle 2013). Third, the chapter analyses the social organization and emergence of illegal transport of electronic waste (Bisschop 2012) and the legal-illegal interfaces in e-waste flows. These results are integrated with findings on the push, pull and facilitating factors in these flows to examine the motivations and opportunities that shape the flows of e-waste. Fourth, this chapter analyses the governance reality of the illegal trade in e-waste (Bisschop 2013). It examines which actors are involved in this governance framework and provides insights into the facilitating and hindering factors for governance throughout the e-waste flows. Besides analysing the governance actors individually, particular attention is given to their interaction.

The Scale of Illegal Transports of E-Waste in Europe and Belgium

Measuring environmental crime is complex (Gibbs and Simpson 2009) and measuring illegal transports of e-waste is no exception. This is a phenomenon about which there is little official data, despite this issue being on the international[3]

---

1 This chapter is based on the following three publications, which were used with permission of the publishers. Bisschop, L. (2012). Is it all going to waste? Illegal transports of e-waste in a European trade hub. *Crime, Law and Social Change*, 58(3), 221–49; Bisschop, L. (2013). Go with the e-waste flows. The governance reality of illegal transports of e-waste in a European trade hub. In P. van Duyne and J. Spencer (eds), *Organised Crime by Hindsight, Corruption and Crisis in Enforcement* (pp. 393–424). Nijmegen: Wolf Legal Publishers; Bisschop, L. and Vande Walle, G. (2013). Environmental victimization and conflict resolution. A case study of e-waste. In T. Wyatt, R. Walters and D. Westerhuis (eds), *Debates in Green Criminology: Power, Justice and Environmental Harm* (pp. 34–54). Basingstoke: Palgrave Macmillan.

2 See Chapter 2 Methodology.

3 For example, Basel Convention, Interpol, IMPEL, EU.

as well as national[4] policy agenda. Illegal transports of e-waste presents multiple challenges for data gathering and analysis. The Secretariat of the Basel Convention keeps track of the hazardous waste transports of their parties. This information is, however, not always readily available: not all parties to the convention report meticulously and some do not report at all.[5] The European Union has a yearly reporting system for shipments of hazardous and problematic waste, but does not have a common database for waste transports in breach of regulation.

The reported data on e-waste of both the Basel Secretariat and the EU is generally of poor quality (Fischer et al. 2008). Possible reasons for this are: (1) the waste codes are not harmonized and e-waste can be covered by different codes in the system; (2) the codes are interpreted differently across the reporting parties, making country comparisons difficult;[6] (3) e-waste transports are often transported under the heading of 'recyclable electronics' and are not reflected in e-waste statistics;[7] (4) within one country different organizations (inspectorates, customs, administration, police) report to the European Commission leading to possible double reporting;[8] (5) European targets are based on kilograms of waste controlled, which distorts the figures and the effectiveness of the controls in avoiding environmental harm;[9] (6) EU member states' official take-back systems only account for a portion of the discarded EEE.[10] The amount of Used Electric and Electronic Equipment (UEEE) and Waste Electric and Electronic Equipment (WEEE) from corporate consumers is unknown as is the size of the second-hand market (VROM-inspectie 2011). Moreover, the data gathered by the EU and the Basel Secretariat provide information about reported movements of hazardous waste and not necessarily about illegal transports. Existing reports of illegal transports are thus a result of the controls rather than a reflection of the actual illegal transports occurring. As an example, controls by all Belgian inspectorates

4 For example, Belgian National Security Plan 2008–11 (p. 7) and 2012–15 (p. 15).

5 It is sometimes possible however to estimate the hazardous waste transports of non-reporting countries based on import and export data of others (Sander and Schilling 2010; Wielenga 2010).

6 The reporting requirement in e-waste regulation will be detailed later.

7 As an example, only 20,000 tonnes of e-waste is mentioned in the EU 2001–03 statistics. Given that the estimated generation in the EU is 7 million tonnes this seems a rather small figure.

8 This is likely to apply to Belgium, since different federal and regional authorities have their own responsibilities in waste transport matters. Waste transit is a federal responsibility; waste export and import is a regional responsibility; notifications data is collected by the Flemish public waste authority (*Openbare Vlaamse Afvalstoffenmaatschappij – OVAM*).

9 'A fridge weighs a lot more than an iPod, but the latter are the most interesting because they contain the precious metals' (civil society respondent 14).

10 'The collection target of 4 kg per person per year does not properly reflect the amount of WEEE arising in individual Member States' (European Commission 2011). With a 45 per cent share of the e-waste for Flanders, the official take-back system Recupel is amongst the best of the EU class, according to a Belgian government respondent.

are at a maximum since 2007–08 – given the available staff – and therefore the reports might be more a reflection of the limited resources than of the actual flows.

With the above data challenges in mind, it should be understandable that the scope of the illegal transports of e-waste globally, on a European level or within the research setting of the Port of Antwerp, can only be represented by *best guesstimates*. The data on illegal transports of e-waste provided in this chapter are therefore given for illustration purposes and should not be regarded as incontestable figures. Many of these statistics are intangible, because there is no frame of reference. Gathering global data about e-waste transports is therefore necessarily a matter of patchwork. It does, however, provide a general idea about the scope and the directions of the transports. In what follows, a picture is painted of the scope of the illegal flows of e-waste within the EU. This is contextualized with global information about (legal) flows and generation of e-waste.

The EU and (E-)Waste

Shipments of waste within and out of the EU-15 increased from 2.7 million tonnes in 1997 to 8.3 million tonnes in 2003 (Fischer et al., 2008, p. 39). These increases may be a result of additional control efforts and additional reporting by countries and do not necessarily reflect the actual growth in waste shipments. Waste transports make up about 15 per cent of all transports within the EU (Kraan, Nijssen, Dols and Huijbregts 2006; IMPEL-TFS 2012).[11] Most waste transports stay within the EU or take place between member countries of the Organization for Economic Cooperation and Development (OECD). Of total waste transports 83 per cent is meant for recovery and 17 per cent for disposal. However, countries provide very limited information about the amounts or the final destination of goods, making it difficult to assess trends. Based on the Basel Convention reporting, Wielenga (2010, p. 4) concludes that '[t]here is no evidence that significant amounts of hazardous wastes are being transferred from richer countries to poorer countries'. Other findings mention that 51 per cent of shipments to non-OECD countries are illegal (IMPEL-TFS 2006).[12][13] The illegal transports of waste reported to the European Commission increased from 2001 to 2005: between 6,000 and 47,000

11 IMPEL-TFS is a subgroup of the European Network for the Implementation and Enforcement of Environmental Law (IMPEL) that focuses on the inspection and enforcement of Transfrontier Shipments of Waste.

12 This percentage is based on limited action periods by IMPEL-TFS partners across Europe. Belgium, with the ports of Antwerp, Zeebrugge, Ostend and Ghent, was one of the participating member states.

13 Between March and May 2009, 64 countries in Europe, Asia/Pacific and Africa participated in the World Customs Organisation initiative 'Demeter'. This targeted illegal transboundary movements of hazardous waste from Europe to Asia-Pacific and Africa. It resulted in 57 seizures (totally 30,000 tonnes and 1,500 pieces of illegal hazardous waste) of which the majority occurred in Belgium, the Netherlands and Italy (World Customs Organization 2009).

tonnes of illegal shipments are reported yearly. This equals just 0.2 per cent of the notified waste and therefore likely represents only a fraction of the actual transports (European Environment Agency 2009, p. 11). As mentioned earlier, this could well be due to more enforcement efforts or more meticulous reporting by particular member states and does not necessarily imply an increase in shipments.

The most important member states for shipments of e-waste – import, export and transit – are Germany, the Netherlands, Belgium and the United Kingdom and these countries also register the most illegal transports. Part of these flows might, however, simply be a result of economic and geographic realities, because these countries have economically significant ports and function as a transit for inland Europe.[14] Rotterdam and Antwerp have been labelled as hubs for (illegal) waste shipments (de Rijck 2011; Huisman and van Erp 2013), but given that these ports serve as shipping routes to Africa and China, the high number of waste transports to non-OECD countries could – in part – be a consequence of the economic and geographic reality of these ports. According to both corporate and governmental respondents, these ports are victims of their own law enforcement policies: ports in Spain, Italy and France hardly ever exercise any control over illegal e-waste transports thereby reducing their likelihood of having high statistics (van Erp and Huisman 2010).

Note that there is flexibility in the routes the illegal transports follow. As soon as more stringent controls are in place in one European port, the transports move to another port. The major shipping lines have storage facilities in different ports to allow these deviations. According to the respondents interviewed for this research, this happens between the ports of Rotterdam, Antwerp, Hamburg, Felixstowe, Le Havre and Bilbao.

Besides these trade and trade control data, figures about WEEE generation are a source of information. The EU's e-waste generation is estimated to grow 3 to 5 per cent because of increased use of electrical and electronic equipment,[15] adding up to 10.5 million tonnes, or 15 to 20 kg of electronic and electric equipment brought onto the market per capita per annum (Crem 2008). By 2017, an estimated annual volume of 65.4 million tonnes of electronics will be end-of-life on a global scale (Duan et al. 2013). About 7 per cent of this is registered as WEEE exports and up to 33 per cent is separately collected for environmentally sound treatment

14 Geographically, Switzerland, a land without seaports, relies on exports to neighbouring EU countries. It is known to ship waste directly to Belgium, Bulgaria, France, Germany, Poland, Italy, Romania, Serbia, Spain and the Netherlands, but indirectly transports to Africa, Gabon, Nigeria, Brazil and Togo. Germany has an own seaport (Hamburg), but given the size of the country and the distance to Hamburg it is often economically more feasible to ship goods through the ports of Rotterdam and Antwerp from the nearby *Länder* (for example Northrein-Westfalen). These shipments are not necessarily problematic or illegal, but have proven to be worrisome in the past (Espejo 2010).

15 Studies are trying to forecast future global generation of e-waste (Williams et al. 2010).

(Environmental Investigation Agency 2011). 'A part of the other two thirds is potentially still going to landfills and to sub-standard treatment sites in or outside the European Union. Illegal trade of electrical and electronic waste to non-EU countries continues to be identified at EU borders (European Commission 2011).[16] Reports indicate that the flows of WEEE/UEEE go from Western Europe and the USA to West Africa and South East Asia (Crem 2008; Fischer et al. 2008).[17] Transports towards Africa are most likely to be e-waste or low quality second-hand products (European Environment Agency 2009).[18] There are no details available about the final destination of the components or metal scrap, but in Ghana the motherboards of the dismantled computers were found to be sold as a whole for export to Nigeria or China, whereas other recovered metals are used in local industries or sold for export (Prakash and Manhart 2010). Data on e-waste transports are inevitably guesstimates, but provide the necessary contextualization for discussing the Belgian research setting.

Import, Export and Transit on the Belgian E-Waste Market

First, a brief introduction about the role of the Port of Antwerp in (e-)waste transports is provided. Thereafter, the import, export and transit of e-waste in Belgium are discussed in terms of both scope and geographical orientation.

Antwerp is an economically significant trade and waste hub (Baker et al., 2004), but mainly as a port of transit: 80 per cent of all waste is in transit, whereas only 20 per cent of waste is imported into or exported out of Belgium. A lot of the waste in Antwerp is in transit from Germany, Austria, Switzerland, France and to a lesser extent the Netherlands. The most frequent countries of destination in West Africa are Nigeria, Ghana, Cameroon, Togo and Senegal, partially due to Antwerp's trade connections with this region. As an illustration, Ghana, Benin, Ivory Coast, Liberia and Nigeria import about 250,000 tonnes per annum illegally (Schluep et al. 2011). Besides the West African countries, South East Asia is an important destination for e-waste. The transports of e-waste are partially a result of existing shipping routes, in which Antwerp functions as a port of transit for other (EU) countries, rather than Belgium being the sole source of e-waste. A civil society respondent (S10) was of the opinion that Antwerp functions as 'the rubbish tip' for e-waste and end-of-life vehicles destined for Africa.

16 Similar figures are found in the US, where 25 to 35 per cent of e-waste is recycled (Environmental Protection Agency 2011; Gibbs, McGarrell and Axelrod 2010).

17 Lagos in Nigeria is estimated to receive about 500 containers per month (Puckett and Smith 2002), of which 45 per cent originates in Europe (Crem 2008), 45 per cent the United States and 10 per cent Japan, Israel and others (Puckett et al. 2005). These estimates are based on asset tags on the equipment and on other identifiers.

18 They did so by analysing the amount of television sets exported from the EU and checking the value of the shipments.

The documentary analysis provided a number of facts about e-waste transports with a connection to Antwerp. Data from the Flemish environmental inspectorate (LNE 2010) revealed that the controlled e-waste exports towards Asia had 13 per cent of infractions in 2009 compared with 23 per cent in 2008. According to the inspectorate, this decrease is mainly a result of the decrease in transports from particular expeditors. They were targeted in 2008 for their illegal transports of e-waste and tar containing cable waste. There were increased controls after media attention[19] on e-waste transports to West Africa. Twenty-one shipments with destinations in Ghana, Cameroon and DR Congo were controlled in 2009 and 12 of those contained hazardous waste such as monitors and containing fridges containing chlorofluorocarbon (CFC).[20] In 2010, the federal environmental inspectorate found 35 per cent of inspected transit units, containers and vehicles, to be in breach of legislation (Pensaert 2011). A study of hazardous waste seizures in Hong Kong (RILO 2007, p. 20) mentioned three Belgian shipments of 170 tonnes of used computer monitors, two of which were actually meant for Vietnam: 'The seizure of the transit consignment made in June involved nine 40-foot containers of 125,020 kg of used computer monitors. It was the largest seizure of used computer monitors in one single consignment, amounting to nearly 49 per cent of the total quantity of seizures of waste consignments exported from the EU'. This study found Hong Kong to be a transit port, similar to what can be observed about Antwerp. A hazardous waste inspection project in June and July 2010 (Heiss et al. 2011) found e-waste to be the illegal waste type most frequently encountered. These were wrongly declared as second-hand goods and contained CFCs or cathode ray tube (CRT)[21] television sets or monitors while being described as metal scrap. The routes followed were generally from North America to Asia and from Europe to West Africa and Asia. In the annex of this report, INECE lists the shipping routes encountered during the inspections. Belgium is listed there once as a state of export and multiple times as a state of transit.[22]

The amount of EEE that was introduced in the Belgian market is another indicator of the scale of e-waste transports. In 2008, a total of 141,194 tonnes of household EEE and 26,686 tonnes of commercial EEE was introduced into

19 These media reports exposed the dumping or inhumane 'recycling' of exported 'second hand' fridges, TVs, laptops, PCs and so on and labelled the Port of Antwerp as a true waste hub (Holderbeke 2009).

20 CFC stands for chlorofluorocarbon which was used as a refrigerant. The manufacturing has been phased out by the Montreal Protocol because it contributes to the depletion of the ozone layer and is very hazardous.

21 CRT stands for cathode ray tube and these television sets contain a lot of lead (up to 2.5 kg), mercury and cadmium and are thus hazardous.

22 These transit flows originated in France, Germany, Netherlands, Spain, United Kingdom and Switzerland and went to Nigeria, Tanzania, Ghana, Mali, Ivory Coast, Senegal and Burkina Faso (INECE 2010).

the market of Flanders and about 58,638 tonnes[23] were collected (Schmidt 2004). A share of the WEEE is first collected in the legitimate recycling systems (for example *Recupel*[24]) and then properly recycled. This accounts for about 40 per cent and is increasing. According to a corporate respondent (C9): 'The Belgian take-back system is regarded as one of the most effective because the centralized system does away with the risk of a race to the bottom in the separate systems, which are more likely to feed into illegal flows of e-waste'. Although this does not represent the total amount of products introduced into the market, this should not necessarily be regarded as problematic, since the disposal of products does not happen at the same rate. As a government respondent (G14) explained, 'an estimated 10 per cent of Belgium e-waste is unaccounted for, either through the official take back system or in other flows. For other European countries, 10 per cent or more is however known to flow into illegal transports of e-waste'. Now that the scale of e-waste transports has been assessed for both the EU and the Belgian setting, this chapter continues by discussing the harmfulness of illegal e-waste flows.

E-Waste and its Victims

A major share of the EEE that is transported to developing countries never makes it to the second-hand market and is dismantled to extract secondary raw materials. All too often this 'recycling' happens in precarious circumstances, where remainders are illegally dumped or burned, releasing toxic components[25] (Eidgenössische Materialprüfungs- und Forschungsanstalt (EMPA) 2009). These toxics easily disseminate in the soil, air or water, often without notice, but are not easily broken down and thus stay there for many years (Baker et al. 2004; European Environment Agency 2009; Brigden, Labunska, Santillo and Johnston 2008; Kuper and Hojsik 2008). This illustrates that the inadequate treatment of e-waste is an immediate and future threat for human health and ecology, for economy and politics. This is why illegal transports of (e-)waste have been identified as a major form of environmental crime by the international community. The discovery of and media attention to dump sites of toxic waste in developing countries during the 1980s and 1990s led to the adoption of international and European legislative

---

23 This corresponds to about 9.52 kg per inhabitant. The WEEE-directive asks for a minimum of 4 kg per inhabitant so this is largely met in Flanders.

24 The WEEE Directive provides a minimum harmonization for producers to take care of the collection and ecologically sound treatment of their products, which is implemented differently throughout the EU member states (WEEE-forum 2008). Recupel is the official take-back system for e-waste in Belgium. Consumers pay a fee for environmentally sound disposal when they buy appliances. Recupel uses these funds to collect the e-waste free of charge.

25 For example lead, cadmium, brominated flame retardants, beryllium or mercury.

frameworks that regulate (e-)waste transports[26]. In reference to the butterfly effect (White 2011), the harm manifests itself locally, regionally, nationally and globally.

The first environmental harm is the impact of the hazardous components upon ecosystems. A second environmental effect is on climate change through the release of greenhouse gasses they contain and especially through the burning of products. For one device the impact is minimal, but the mass quantity of batteries, monitors and so on makes it problematic (LNE 2010). Moreover, the continued exposure to these hazardous substances can make the impact much greater than initially experienced. In merely referring to the effects on the quality of water, air and soil, we risk ignoring the human victims of environmental harm. Speaking in terms of the impact of ecosystems and climate change runs the risk of the phenomenon becoming so-called 'victimless', a term so often related to corporate crime. This seems to 'exempt' the responsible actors from caring for the victims or restoring the harm (Fattah 2010). Victims of the e-waste dumping often do not know they are harmed or accept the harm because they need the e-waste business to survive (Bisschop and Vande Walle 2013). Environmental victimization is not always immediately visible or identifiable, but victims of environmental crime and harm do exist (Hall 2011).

The improper dismantling and recycling of e-waste has a detectable impact on the health of workers. The precarious working circumstances in recycling facilities in Africa and Asia in terms of health, safety and working standards have been illustrated multiple times (Puckett, Westervelt, Gutierrez and Takamiya 2005; Puckett and Smith 2002; Brigden, Labunska, Santillo and Johnston 2008; Kuper and Hojsik 2008; Sepúlveda et al. 2010). In the West African countries of Ghana, Togo, Nigeria and Ivory Coast, adults and children go through heaps of dumped electronic and electrical equipment (EEE) in search of valuable materials, often

---

26 Basel Convention on the control of transboundary movements of hazardous wastes and their disposal (adopted on 22 March 1989, entered into force on 5 May 1992); Basel Convention Ban Amendment, 22 September 1995; Montreal Protocol on ozone-depleting substances, 16 September 1987 (entered into force 1 January 1989); and OECD Decision on control of cross-border movements of waste destined for recovery operations (Decision of the Council C(2001)107/Final (as Amended By C(2004)20)). European Waste Shipment Regulation (Regulation (EC) No 1013/2006 of the European Parliament and of the Council of 14 June 2006 on shipments of waste (OJ L 190, 12.7.2007, 1–98); Directive 2002/96/EC of the European Parliament and of the Council of 27 January 2003 on waste electrical and electronic equipment (WEEE) (OJ L 37, 13.02.2003, pp. 24–38); Directive 2006/12/EC of the European Parliament and of the Council of 5 April 2006 on waste; Directive 2005/32/EC of the European Parliament and of the Council of 6 July 2005 establishing a framework for the setting of eco-design requirements for energy-using products and amending Council Directive 92/42/EEC and Directives 96/57/EC and 2000/55/EC of the European Parliament and of the Council. Bamako Convention on the ban of the import into Africa and the control of transboundary movement and management of hazardous wastes within Africa (Signed 30 January 1991, entered into force on 22 April 1998).

barehanded, and dismantle them without protective equipment. Asia seems to have a somewhat better reputation with (recently) installed treatment facilities, but a corporate respondent (C15) said '[o]ften the façade in Asia is good, but you should not look too far inland'. A Swedish study (Nordbrand 2009) found that e-waste flows are moving to the north of China or to Vietnam and Cambodia, likely as a result of more stringent environmental policy in Southern China. E-waste workers in developing countries, whether in Africa or South East Asia, generally do not have the cultural nor the economic capital to adapt to the environmental harms they face (South 1998). As an NGO respondent explained, many of the e-waste workers, often minors, work at Agbogbloshie for three to five years, after which they return to their families in the North of Ghana, because they can no longer work due to their illnesses, basically returning home to die.

Individuals outside of the e-waste business are also affected by the harmful substances. This includes those living nearby using water contaminated by the dumping or burning, inhaling the toxic smoke of the burning e-waste or eating the crops grown on the toxic soil (Applied Research Institute – Jerusalem (ARIJ) 2012). CRT monitors for example contain lead, which is known to damage the nervous, kidney, blood and reproductive system and affect children's brain development. The monitors contain barium as well, causing brain swelling, heart damage and increased blood pressure (Puckett and Smith 2002). The gathering of soil and water samples through longitudinal studies is pertinent to demonstrate victimization. Through contaminated water, air and soil, environmental victimization travels across local and national borders and may be found in imported fruits and vegetables. Although the quantities are likely to be minimal, the Northern 'not in my backyard' viewpoint backfires in these instances.

An important element to take into account here is the link of illegal e-waste transports to social and ecological inequalities. Vulnerable groups are also those most likely to suffer, because they have a bigger chance of working or living near the polluting factories or landfills (Stretesky and Lynch 1998). Their social, economic and political characteristics make them vulnerable to victimization, resulting in e-waste flowing to the poorest nations (Pellow 2007; White 2011). This differential victimization occurs due to differences in cultural capital and in information about the harmful effect of working and living in a highly polluted environment. Several Ghanaian respondents explained that importers and sellers of second-hand goods constitute an important group of voters, causing politicians to hesitate in drafting more stringent regulation. Moreover, those most severely harmed by the burning and dumping, to be precise those informal workers at the Agbogbloshie dump site, constitute a minority group who travelled to Accra from the north of Ghana in search of alternative sources of income which their region could no longer provide. They are also a religious minority and therefore not the biggest concern for politicians in Accra. This concerns to a certain extent a deliberate neglect of the environmental victims and can even be called environmental racism (Stretesky and Lynch 1998).

Economically and politically these illegal transports of e-waste can also be harmful. The clean-up of dumps is a heavy burden for developing countries. Illegal transports also have economic advantages over legitimate transports due to lower processing costs and therefore adversely affect trade and competition. Facilities that do 'environmentally friendly' collecting and recycling work experience these illegal transports as false competition. Moreover, the informal 'recycling' sector has a lower recovery rate of (precious) metals, which negatively impacts the availability of natural resources. Politically, this illegal trade also undermines the often already weak law enforcement of developing countries through corruption and fraud and mocks international policy-making (Quadri 2010). Finally, there is victimization of Belgian (and other European) consumers because upon buying new electronics they are charged a fee for recycling.

Emergence and Social Organization of Illegal Transports of E-Waste

Factors at different levels and segments of the trade flow have the potential to shape illegal transports of e-waste. Profit is an important etiological factor, but requires further contextualization. Explanations reside at individual, organizational and societal levels of analysis (Gibbs, McGarrell and Axelrod 2010; Clinard and Yeager 1980; Slapper and Tombs 1999). Both in exporting and importing countries and in supply and demand there are motivations and opportunities for illegal e-waste transports. Their nature and scope is impossible to grasp unless the economic, political, cultural and social context are taken into account (van Erp and Huisman 2010). In this study, these are referred to as push, pull and facilitating factors, which together provide the motives and opportunities for actors involved in illegal transports of e-waste. In the analysis of the actors involved, this study follows the flow of the supply chain from producers and consumers through collection and transport to destination. The actors involved can be producers, distributors, consumers, collectors, refurbishers, waste brokers, shipping companies, recyclers, downstream vendors and actors responsible for final disposal (Schluep et al. 2008). Figure 5.1 illustrates the actors that were identified in this case study of e-waste transports in Belgium.

The following explains which of these actors can be a source of leakage into illegal transports of e-waste. This illustrates how illegal e-waste flows start with consumers seeking methods to get rid of their no longer functioning television sets, computers and so on, but extends to e-waste collectors, recyclers and refurbishers in developed as well as developing countries. First, the push factors in production and consumption and in e-waste collection are discussed. Next, the facilitating factors in transport are up for discussion. The analysis then moves across international boundaries and discusses pull factors in countries of destination. For each of these dimensions, this study analyses whether the legal-illegal interface is antithetical or symbiotic (Passas 2002). This analysis will also illustrate how the actors' motivations shape the flows of e-waste on a thin line between legal and

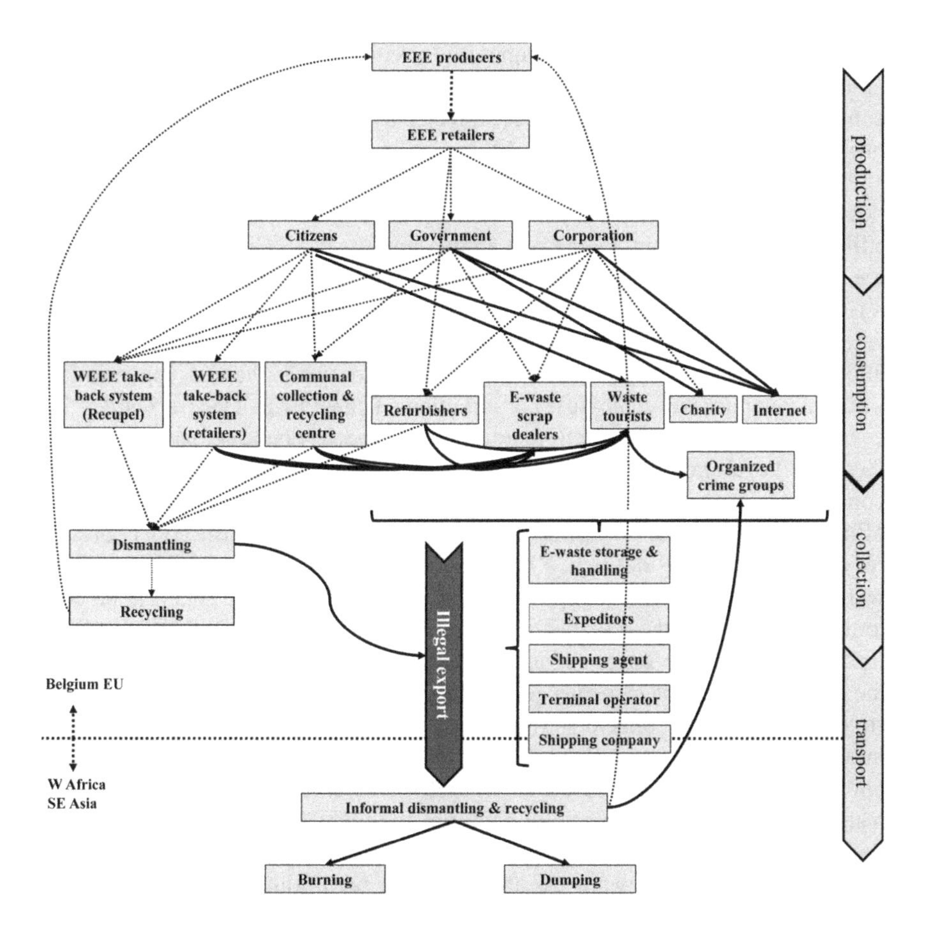

Figure 5.1 Actors involved in e-waste transports

illegal. The analysis of the emergence and social organization of illegal transports of e-waste is thus integrated, because they are inherently intertwined.

Production and Consumption

The historical development of the (e-)waste problem is the first push factor. The volume of waste has grown due to increased production processes and increased consumption of synthetic products. The digital (r)evolution has resulted in a significant increase in the quantity of e-waste, but also the quality has changed given that hazardous substances are used in EEE (Pellow 2007). E-waste is one of the fastest growing waste markets and is likely to increase in the coming years given the exponential consumption of EEE (Environmental Investigation Agency 2011). As a consequence of more stringent waste regulations, waste management prices have risen in industrialized countries, which caused waste to become a global market commodity (Bruinsma 1996; Sanax 1996). Exporting the waste is a way to externalize the harm and create a distance between producers and consumers, on the one hand, and those affected by the dumping or recycling of the products, on the other hand (White 2011).

Rapid, high-tech developments lead to regular replacements of EEE. Many people already have a laptop, personal computer and tablet computer, and might still feel the need to buy the newest edition upon release. Consumption patterns are thus contributing to the e-waste problem. Both producers and consumers have a responsibility in this. Producers can first of all ensure the recycling of e-waste is less harmful by phasing out hazardous components[27] and through eco-design to allow for updates instead of discarding of EEE. Consumers have a responsibility in the economic and ecological consumption of their EEE. Once discarded by consumers, e-waste follows different routes. The motivations and opportunities to feed into illegal transports of e-waste differ for each group of consumers (citizens, corporations, governments). A major part of e-waste from citizens follows the official take-back system (*Recupel*) or goes to the communal waste collection and recycling centres. Besides that, a lot of electronics are collected through retailers who are obliged to take in old products when selling new ones. This is at no cost to the retailer, since the take-back system (*Recupel*) picks up the discarded EEE for free. The costs are integrated into the retail price of the goods and thus paid by the consumer. Citizens may also give e-waste to 'charities' or have it picked up by small-scale informal collectors. Moreover, they throw small electronic appliances into the household waste instead of disposing of them separately.[28] This study did not interview citizen consumers about their involvement in e-waste flows. For insights into their motivations and opportunities, this chapter therefore relies on findings of other studies (Espejo 2010). Citizen consumers are found to be mainly influenced by a lack of awareness about both the harmfulness of e-waste and the existence of environmentally sound recycling systems. Moreover, they might not know about their legal rights and responsibilities. In giving the UEEE to charity, or to someone who offers to pick it up, they most likely choose solutions that seem most comfortable, helpful or profitable for them.

Besides individual consumers, governments and corporations are important consumers of EEE. This commercial WEEE/UEEE is hardly ever collected by *Recupel*, since the owners can make money out of it or sell it through other channels which guarantee data wiping. Moreover, these actors have a financial incentive to regularly renew their equipment. Both governments and corporations who regularly update their equipment work with contractors who take care of the

27 This is the subject of the EU's Restriction of Hazardous Substances (RoHS) Directive (2002/95/EC).

28 According to a government respondent, the amount of that is difficult to assess, but analysis of household waste has shown to contain small electric and electronic devices (such as computer mouse, earphones, iPods, mp3 players and so on). The report of this analysis is not public yet.

data wiping, refurbishing and replacement of their equipment (Babbitt, Williams and Kahbat 2011). Older equipment is discarded and disposed of using *Recupel* or waste collection and recycling centres. Sometimes, however, such contractors feed into illegal transports of e-waste. One of the corporate respondents (C20) explained how their awareness of sustainable WEEE solutions was raised as a result of the discovery of their equipment in illegal transports, exposing their corporation to bad publicity. Another corporate respondent (C22) explained how it is vital for them to 'not only provide a box to collect e-waste, but make sure you know where the box goes to'. According to some corporate respondents the 'major threat is with the business and government staff who might be tempted to feed into alternative flows of e-waste' (C18). Because these corporations allow this to occur, through a lack of security checks or due diligence, they are *facilitating interfaces* (Tijhuis 2006).

The following testimony of a corporate respondent (C19) further illustrates how corporations and governments lack awareness or due diligence in matters of e-waste:

> It has happened that I arrive somewhere to buy second-hand computers a government or corporation wants to dispose of. I offer a certain price they have to pay for the refurbishment, with certified data wipe. Sometimes I can offer them money depending on the quality of the equipment. Many times however these computers or other e-goods are bought for high prices by competitors. I know it can never be profitable to treat or refurbish them in Belgium for these high prices, so it is likely they end up in illegal transports. Their prices are so high that they should ring alarm bells, but in the end it is the consumer who decides who to sell to.

A report by the Dutch inspectorate assumed mainly small- and medium-sized enterprises to be involved in this because major corporations are afraid of the reputational damage (VROM-inspectie 2011). The respondents interviewed in this study, however, referred to both small and large-scale corporations. If it does concern large corporations, the quantities are of course likely to be substantially larger. As is evident from the above quotations, the motivations for corporate and government users of EEE to feed into illegal transports of e-waste are profit and a lack of awareness about both the harmfulness of e-waste and the untrustworthiness of some e-waste collectors.

With reference to the legal-illegal interfaces in e-waste flows (Passas 2002), legal consumers can feed into illegal transports of e-waste, since they interact with actors who offer to treat their e-waste for low prices. These actors can have legitimate business structures (refurbishers, brokers), but could well be *waste tourists* (see below). Consumers are clients of these illegal actors and therefore have a symbiotic relationship with them. It is unclear, however, to what extent this is motivated by a search for cheaper disposal and a lack of awareness about the harmfulness of e-waste and the untrustworthiness of particular e-waste collectors or, on the contrary, by an intentional choice for illegal disposal. When they are unaware about the illegality of it, this could then refer to the synergy interface. When it concerns an intentional choice, this equals the interface of outsourcing, because the dirty work of disposing of the e-waste is done by an illegal actor for a legal actor. Outsourcing is particularly relevant for waste, because it allows legal actors to externalize the harm.

Collection of E-Waste

The negative value of waste is deemed to be a key criminogenic characteristic of this economic sector (van Daele, Vander Beken and Dorn 2007; van Erp and Huisman 2010; Vander Beken 2007). For a normal commodity, a producer provides the consumer with the product and in return gets the money. For waste, the waste producer gives the waste treatment facility the product as well as the money. This inverse incentive structure is therefore a push factor for illegal disposal (van Duyne 1993). However, for e-waste, the picture is more complex and holds a double profit motivation. E-waste includes devices with treatment costs, but some products hold enough valuable components to make recycling or treatment profitable (LNE 2010). For the former, exporting them as second-hand products saves the costs of treatment. The latter is a motivation for having the goods dismantled as cheaply as possible to sell the raw materials (Sander and Schilling 2010). Corporations that treat the e-waste legally and have environmentally sound management systems are few and their prices can be high. This makes it attractive to look for cheaper, less environmentally sound alternatives. The corporate respondents of this study, however, claim it is difficult to make profits when dismantling activities happen in Belgium given high labour costs. Therefore, they said, it was unlikely for actors to make a profit from e-waste recycling even when the e-waste is accepted for free. When money is offered for e-waste, some believe this to be suspicious and likely to lead to illegal exports. One corporate respondent (C13) explained that: '[y]ou can make money by 'recycling' e-waste in poorer environmental and social conditions, since this provides you the precious metals with lower labour costs'. Similar results were found in previous research (Interpol 2009).

Another push factor for illegal transports is the complexity of the e-waste flows and the competitiveness of the market. Many sub-streams of waste arise from the dismantling of these products and there are multiple actors involved in e-waste collection. It involves metal scrap dealers, urban recycling centres, official take-back systems (for example *Recupel*), registered metal collectors (for example picking up disposal skips from electronic hardware stores) and informal actors (for example waste tourists, internet or charities; see Figure 5.1). Many of these e-waste collectors and recyclers live up to their espoused environmental and ethical standards and regard illegal transporters of e-waste as their biggest competitors. Other organizations that claim to recycle EEE are less honourable and engage in direct or indirect export – often through brokers – to developing countries. 'E-waste is prone to fraud, because many actors can buy and sell, often as their sole means of income' (corporate respondent C11). The potential leakages in e-waste collection identified in this case study are now discussed in turn.

In communal waste collection and recycling centres some might be tempted to sell an e-waste load outside the official system. Similarly, retailers could be tempted to sell a container instead of having it picked up for free by *Recupel*. These retailer collection points do not keep accurate waste registers, which makes it difficult to determine the exact amount of e-waste collected. Whether these buyers of e-waste follow the efficient and registered recycling flows is unclear. Both retailers and communal waste collection and recycling centres could also fall victim to e-waste theft.[29] These are grey areas which could result in illegal transports of e-waste towards developing countries.

The Belgian take-back system is perceived as an effective system that guarantees legal disposal and recycling. However, respondents mentioned that there is a parallel flow of particular products (for example mobile phones) that is completely out of sight of the official take-back system. Other European countries moreover have different take-back systems, which are not monopolies as is the case in Belgium. According to government and corporate respondents, these take-back systems are not as effective because they require producers and retailers to take care of the recycling, hence they are more likely to choose cheaper alternatives. This partially explains why 80 per cent of the e-waste that passes through Antwerp originates outside Belgium.

Refurbishers are other actors that take care of e-waste collection. This sector buys electronic devices from firms or government agencies – or universities for that matter – that change their computers every three to five years. Retailers deliver damaged goods to them directly. These goods are repaired, refurbished and the remains are recycled. Refurbished goods are sold to schools or development projects in industrialized and developing countries or simply sold to individual consumers who do not need the latest technology. These goods are shipped legally to countries outside the EU, mostly in large mono-consignments. In this way, refurbishers try to make their business in a niche sector: 'The business model of retailers is focused on selling, not on the reverse logic of take-back. This is where we try to make a difference' (corporate respondent C21). These professional refurbishers are keen to show they work legally and therefore have a policy of transparency. This allows responsible authorities to check them whenever necessary. Not all refurbishment companies choose these environmentally and socially just paths, however. A proportion of this equipment for refurbishing disappears through networks of scrap dealers, waste tourists and e-waste brokers. Even Belgian government computers are thought to have ended up in developing countries illegally (Puckett et al. 2005).

Some EEE is donated to charity and sent to development projects abroad. Whether these computers arrive there or whether these transports answer to the quality requirements is unclear. Other initiatives collect mobile phones and

29 The corporate respondents told me that containers are regularly emptied by thieves.

donate, for instance, 1 euro per phone to charity, but once again it is not clear where the collected UEEE/WEEE goes. Some websites also offer to buy UEEE (for example mobile phones) for a small price or offer to pick WEEE up for free. Sometimes these websites link back to known refurbishers or collectors, other times the organizations or individuals behind it are unknown.

During field visits to Ghana, several importers and UEEE shop owners explained how they guarantee supplies. What happens is that *waste tourists* buy or collect the e-waste. These informal actors might be EU residents or have a tourist visa. They collect the 'second-hand' goods, load a container or a truck and travel back to the country of destination to wait for their shipment (VROM-inspectie 2011). Some of these waste tourists live in the countries of origin and cooperate with relatives in the countries of destination to pick up the transport. According to corporate, government and civil society respondents, these waste tourists can be more organized than they might seem: the same people re-emerge and are interconnected through business-like structures of collectors in European countries, transporters and recyclers or sellers of second-hand goods in West Africa. A Ghanaian terminal operator revealed he has several clients that ship approximately 20 containers of UEEE/WEEE per month. According to the Belgian government respondents, it is difficult to track them down because they usually have false passports under different names. Some of the government respondents expressed their concern that this might be linked to organized crime and Ghanaian civil society respondents mentioned Chinese, Nigerian and Eastern European organized crime in particular. This is consistent with the findings of Europol's latest organized crime threat assessment (Europol 2011) which explains how illicit waste trafficking is often facilitated through the cooperation of organized crime groups with legitimate businesses and how both northern and southern European ports act as hubs for illegal waste.

In the last few years, the respondents have witnessed the increasing importance of the internet for e-waste collection. The same goes for new-for-old swaps in stores. A government respondent (G15) explains: 'E-goods collected over the internet and in stores may end up in good treatment or recycling facilities, but a share of it gets lost and transported to Africa. It is difficult to know whether the good quality or bad quality goods end up in Africa'.

Metal scrap dealers play a role as intermediaries in the collection of e-waste. They buy discarded electronics and often already disassemble those to sell the metal content. These might then still end up with the same recyclers the official take-back system uses. However, because the threshold to collect WEEE within the official system is high (for example licenses, equipment), small-scale scrap dealers now risk flowing into illegal transports. 'They aren't all criminals but they sure do facilitate a lot', according to a government respondent (G14). Sometimes the recycling facilities in Belgium are intermediaries when components require manual separation after passing through the smelter (Sander and Schilling 2010). Both government and corporate respondents have confirmed that these are shipped to Asia for manual dismantling after the smelting process is complete. These transports are legal because this is a non-hazardous activity.

Other intermediaries are facilities for waste storages and handling. These storage facilities receive e-waste or used goods of different quality and mix those up in the overseas shipments. Once again it is important to stress that 80 per cent of all e-waste that passes through the Port of Antwerp originates in countries other than Belgium. Located in the Brussels area and locations closer to the Port of Antwerp, these brokers receive e-waste by rail or road transport from other countries (for example Germany, the Netherlands or France). According to a government respondent (G27), these businesses and their suppliers re-emerge: 'The invoices that are meant to prove the origin of the goods are often identical and contain hardly any information, with the intent to hamper controls.[30] These waste storage and handling facilities buy and sell the waste and are actually already a transport actor, which is the topic of the next section.

E-waste collection by waste tourists, for charity and over the internet, could all be perceived as the activities of illegal actors who compete with the legal market, thus constituting an antagonistic interface. Similarly illegal e-waste brokers are competitors and they might even aim to put other collectors out of business (predatory). Some of the e-waste collectors are however intermediaries in legal transactions as well and therefore promote similar interests to the illegal collectors of e-waste. This fits a symbiotic nature of the legal-illegal interface. When there is an unconscious involvement in illegality, it is an interface of synergy. In case they do know about the illegality, this interface is either one of collaboration in the case of long-term links or one of reciprocity for shorter term but still mutual benefits. One last leakage and illegal-legal interface occurs when retailers as well as communal waste collection and recycling centres are the victims of e-waste theft. This could be perceived as an injurious legal-illegal interface.

Transport of E-Waste

Containerization saves cost and time and has facilitated the rapid growth of legitimate international trade in recent decades, but the anonymity of containers offers particular advantages for organizations wishing to transport illicit commodities (Griffiths and Jenks 2012; UNODC 2011; Levinson 2006). Shipping a container to Africa or South-East Asia is cheap, making it a low threshold for illegal transports, as illustrated by the following quote from a corporate respondent (C1): 'These ships are so to speak waiting in the port to be loaded again after unloading all the processed goods (e.g. clothes, electronics, cars, etc. from China) and raw materials (e.g. cocoa, fruit, metals, timber, etc. from Africa)'. Different actors have a role to play in the transports and can thus be tempted by these facilitating factors (see Figure 5.1).

30 van Duyne (1993) observed similar structures for invoicing and transportation in a Dutch-Belgian case of illegal waste transport and dumping.

Port authorities play a role. On the one hand, they are mainly interested in filling the containers and sending them back to Africa and Asia. On the other hand, they are responsible for port safety and can in this way indirectly influence e-waste transports. As an example, the Antwerp port authority, harbourmaster's office, the waterway police and inspectorates have drafted a regulation[31] for the transport of additional cargo in second-hand vehicles and imposed stricter controls. One of the reasons for this was that e-waste smugglers had started using cars, vans and trucks to transport waste as a countermeasure to the increased controls on containers[32]. The new regulation requires a bill of lading for the extra load in vehicles and there are stricter loading instructions. This new regulation is, however, under pressure because the end-of-life vehicles are a major commodity for the port, which might see this economically significant activity relocated to other ports. The port authorities and state actors might simply be shaping the structural context for these flows, but could be interpreted as facilitating illegal activities (Kramer, Michalowski and Kauzlarich 2002).

Terminal operators load and unload the goods on the ships. They are generally not concerned with the legality of the goods, but merely with the safety of the operation. Shipping lines are in a similar position (Sander and Schilling 2010). A government respondent (G19) sees it as follows: 'The shipping lines will often go with 'I don't know, no idea what's inside', but they know many of their customers and could be more responsible about who they allow through a use of black lists'. Some civil society respondents have revealed that the Port of Antwerp logistics is thriving on mafia business, but it is hard to interpret these comments. Certain shipping lines are allegedly connected to the Italian mob, but hard proof is lacking.

An important role is played by shipping agents. They arrange the transports over road or inland waterways to the nearest port and take care of the handling of the goods in the port. Those expeditors are not always brokers because they do not necessarily buy the waste, but might simply arrange the transports. Shipping agents usually do not engage themselves with the content of the transports and merely arrange the paperwork. Through this activity, however, they facilitate illegal transports. This is explained in the following quote from a government respondent (G14):

> Despite the requirement in the WSR for expeditors to provide information about the destination of the goods, the expeditors hide behind commercial secrecy and

31 Regulation of 24 November 2011 for handling of second hand vehicles in the Port of Antwerp (*Reglement voor het behandelen van tweedehands voertuigen in de haven van Antwerpen*) – entered into force 1 January 2012.

32 A baseline assessment of the cars shipped from the Port of Antwerp found out that 5–10 per cent of vehicles contained e-waste. With about 400,000 vehicles shipped annually and 10 per cent of those originating in Belgium, this means 4–8,000 vehicles are loaded with e-waste in Belgium each year.

> are hesitant about giving away the information about the destination[33]. They only fill out [the shipping documents with] the information they get, not all they know and in this way they keep the traffic in place. Their clients deliberately withhold information about the address of the disposer, but expeditors allow them to.

Shipping lines and terminal operators have e-waste smugglers as clients, either in container or in vehicle transports. This fits the symbiotic nature of the legal-illegal interface (Passas 2002) because legal actors work for illegal actors, but it is unclear to what extent the former knowingly collaborate. In case they do not know, this interface is one of synergy. In case they do know, this interface is either one of collaboration in case of long-term links or one of reciprocity for shorter term but still mutual benefit. Similar to shipping lines and terminal operators, expeditors and shipping agents have smugglers as their clients, but their involvement is deemed to be more deliberate. 'If the shipping agent fills out the waste goods codes correctly, it will never pass the customs system without a check', according to government respondent 22. They can at least be accused of a lack of due diligence or of culpable negligence by withholding information. Similarly the synergy, collaboration or reciprocity interfaces apply.

Countries of Destination

A fourth segment in reference to the e-waste flows (see Figure 5.1) is of a different nature. Rather than factors that push or facilitate the flows of e-waste, factors that attract e-waste flows are analysed. Although this should not be overplayed, the institutional framework in countries of destination – or lack thereof – is a first pull factor (Schluep et al. 2008). Although some studies (LNE and Haskoning 2010)[34] perceive this to be of low risk due to its clarity, consistency and good quality, others believe the massive amount of regulation on waste indeed leaves only limited blind spots, but does hold a risk of causing confusion and liability problems (Bruinsma 1996). A corporate respondent (C15) adds: 'stringent regulation and control creates extra motivation for bypassing the law and often provides those crooks with bigger profits'. This refers not only to their weak regulatory system or government, often as a result of wars or conflicts, but also their precarious socio-economic situation. This causes them to allow e-waste shipments to be imported into their country, because of their financial attractiveness (Puckett and Smith

33 Annex 7 to the WSR is problematic here, since this allows the original sender and receiver of the goods to be disguised.

34 A 2010 study commissioned by the Flemish Inspectorate for the Environment analysed different waste streams and their risk profiles. To arrive at the risk profiles they weighted risk factors (legislation, market and context, technique, costs, criminogenic factors) on a scale from 1 to 5, 1 being the lowest risk, 5 the highest.

2002). Imports of e-waste are a way to increase their revenue (through taxes), which is referred to as garbage imperialism (Pellow 2007).

EEE discarded by industrialized countries may represent the sole secure source of livelihood for many people in developing countries, constituting a second pull factor. These economies-in-transition and developing countries have a massive formal as well as informal economy thriving on the repair, refurbishment, dismantling and recycling of second-hand EEE. These informal actors are wary of the term 'e-waste', because these 'used goods' are the only guarantee of livelihood for many (Amoyaw-Osei et al. 2011; Prakash and Manhart 2010). As I witnessed in the field (Agbogbloshie dump, Accra) many devices or cables are simply burned to remove the plastic casing and collect the metals. Scrap collectors – known as scavengers – collect valuable waste on the streets and the well-organized informal recycling sector dismantles the devices and sorts valuable and non-valuable components (Odeyingbo, Deubzer and Schluep 2011). In Ghana, the informal sector is estimated to generate 100 to 250 million US dollars per annum and employs 22,000 people in Accra alone (Prakash and Manhart 2010).[35] An estimated 0.82 per cent of the total Ghanaian population have informal WEEE repairs or refurbishing as their sole means of livelihood. Second-hand – but also non-working – television sets, computers, mobile phone (batteries) and so on are sold on many street corners. In China, the millions of jobs in the informal sector are a motivation for the government not to tackle the illegal shipments of e-waste too harshly, according to an NGO-respondent (S12). Stopping the flow of e-waste would take away the supply for these informal sectors and might cause social unrest. One corporate respondent (C18) said: 'The big recyclers in Europe are likely to disagree, but some recyclers abroad are equally well equipped and exports to these countries are more economical given the proximity of the production sites'.

Besides guaranteeing a livelihood for many people, the digital divide creates a hunger for technology in developing countries. This is a third pull factor. E-waste transports can help bridge this divide since computers, mobile phones and other electronic devices allow people to catch up with global developments in knowledge and communication. 'Importers seem willing to bring in containers mostly filled

35 Formally registered businesses import EEE on a regular basis and mostly focus on a particular product (for example refrigerators, PCs and so on): 70 per cent of the imports work, 20 per cent can be repaired (but often only functional for another one or two years) and 10 per cent do not function. Informal importers are unregistered business owners, mostly residents of foreign countries who import one or two containers per year. Some of this EEE is bought from refurbishment companies and tested for functionality; other EEE imports are not tested however. Of these informal imports, 60 per cent are functioning, 20 per cent can be repaired (once again with a short lifespan remaining) and 20 per cent is simply e-waste (Prakash and Manhart 2010). Another way EEE enters the country is through private imports (in the luggage of individuals) or through donations (which are exempt from tax).

with e-waste because the demand for electronics is so high that buyers are prepared to purchase untested items'. (Environmental Investigation Agency 2011, p. 2). It is, however, important to be mindful about the consequences of bridging this digital divide. Inadequate treatment of e-waste flows can have detrimental effects for environmental and human health as well as for the economy and politics. The developing countries end up with the old technology and with the waste. One of the Ghanaian civil society respondents (S16) referred to this as 'bridging the digital divide by creating a digital dump'.

The informal e-waste collectors and dismantlers feed into the legal e-waste industry through the increased demand for secondary raw materials, which is a fourth pull factor. The pressure on natural resources plays a role in market dynamics and is likely to become increasingly important in future geo-politics. One way of guaranteeing the inflow of (precious) metals into natural-resource poor Europe is by exploiting the resources of the urban mine[36] to their full potential. There is, however, a major pull for e-waste transports to Asia. The spotlights have been on China and India, and the situation in terms of illegal e-waste transports seems to have improved somewhat. China has stricter laws[37] on e-waste, which prohibit import unless it is useable as raw materials and unless the requirement of prior consent is met. In practice however these imports are still tolerated and sometimes documents refer to unknown or unlicensed treatment facilities. The extracted components or metals still end up with the same producers, mainly in India and China, after dismantling in Africa, Vietnam, northern China and Cambodia. Repair, refurbishing, reselling, recycling and dismantling happens in small workshops which are supplied by informal collectors (hawkers, pedlars, individual vendors) (Veenstra et al. 2010). Although these recycling facilities are increasingly well equipped, the limited number of official recycling facilities in China does not provide enough materials for their smelters. However, informal dismantlers in some regions (for example Accra) are improving both environmental and labour standards, as a civil society respondent (S21) explained: 'moving away from the one-sided bad story, because a lot of progress has been made'. Local NGOs in Ghana motivate dismantlers not to burn the e-waste by not buying the burnt copper. Other actors however, accept all metals, burnt or not, and this perpetuates the burning.

Similar to their involvement in countries of origin, organized crime groups were mentioned to be involved in the collection of metal scrap in West Africa. In particular, respondents referred to organized crime groups of Nigerian, Italian, Eastern European and Chinese origin who collect the valuable materials from

---

36 The urban mine is a mine of (raw) materials from products, buildings and waste in a society. Urban mining is the idea of using those compounds and elements as resources for new production, thereby avoiding these materials from going to waste. E-waste exports can thus be seen as a loss in raw material.

37 SEPA Document No. 19/2000 of 24 January 2000 'Notification on import of the seventh category of wastes'.

informal workers on the dump and sell them as secondary raw materials on the global metal market. This is consistent with findings by Gonzales, Schofield and Hagy (2007) which state that Asian organized crime groups are expanding their influence to legitimate business such as waste disposal. As an Agbogbloshie worker put it: 'I sell copper to Chinese men and mother boards to a white man from Europe'.

The interface in countries of destination is one of legal and illegal and of formal and informal networks. Informal collectors and dismantlers compete on the same market as formal actors, and even organized crime. This implies an antagonistic interface and might even be aimed to extort (parasitical interface) or destroy (predatory interface) other actors. There is another legal-illegal interface that presents itself. The raw materials that were extracted by informal actors feed into the legal production. Sometimes organized crime acts as a go-between in this. This constitutes an interface of reciprocity or collaboration between legal, illegal and informal actors. On the supply side, these informal dismantlers as well as sellers of second-hand e-goods cooperate with both illegal (e-waste) and legal (used goods) transporters. It is not easy to determine whether this last category of actors is legal or illegal. Legal recycling actors face competition (antagonistic interface) from governments that tolerate the imports of e-waste (against national or international regulation). These governments support informal or illegal dismantling or recycling actors, constituting a (non-financial) funding interface. Legal actors might thus be facilitating and even initiating crime (Kramer et al. 2002), but the line is difficult to draw. The transports of e-waste are not allowed, but they do provide a stable (and sole) source of income for many. Throughout the flows, the status of e-waste can actually change between legal and illegal multiple times. Once EEE is dismantled, refined or comes out of a smelter, there is no way of tracing where it came from, which implies it may feed into the legal industry again.

Governance of Illegal Transports of E-Waste in a European Trade Hub

The field of crime was long dominated by state institutions, but in face of the complex problems the world faced, a shift was required moving beyond the nation state paradigm to the transnational level, away from a single government actor to governance arrangements in which different actors are involved (Loader and Sparks 2002; Sheptycki 2007). In response to ecological challenges the world faces, many multilateral environmental agreements (MEAs) and national environmental regulations have been drafted. These attributed a focal role to the state and corresponded to the so-called command and control regulation (Holley et al. 2012). Environmental issues are one global dynamic that involves new actors taking up responsibilities formerly reserved for the nation state. These new actors can be legal entities such as (multinational) corporations or non-governmental organizations. Over the years, corporate actors have developed environmental self-regulation, which sometimes goes beyond the requirements set in legislation (Bartley 2007; Gunningham et al. 2003). This resulted in various regulatory hybrids where responses to (transnational) environmental issues can be found within government institutions such as the criminal justice system, but also involves regulatory initiatives in interaction with corporate and civil society actors. Governments as well as business, civil society and international organizations shape governance and regulation, but it is not clear what governance frameworks this led to in practice (Braithwaite 2008). This chapter continues by analysing the governance reality of e-waste flows and provides insights into the facilitating and hindering factors in these governance arrangements, for each actor on its own and in interaction. The frame of analysis used for this is a nodal-networked analysis (Shearing and Johnston 2010). This analysis relates back to the models of the responsive regulatory pyramid and networked governance.[38]

A range of actors govern illegal transports of e-waste from countries of export and transit – in this case Belgium – to countries of import – in this case Ghana. A first section provides the results of the *nodal governance analysis*, the examination of the governance reality of the separate governance nodes. Thereafter, the role of corporate and civil society actors is examined. Attention is paid to their roles and responsibilities, strengths and weaknesses in dealing with e-waste.[39] The following networked governance analysis examines the interactions within the governance reality of illegal e-waste flows. The findings show how the governance reality of illegal transports of e-waste answers to several characteristics of these ideal-typical models, but is at the same time faced with the complexity inherent to governing the illegal trade in e-waste.

Government Actors (Together) in the Director's Chair

The control and prevention of illegal e-waste transports involves a diversity of government actors. Environmental administrations and inspectorates, customs, harbourmaster's office, police and judiciary each play a role in Antwerp and Belgium. The following discusses the governance reality of these government actors. The role of the Ghanaian government actors is discussed separately.

Environmental administrations

The Flemish public waste authority (*Openbare Vlaamse Afvalstoffenmaatschappij – OVAM*) is responsible for Flanders' waste policy and coordinates all Belgian statistics (for example for European Commission). OVAM is responsible for notification procedures of Flemish waste exports and imports. The notifications for transit are with the environmental inspection. Licenses are also a responsibility of OVAM, which is executed in close cooperation with the regional inspectorates. The most

38 A detailed explanation of the theoretical framework can be found in Chapter 2.

39 In the scope of this study, it is impossible to discuss all governance characteristics of these actors. Therefore, this is focused on those elements relevant to the e-waste case.

important function of OVAM for e-waste is in policy preparation, implementation and advice. They have an advisory function for authorities across Flanders. OVAM's policy preparation has influence across the regional borders. According to a government respondent (G25), this coordinated policy is deemed valuable compared to 'other countries (such as the Netherlands) where these responsibilities are fragmented (e.g. city, province and inspectorate)'.

Environmental inspectorates

The Belgian responsibility for environmental inspection of waste transports is divided between the federal and regional levels.[40] The control for transit is with the Federal Environmental Inspectorate (FEI/FLI/IFE) and the control for import and export is with the Flemish Environmental Inspectorate (EID/MI), Brussels Environmental Inspectorate (IBGE/BIM) and Walloon Environmental Inspectorate (DPE/URP).[41,42] For e-waste transports, 20 per cent of containers and 10 per cent of second-hand vehicles originate in Belgium, with the rest in transit. The responsibilities of these inspectorates were updated in order to stimulate a coherent policy and determine effective, proportionate and deterrent sanctions for breaches of the EU waste legislation.[43] The Belgian institutional reforms planned for the regionalization of all inspection tasks for waste transports several years back, but at the time of research and writing both the federal and the regional levels still had their own responsibilities.

---

40 Special Law for the Institutional reform of 8 August 1980 (Bijzonder wet van 8 Augustus 1980 (Consolidated version of 22 December 2010); Law of 12 May 2011 amending the law of 9 July 1984 on the import, export and transit of waste. (*Wet van 12 mei 2011 tot wijziging van de wet van 9 juli 1984 betreffende de invoer, de uitvoer en de doorvoer van afvalstoffen*). Explanatory Memorandum for the draft law amending the law of 9 July 1984 on the import, export and transit of waste (*Toelichting bij het Wetsontwerp tot wijziging van de wet van 9 juli 1984 betreffende de invoer, de uitvoer en de doorvoer van afvalstoffen*).

41 In view of the research setting in the Port of Antwerp, the Flemish (FLI) and Federal inspectorate (MI) are most relevant. The other inspectorates are not discussed separately, but were contacted for interviews. FLI and MI, the Dutch abbreviations, are used.

42 As part of the reforms of the Belgian state, policymakers have discussed the transfer of the federal responsibilities for inspection to the level of the regional authorities. This would imply that the transit of waste becomes a regional responsibility, but the legal changes have not been voted nor implemented (August 2013).

43 This refers to: (1) Regulation (EC) No 1013/2006 of the European Parliament and the Council of 14 June 2006 on shipments of waste; (2) Regulation (EC) No 1774/2002 of the European Parliament and the Council of 3 October 2002 laying down health rules concerning animal by-products not intended for human consumption; (3) Regulation (EC) No 2037/2000 of the European Parliament and the Council of 29 June 2000 on substances that deplete the ozone layer; (4) Directive 2008/99/EC of the European Parliament and the Council of 19 November 2008 on the protection of the environment through criminal law; and (5) Directive 2008/98/EC of the European Parliament and the Council of 19 November 2008 on waste and repealing certain Directives.

The Federal Environmental Inspection (FLI) is responsible for transit of waste. Four FLI inspectors focus on the Belgian harbours, two of which work in the harbour of Antwerp and focus on all waste issues, e-waste being one of the waste types they focus on. Their powers include stopping transport vehicles in view of controls of loading, requesting to see books and transport documents, entering premises where waste in transit is temporarily stocked and interrogating persons about facts they deem necessary for their controls. With the new law on the transit of waste,[44] they became judicial police officers, which allows them to give warnings, administrative fines, determine a deadline for compliance with the law and block, secure, send back, take into custody or destroy goods and transport vehicles of goods without cost.[45] For vehicles, a selection is made by walking the quays and selecting vehicles based on origin, destination and shippers.[46] They look inside the vehicles to see whether there is something suspicious such as CFC-containing refrigerators or poorly stacked and packed UEEE. For containers, the selection is based on the transport documents, where similar criteria apply.[47] Selected containers and vehicles are scanned by customs using fixed or mobile scanners.[48] The inspectorate interprets the images and unblocks the unit when the equipment is legal. In case of further suspicions, the units are physically inspected.[49] When unloading these units, there is close contact with the terminal operator as well as with the shipping agent, but the shippers will not be involved in order to avoid them from negotiating or hampering the controls. When controlled transit shipments turn out to be illegal, states of origin are required to take these shipments back and decide whether to prosecute. However, this is often to no avail. Therefore, if it is environmentally irresponsible to send the shipment back or if no responsible owner is found within reasonable time, the FLI makes sure the waste is treated in nearby licensed facilities. FLI can also impose fines on shippers.[50] Given the limited staff available, the inspectors limit controls of containers to those for which they can provide administrative follow-up. For instance, a maximum of

44 Law of 9 July 1984 on the transit of waste (*Wet van 9 juli 1984 betreffende de doorvoer van afvalstoffen*), changed by amendment of 12 May 2011, that entered into force 2 June 2011.

45 Article 15 and 16 of the Law of 9 July 1984 on the transit of waste.

46 For sake of clarity, the shipper is the owner of the goods who pays shipping agents and shipping lines to ship the goods to their destination.

47 Selections based only on the goods classification of waste are ineffective, because only a limited number of shipments are actually notified as waste shipments.

48 The fixed scanners provide both horizontal and vertical scan images, whereas the mobile one only scans vertically. Nevertheless, both provide quite good images of what the units contain.

49 The costs can be as high as 3,000 euro in case a container needs to be unloaded and forbidden equipment needs to be treated (at appropriate recycling facilities). This needs to be paid by the shipping agent who recovers this from the shipper.

50 This measure was new at the time of the field visits and interviews and their impact could thus not (yet) be assessed.

approximately 10 units[51] will be selected for scanning and inspectors might not unload scanned units that contain only few electronic devices.[52] The administrative follow-up of the units is often very time-consuming and shippers are often hard to trace.[53] FLI cannot fine or send back every unit that is in breach of legislation and inspectorates choose the units which they deem to have the biggest chance of becoming successfully fined or prosecuted.[54]

The Flemish environmental inspectorate (MI) is crucial in addressing governance earlier in the supply chain, because they deal with (import and) export of e-waste. They have the same powers as the federal inspectorate and in addition give advice about the sanitation of the premises. MI mainly focuses on checks early in the chain through certification, licensing and compliance of companies. They do checks of vehicles and containers in the port as well, but mainly upon the request of other actors such as customs, maritime police or FLI or during joint action days.[55] In cases where other actors come across illegal imports or exports of waste the administrative follow-up is for MI (LNE and Haskoning 2010). Based on the discovered illegal transports, the MI will follow up with inspections further down the chain, going back to the source. They check whether the scrap dealers and refurbishers have a license and waste registry. When the facility is outside the Flemish territory, other Belgian or European authorities need to follow up. Road controls, controls in the harbour and site inspections of waste facilities are the job of two full-time inspectors (LNE 2011).[56] Approximately 5 to 6 per cent of MI inspections result in police reports, but the core of their activities is in the administrative legal procedures. Prosecution of waste cases is very difficult (see below) and therefore MI often chooses to address the license.

As illustrated above, the limited amount of staff requires inspectorates to be selective about which cases they follow up. As will be explained in the following sections, they are also the go-to agency for advice, expertise and administrative follow-up up if other government actors detect suspicious units. Several respondents deemed this to be the most important bottleneck in the control of illegal transports of e-waste. One of the corporate actors (C21) added the following critique on the inspectorates:

---

51 Units can either be containers or vehicles.

52 Another factor they consider for physical checks is whether the suspicious unit was identified by other authorities (within Belgium or in countries of export).

53 They might well have left for Africa already or operated under false passports.

54 When a unit is clearly problematic the choice will be made to act upon it. As an example a truck was sent back in which 10 out of 16 refrigerators contained CFCs and 8 out of 12 CRT TVs were not functional or had no electric cable. Moreover, the truck itself proved to be a refrigerated truck which was not degassed. Another truck contained only 2 CFC fridges and the choice was made to oblige the shipping agent to recycle those and allowed the rest of the truck to be shipped.

55 Several times a year there are 'action days' in the ports. FLI, MI, customs, HMO and police then particularly focus on illegal waste shipments.

56 In comparison, the Dutch inspectorate has 23 FTE responsible for waste matters.

> Inspectorate controls target the corporations that come into the media, whereas others might try to copy our business, but disregard the management and compliance system behind it. If I can 'google' them, they should be able to as well. I don't mind being checked, but they need to check competitors as well, also those they can't find that easily.

Customs

Customs authorities, whether in the country of export or import, are responsible for the clearance of goods. Their core function is taxation and they therefore need to check whether the goods correspond with the declaration. Though fiscally oriented, they also have other tasks such as the protection of society's health, environment and safety.[57] A government respondent (G18) explained how 'the pressure to focus on taxes is decreasing. [...] This leaves room for customs to focus on tasks that were long-time not regarded a customs' priority, although in se it was always part of the mission'. The renewed focus seems to have repositioned customs within the security framework, which also has implications for their role in the governance of illegal e-waste transports.

Faced with an enormous trade volume and a limited number of customs officers, most customs controls are paper controls and are informed by a risk analysis system. Currently less than 1 per cent of shipments are controlled and even a marginal increase would require a significant increase in staff. Automation and informatization recently reoriented the customs' system from a transaction based to a system-based control, which was meant to address both the growing flow of goods and the need to safeguard security. The system-based control uses the management system of the corporation to determine the frequency of controls of the shipped units with the intent to limit the hindrance for the international logistics chain.[58] This changed focus on the quantity of controls and had implications for the quality as well (Sluis et al. 2012). The former system of transaction-based control distrusted and stopped all goods to check for irregularities. System-based control deems the large majority of transactions as trustworthy and uses 'green lanes' with limited checks. Automatic Economic Operators (AEO) are the core of the system-based control. Producers, exporters, shipping agents, storage facilities, transporters and importers can all be granted the AEO certificate.[59] It aims to

57 Missie: http://fiscus.fgov.be/interfdanl/nl/publications/missie.htm [last consulted on 29 December 2011] and European Customs Information Portal: http://ec.europa.eu/ecip/ [last consulted on 21 January 2012].

58 The goals were set out in the 2000–01 Belgian government reforms, but only became fully operational in 2008.

59 These conditions are a good customs track record, trade and transport administration that allows for sound customs controls, financial solvency and sound safety provisions. A system audit is required (by means of a self-assessment) before AEO is granted. There is regular follow-up through self-assessments and there are limited random controls.

stimulate self-regulation by rewarding integer behaviour with quicker processing.[60] In practice a large amount of traffic falls under AEO and goes through the green lanes, although there can still be random checks. Government respondents told me this AEO certification is not an air-tight system because waste handlers who were fined in Belgium received an AEO certificate in other EU countries, which grants them trade priorities across the EU.

Customs also does a risk analysis on the customs declarations, which contains information about the origin and destination of goods, goods codes, value and so on.[61] For (e-)waste, the system checks for particular countries of destination, descriptions of the goods, VAT-numbers, text selection (for example suspicious streets) and the value[62] of the goods. These criteria are informed by legislation, by Risk Information Forms (RIF)[63] and further refined based on the past experience of customs in negotiation with environmental inspectorates and administrations. Selected units are subjected to further document control, scanning or physical verification of the goods. Note that this system applies only to import and export and not to transit data. Particularly for e-waste this is problematic because 80 per cent of e-waste shipments are in transit in Antwerp. For goods in transit, customs trusts the export checks of other EU states, as foreseen in the European waste legislation.

Another critique of the system is that the customs' scanners are not used to their full potential. It may be surprising, but this was mentioned by both government and corporate respondents. As an illustration, in 2010, 30,529 containers were scanned whereas the total capacity is 70,000 containers per annum. A corporate respondent (C4) added: 'If you ask me, it's merely a matter of good logistic planning to use this tool to its full potential. The only costs you have are the customs' staff and that's where the shoe pinches. As long as this does not cause delays in shipment, we applaud the use of scanners'. Some respondents called these mere 'teething problems' and found other critiques more fundamental. For instance, a government

60 Holders of AEO certificates get certain advantages such as quicker customs simplified procedures, less physical verification and other controls. In case of controls, AEO certified companies get priority and can ask for a physical check of the goods at a particular location. AEO – Wat. Douane and Accijnzen: http://fiscus.fgov.be/interfdanl/nl/aeo/wat.htm [last consulted on 8 February 2012].

61 For waste transports, the necessary documentation (attachment 7 and notification documents) is required.

62 In case a container of electronic equipment is reported with a value of 500 euro this will give a warning, because it is likely to be of low quality.

63 The European communications system for customs uses Risk Information Forms (RIF) as a source to exchange risk information dealing with routine customs controls. This system gives warnings about suspicious transports to other customs organizations in order to allow for focused controls. A RIF can be issued following an irregularity in customs declarations or might contain the results of the customs control. The RIF aims to support simple and effective targeting and risk analysis at the external frontier (European Commission – Taxation and Customs Union 2012).

respondent (G17) explained that the system does not allow enough discretion to determine these checks from the bottom up. 'Personnel on the ground know the flows very well and are able to assess whether or not to expect trouble. Practical knowledge and experience seems to be referred to playing the second fiddle'. The risk analysis system, however, still allows input based on practical experience and leaves room for individual choices. Officers on the quays can often decide whether a transport requires document, scan or physical control. In essence, this system tries to strike a balance between allowing enough discretion and avoiding the controls from being perceived as too subjective. Related to that, there is a lack of customs' expertise and training as well as autonomy on waste issues. Customs have a stop-function for illegal waste transports, but are not a first-line service that acts autonomously for environmental issues. The administrative follow-up is for the inspectorates. The reality is of course that customs has many more employees, many more eyes and ears than inspectorates, police, judiciary and environmental administration. Work-to-rule actions by customs have already illustrated that a lot more waste transports can be intercepted when customs focuses on this more intensely. A civil society respondent (S10) added:

> In practice, the controls fall back on people who are interested in and passionate about the topic. However, they are not applauded for doing this, because customs is primarily a financially oriented institution. Hierarchical leaders will often tell them not to focus on non-fiscal matters too much, because it is not their core priority. Too many seizures by customs give a country a bad name.

A final but fundamental critique of the customs system in Antwerp is the possibility of having a late bill of lading – which in practice means you can deliver the goods in the port and provide the necessary documentation afterwards. Although the respondents gave mixed messages about this – some said it was everyday practice while others said it was not possible – it did seem part of Antwerp's charm and harm.[64]

Harbourmaster's Office

The Harbourmaster's Office (HMO), part of the Antwerp Port Authority (APA),[65] has the responsibility to safeguard the safety, peace, public order, integrity and environment of the port. The Harbourmaster and his deputies are judicial police officers and have the authority to investigate criminal offences and submit police reports (Verstraeten 2007). The policing authority of HMO is limited to the nautical

---

64 Antwerp is known as a flexible port where 'you can put a container on the ship of yesterday' (civil society respondent 10). This and other respondents explained how containers can be shipped and documents can be provided afterwards. For instance, particularly units that arrive on Friday afternoon have a high change of being on the ship without checks.

65 The Antwerp Port Authority is discussed later, as one of the private actors.

context and to the territory of the harbour.[66] HMO handles about 550 offences each year and 75 per cent of those result in police reports. Most of these offences are breaches of environmental legislation, the vessel traffic system or dangerous goods regulation. As part of the APA,[67] HMO has the difficult task of uniting both economic and safety rationalities. Economically they advertise the flexibility of the port in Antwerp which does not always coincide with the governance reality of preventing and controlling illegal e-waste transports. Other respondents feared the fragmented policy at the terminals[68] in Antwerp stimulated criminal activity. 'There are currently vehicles that are driven from Greece or Italy to be shipped in Antwerp, so there has to be a reason for making this trip worthwhile', as a government respondent illustrated (G15). Of particular importance for the case of e-waste, is the 2011 police regulation[69] that was issued by HMO to address worries about the Port of Antwerp's reputation as a waste hub in second-hand vehicles and their cargo. The extra cargo in the vehicles now requires a bill of lading and needs to be accessible and controllable. It stipulates that CFC-holding equipment is not allowed and all used electric and electronic equipment (UEEE) has to be functional. Eight extra employees of HMO will be responsible for the enforcement and will be allowed to block vehicles until the responsible authority unblock them. Inspectorates worry this will result in an overload of requests for checks of docked vehicles. The coordination of the different authorities involved is thus crucial. A particular advantage of this new regulation is that it allows for immediate fines in the case of breaches. These fines can be as high as 1,500 euro per unit. It remains to be seen how the new regulation will work in practice, since the newly hired staff members were not in function at the time of this research. Transport corporations fear the effect of increased controls on trade, as the following quote (corporate respondent 4) illustrates: 'We have enough traffic now, but it would be bad to see that disappear. Illegal and legal traffic tends to go down and shifts to ports where one feels less targeted. It is better to increase controls in the EU hinterland by means of harmonized legislation and enforcement'.

66 Article 7 of the Law of 5 May 1936 establishing the statute of the harbourmaster (*Wet van 5 Mei 1936 tot vaststelling van het statuut der havenkapiteins*) (consolidated version of 15 June 2011).

67 Port Glossary, available at: http://www.portofantwerp.com/portal/page/portal/POA_EN/Havenhandboek/Havenlexicon [last consulted on 28 December 2011].

68 The terminals have different policies, whereas other European ports (for example Rotterdam) have an integrated policy for the entire port area.

69 Regulation of 24 November 2011 for handling of second hand vehicles in the Port of Antwerp (*Reglement voor het behandelen van tweedehands voertuigen in de haven van Antwerpen*) – entered into force 1 January 2012.

Federal environmental and maritime police

Waste fraud has been listed as a police priority in the national security plan.[70] This implies that the police can focus on this topic proactively and reactively. In practice, the police focus is on serious environmental crimes, which means they are organized, linked to a corporate environment, involve high profits, are international, repetitive, related to other criminal behaviour and have an impact on the environment as well as citizens' health. Of particular importance to the case of Antwerp, is the role played by the maritime police (*Scheepvaartpolitie Antwerpen – SPNA*).[71] They are responsible for protecting goods and persons in the harbour, for public order and security[72] as well as for environmental issues.[73] The environmental team consists of one full-time and one part-time officer and (e-)waste is one among many other environmental responsibilities.

The governance reality holds different challenges for the police in preventing and controlling e-waste transports. First of all, there is the limited staff and resources available, especially in the districts responsible for the Port of Antwerp. Many of the respondents, also in other government agencies, were worried about the potential implications of future priority changes. A government respondent (G18) explained: 'It would be a pity for all the efforts of an already resource-wise challenged network of authorities to go to waste. Many of us work in difficult circumstances, often without hierarchical support within our own organisation'. Given the limited resources, it should come as no surprise that proactive controls are limited.[74] The police mainly focus on major criminal cases in which the federal judicial police are responsible for gathering information. In these investigations the police try to target the offender and attempt to calculate the profit made with the illegal transports. It is often very difficult to retrospectively prove that earlier waste transports were illegal as well. A government respondent (G23) added:

---

70 National Security Plan 2008–11 and 2012–15. Other environmental crimes, such as smuggling in endangered species are not listed as a priority and therefore only focused on reactively.

71 The local police of Antwerp, Beveren and Zwijndrecht are not authorized for environmental law implementation in the harbour, but they can work on road transports of waste and check for illegal transports. The local police can also support the federal police in case of controls and inspections of shipments towards non-OECD countries that require extra capacity.

72 This responsibility is with SPNA since the police reform of 2001. Because port areas were a federal priority in the past this was continued after the police reform (Ponsaers et al. 2008).

73 De Scheepvaartpolitie, available at: http://www.polfed-fedpol.be/org/org_dga_spn_nl.php [last consulted 21 January 2012].

74 In road transport controls, police officers check for waste. Information about these is gathered in the 'ecoforms'. These contain information about weight, date, origin and destination of waste. 'It is important to then check whether the followed route is logical or whether it is suspicious. Transports in weekend or overnight and those with rental trucks are generally deemed suspicious' (G1).

'for minor cases, the police have limited possibilities. It is important to trace those back to the source in order to inform and sensitise, but that is outside the police scope of action'. A third challenge is that the environmental police officers are experts on police investigations, but not on environmental issues. Similar to customs and HMO, they need expert knowledge of environmental administrators and inspectors, whose reports are added to the police files. When checks by SPNA point towards illegal shipments the container can be blocked. The follow-up is for the responsible authorities.

Judicial authorities

The Port of Antwerp is located on the left and right banks of the Scheldt estuary, which translates into separate judicial and municipal districts each with its own law enforcement priorities.[75] Depending on the *locus operandi*, the judicial authority has prosecutors in either the districts of Antwerp or Dendermonde. The judicial authorities of Antwerp took the initiative to set up a project approach for waste fraud in the Port of Antwerp.[76] This plan[77] stipulates that not all environmental offenses should be subject to criminal prosecution. The priorities are with those offenses that are so serious that available administrative sanctions or procedures to regulate the issue are insufficient. Moreover, these need to involve either criminal intent by the perpetrator, hold a real risk for the environment, be a danger for public health, cause abnormal hindrance for the surrounding area or result in significant financial benefits. This plan stresses the importance of partnerships and follow-up of cases through the (criminal) justice chain. It lists both quantitative and qualitative micro-indicators to follow up the actions taken by the different partners, although they cannot hold each other to account. Follow-up is the responsibility of the working group on waste fraud. Preventive aspects are not part of this plan. Despite the good intentions of the project, each actor in the network needs to be conscious about the added value of the information other actors in the governance network can provide. The success of the judicial approach, therefore, to a certain extent depends on the information provided by other actors, gathered with other intentions in mind.[78] According to a government respondent (G19): '[t]hey undoubtedly have the technical expertise and knowhow, but the information

---

75 This includes the city of Antwerp and the municipalities of Beveren and Zwijndrecht. This means that the port is not only a territory of the province and judicial district of Antwerp, but also of the judicial district of Dendermonde and the province of East-Flanders.

76 In the port of Zeebrugge, a similar network was set up, inspired by the Antwerp example.

77 District Action Plan of 19 January 2012 'Approach to severe environmental crime with a focus on organized waste fraud' – Integrated plan of objectives 2012 (*Arrondissementaal Actieplan Aanpak zware milieucriminaliteit met focus op. georganiseerde afvalzwendel, Geïntegreerd Doelstellingenschema 2012*).

78 This relates to the 'administrative dependence of the environmental criminal law' (Faure 1991).

they gather is not necessarily useful in criminal cases'. Information from different relevant sources such as maritime police, inspectorates and so on is gathered by the prosecutor. 'So in fact it is at prosecutor's level that someone needs to have the insight that similar names recur', according to a government respondent (G23). In principle, all possible means will be used to prosecute import and export cases and also transit issues will be met with sanctions. In practice, however, prosecution of transit cases is problematic and the focus is mainly on export. Out-of-court settlements are given whenever possible. A government respondent (G19) illustrates this:

> The objective is to investigate the potential criminal networks involved in it and find those 'big fish', but there are many intermediaries in different (international) locations. There is cooperation needed with different actors and it is a very media sensitive topic. Moreover, in everything we do, we feel the threat of the economic lobby. An enforcement actor who wants a new regulation to be imposed in the harbour gets a lot of critique. Economic actors are often protected by powerful people up in the government hierarchy.

In practice the cases thus hardly ever result in successful court cases, while fines[79] are too low and prosecution is too slow to be effective, similar to other environmental cases (Faure 2012). This is a problem not limited to Belgium, but applies throughout Europe, as the following quote from a civil society respondent (S20) illustrates: 'If you get fined for a WSR-breach, a fine of 1,000 euro is very unlikely and hardly ever imposed. If you are in the illegal waste business, you can make that part of your business plan'.

A corporate respondent mentioned that a client who has units inspected in the harbour will generally not ship waste again, because that costs them about 3,000 euro. Government actors doubted that and one quote (G14) illustrates how they see the same people and the same names reoccurring: 'We might come across 20 of their shipments yearly, whereas 200 might have gone through without trouble'. Those WSR cases rarely go to trial and hardly ever result in convictions, often because it is too technical to prove criminal intent. In fact, no major cases have made it to trial successfully in Belgium, making it, according to a government respondent (G14) 'much more lucrative to ship waste illegally than ship drugs, because the sanctions for drugs are both more severe and more likely'.

79 Sanctions can be as high as eight days to three years' imprisonment and/or a fine of 52–4,000.000 euro for breaches of Articles 7 and 9 of the Belgian law on transit of waste and breaches of WSR articles and other EU regulations. Breaches of Articles 10, 16, 17 and 18 of the WSR and other EU laws are met with imprisonment of eight days to one year and a fine of 40–120,000 euro.

Government actors in Ghana as a country of destination

In this section I analyse the role of government actors in Ghana as a country of destination of many of the WEEE/UEEE shipments. Despite signing the international conventions, there is currently no Ghanaian legislation that regulates e-waste or second-hand transports. As long as that is not in place, checking transports is to no avail since no fines can be imposed. A civil society respondent (S22) adds: 'Many politicians fear they will lose voters' support. The importers and UEEE shop owners are more important to them than the Agbogbloshie workers from the North. We might even call it environmental racism'.

The Ghanaian Environmental Protection Agency (EPA) aims to play a similar role as the inspectorates in countries of origin or transit, but is very limited in staff. Two full-time employees work on waste issues. In lack of a legal basis to act, their main concern is with raising awareness of government actors about the dangers of e-waste since many consider them as profitable second-hand products, as the following quote from a government respondent (G29) illustrates: 'The e-waste situation was alerted by a Belgian inspector who said there was a problem. It was difficult to understand what the problem was. Since then, e-waste has been a real nightmare. It comes in on a daily basis'. The EPA's current enforcement focus is on licensing recycling facilities and analysing where WEEE/UEEE is sold and refurbished. However, these actors are numerous, very flexible and spread out across Ghana. Other actors think this licensing by means of environmental impact assessments is too high a barrier for many recycling facilities, pushing them into informality. This was observed in Belgium as well, where small-scale collectors could not answer to the high standards imposed. The EPA therefore reaches out to these informal actors and shows them how to improve the working conditions with simple tools similar to what local NGOs do. In this way, they intend to support them instead of criminalize them.

Ghanaian customs are less concerned with e-waste. Local NGOs think customs as well as port authorities have real governance potential in tackling the illegal e-waste transports. I observed how containers of WEEE/UEEE are inspected and unloaded by customs. E-waste is not their first concern, especially because they can impose high taxes on imports of electronics and also given the low level of training. The scanning facilities are present, but only homogenous shipments are inspected. In face of this governance reality, customs will need more incentives to control for illegal e-waste shipments (for example rewards for seizing low quality goods). A government respondent (G28) explains: 'Customs are paid very low wages so they want a piece of the cake for themselves. And how can you blame them?' In case a law is passed, awareness raising and training of these enforcers will be crucial. Even then, the problem remains that seized goods will have to be recycled locally, often ending up in the same system. The Ghana Ports and Harbours Authority (GPHA) focuses on environmental safety in the port. Mainly the dumping of waste and release of waste water is their concern. A few of their employees are concerned about e-waste, but this depends on their own interest in the topic. Ghanaian police do not work on environmental issues. Based on the above, it should come as no surprise that – in absence of national legislation– cases do not go to court.

Corporations as (Passive) Governance Actors

This section examines the governance reality of corporate actors in e-waste flows. The roles of shipping agents, shipping lines and e-goods producers and recyclers are analysed. This will make clear that the governance of the flows is not really a priority for these actors, since their role is often limited to responding to requests of government actors. Others take more initiative, mostly when it coincides with their core business (Gunningham, Kagan and Thornton 2003).

Shipping agents

A shipping agent is paid by the buyer or seller to organize the transport. Their tasks can involve drafting the bill of lading, taking care of the transport documentation and arranging the payments and deposits. When looking at the governance reality for shipping agents a number of observations can be made. Goods handlers in Antwerp recognize they have a responsibility in transports of second-hand vehicles containing e-waste, as the following quote from a corporate respondent (C2) illustrates: 'In the past, some of these vehicles were definitely filled with goods, amongst others e-waste. But meanwhile, a code of conduct was drafted which was later used as a basis for the new regulation'. As witnessed in the field visits, not all shipping agents agreed the shipments were a bad thing, with one corporate respondent (C23) stating: 'Inspectors themselves should go to Africa to see how difficult life is'. The fact that many shipping agents are unaware of the issue or even facilitate regular illegal transports was made obvious by a terminal operator (corporate respondent 19) in Ghana as well: 'One of our clients ships 15 containers of e-waste every 2 months. We have about 20 similar clients'.

The shipping agents' business is based on trusting the shippers, as the following quote (C23) explains: 'The papers are faxed and I don't know what's truly inside the containers or vehicles. I'm not there when they are loaded'. The responsibility is shifted to actors earlier in the chain: the shipper. Shipping agents, and especially those that do the handling and storage as well, have a possibility to know the content, at least according to a civil society respondent (S11). 'Many of them take care of the documents and book the container and therefore know their customers'. Some shipping agents take initiatives to inform their clients about what is allowed and warn them about possible fines.[80] Some even anticipate potential trouble and ask their customers for a warranty (for example 3,000 euro), because the terminal

80 They do this by providing the port regulations of Antwerp to their clients (translated in English, French or German) and by distributing ads and warning notices in their office and on their website which explain what is allowed and what is not (for example CFC, missing cables).

will charge the shipping agent for the costs of unloading.[81] Some shipping agents take measures to know their clients, refusing to work with them when a problem has already occurred. Others, however, work with whatever clients they can get. Both government and corporate respondents therefore suggested installing a system of 'minimum prerequisites for shipping agents. You would quickly see who is willing to go the extra mile, and then you know enough to target controls. This would have to be EU-wide to avoid economic consequences of stricter controls in Antwerp', as a corporate respondent (C2) said.

Shipping lines

The sector of international maritime transports and trade through ports is known for its somewhat non-transparent way of communication (Denoiseux 2010). A corporate respondent (C5) explained '[a]lthough environmental issues could be part of this broader denominator of security, it is still not a major concern'. It is indeed true that contacting shipping lines for this research was challenging. One major shipping line was, however, willing to talk. Together with the interviews of other governance actors, this allowed me to analyse their role with the governance reality of illegal e-waste flows.

Some shipping lines take initiative to self-regulate and several incentives stimulate this. This, however, does not necessarily mean that the entire shipping industry is influenced by these incentives. Economic, ethical and political considerations guide them to refuse certain shipments (Bartley 2007). A first motivation is the concern to be a sustainable and responsible actor. The reputational risk plays an important role. Shipping lines do not strictly have a legal responsibility in illegal e-waste flows, but they feel subject to criticism from their stakeholders. Being recognized as a responsible actor is seen as economically beneficial. They also face the financial risk of fines and of costs of transports not being refunded. For a shipping line, the container itself (not the content) is its asset and it is important to get this back. Moreover, shipping lines are sometimes targeted by judges in countries of destination for a case of illegal waste transport, as the closest actor in proximity, chaining their vessels until the costs are paid for. The shipping lines' involvement (or rather some shipping lines' involvement) is also guided by both the society's tendency to increasingly challenge shipping lines on legal and ethical issues and the fact that the 21st century is a hyper-transparent community. Shipping lines, however, worry how much they can engage without taking up a responsibility that is not theirs. To a certain extent, they choose their battles based on practical considerations. The following quote from a corporate respondent (C5) illustrates this: 'recently the choice was made to focus on suspicious trades of big volumes and look at potential hotspots and partnerships to deal with this. Waste is a big concern, but the battle is not solely ours'. Similar to the shipping agents, shipping lines do not have the authority to open containers and they are even at

81 In addition, port authorities can block their financial warranty and revoke their license. The Belgian judicial system also tries to deal with them as accomplices.

a greater distance from the initial shipper. They rely on the trustworthiness of shippers and shipping agents. Other respondents, however, believed the shipping lines know all the tricks to hide behind their commercial practicalities and know they transport illegal waste, but until recently were not challenged by their stakeholders on these issues. 'Many shipping lines are not intrinsically motivated to know what is inside containers', as a civil society respondent (S20) added.

European producers and recyclers

Transport corporations are not the only kind of corporation involved in the governance framework for e-waste. European recycling corporations are increasingly involved in the e-waste discussion albeit that their motivations are linked to the raw materials discussion rather than they are necessarily environmental. Their core incentive is guaranteeing the inflow of metal scrap for the European recycling facilities. Therefore they try to influence EU policy and aim for the continued criminalization of transports of e-waste in protection of the 'urban mine'.[82] This economic factor is a major part of the current policy discussion and is critical for success, together with addressing corporations on their reputation. Many corporations will do everything to work within the contours of the law. Some might even set standards that surpass legal requirements, especially because customers increasingly ask for follow-up about where their equipment ends up. Corporations seem to be particularly willing to go the extra mile if this fits their core business. Some choose environmental friendly initiatives that enhance the corporate image and might not be profitable for years to come. Recyclers are setting up take-back initiatives in West Africa (and other African regions). This is partially out of concern for the environment, but there is a clear business incentive given the low labour costs for dismantling the equipment. Monitoring is therefore important. This could be connected to formal collection and dismantling initiatives that have emerged in Ghana. It is also useful to connect these initiatives to the informal sector, because they collect 90 per cent of e-waste. 'The fact, that there is an efficient and effective collection system in place in Ghana has to be strongly considered, when starting new initiatives and for avoiding, that e-waste is still being sent to Agbogbloshie' (Rufener 2012, p. 9).

Recycling corporations across the EU have difficulty focalizing efforts because they suspect competitors of feeding into illegal transports. Others believe self-regulatory initiatives to be promising. A central concern for recyclers is with the establishment of a level playing field, as the following quote from a corporate respondent (C12) illustrates: 'Harmonized legislation and enforcement practices within the EU should be increased together with raising public awareness, but not at the cost of increasing administrative burdens for corporations and

82 The urban mine is a mine of (raw) materials from products, buildings and waste in a society. Urban mining is the idea of using those compounds and elements as resources for new production, thereby avoiding these materials from going to waste. E-waste exports can thus be seen as a loss in raw material.

decreasing the competitiveness'. Currently, EU countries are perceived to protect their own market and hamper the enforcement of the EU waste legislation. The European recycling industry therefore proposed a scheme for controls on e-waste transports, in which the percentage of controls is tailored to both the destination (low-medium-high risk) and the exporter (low-medium-high risk) (Euromettaux 2012).[83] It proposes that controls should take place at the EU port of departure at the exporter's costs and that second-hand equipment should be identifiable in the customs documents, which would give specific reasons for customs to check those transports more thoroughly.

Producers of EEE could also choose to self-regulate. They are required to take steps because of their extended producer responsibility as determined by the Waste Electronic and Electric Equipment Directive, which makes producers responsible for take-back and recycling of their products, and the Regulation on Hazardous Substances (RoHS) that requires manufacturers to phase out the use of the most hazardous components. However, '[t]he traceability of products remains an issue for everyone involved', according to a government respondent (G20). Several respondents would prefer producers to set up a take-back system for their products which would make all other take-backs uninteresting. Some producers are currently tying into that niche, similar to refurbishers on the other end of the supply chain. In countries of destination, some producers take their extended producer responsibility seriously, while others claim no responsibility and blame the shippers. A Ghanaian waste collector (C25) puts it as follows: 'currently producers are cherry picking what they will and won't take back. They should not be allowed to get away with that. Producers should be encouraged to take back their equipment, to take the metal, circuit boards and plastic casings. The main problem is that they don't care about their image on these issues'.

Civil Society Actors as Crucial (but Waning) Support

Besides the role for government and corporate actors in the governance reality of illegal transports of e-waste, the question remains what role is played by civil society actors. It seems rather clear to most of the respondents that NGOs continue to have a crucial role to play in distributing information and continuing to raise awareness. In the 1970s and 1980s, NGOs scandalized illegal waste shipments and played an essential role in negotiations for the Basel Convention. Their

83 Low-risk exporters, which are those with AEO certificates, should have 0.0001 per cent chance of control when they ship to low-risk countries (OECD), 0.001 per cent chance when they ship to medium-risk (other non-OECD) countries and 0.01 per cent when shipping to high-risk (West-African) countries. Medium-risk exporters are manufacturers, producers and important traders and they should respectively have a 0.01 per cent, 0.1 per cent and 1 per cent chance of control when shipping to low-, medium- and high-risk countries. High-risk exporters (all other) should respectively have a 1 per cent, 10 per cent and 100 per cent chance of control.

contemporary importance is in continuing to report about current evolutions, by which they keep up pressure, as a civil society respondent (S16) illustrated:

> Consumers, especially corporations and governments, get more aware of their 'e-waste flows' once their equipment has been discovered in a waste dump and that's why NGOs should continue to look for tags and check the hard drives for data. They should keep this up and also follow-up on earlier cases to see whether the situation has improved.

NGOs like Greenpeace have already used GPS trackers to follow e-waste around the world and to bring the topic to the public attention.[84] Similarly, NGOs publish tags that were found on dumped e-waste or confront previous owners with their old data. This technique could be used to track containers as well (Auld et al. 2010). One of the Ghanaian government respondents (G28) explained that they saw fluctuations in transports depending on the amount of attention for e-waste in countries of origin.

For NGOs based in Western countries, their role seems to be one of contributing to the achievements of other governance actors (Young 2009) and they struggle to combine collaborating with industry and meanwhile continuing their environmental advocacy (Holley et al. 2012). These NGOs however continue to be involved as stakeholders in policy-making on both EU and UN levels. By their presence on these levels, they can help to broaden the criminality scope of trade to include more than narcotics or terrorism. Similarly, they could play a role in transposing the international legislation to national laws in countries of destination, while furthering the often neglected implementation.

Several of the respondents raised concern that NGO portrayals are a way of marketing to a certain extent and portray their (Western) views on reality, disregarding the local context. A civil society respondent (S21) agreed and stressed that '[i]nvolving the informal collection and dismantling sector can help towards lowering the environmental harm. Stopping the inflow of e-waste is then only secondary to teaching them how to recycling more environmentally and health friendly'. NGOs based in the local settings have a good chance of involving those communities affected by illegal e-waste flows – but not recognized as such – and getting them involved in the governance process as a complement to the conventional strategies (Braithwaite 2000; Holley et al. 2012). This is true for the local Ghanaian NGOs working on e-waste. They try to involve informal actors as well as reach out to recyclers for support. The intention of these NGOs is to

---

84 A labelling initiative also emerged for e-waste: 'e-stewards'. This aims at the recycling and refurbishment of electronics. This was created by the Basel Action Network (BAN), a USA-based NGO, supported by several recyclers. Besides the safe handling of e-waste, it aims to prevent illegal transports and aims for adherence to Basel standards. This is not very prominent in the EU, maybe because the legal framework is more stringent than in the USA.

reduce the illegal imports, but even then recycling the domestic consumption of new products will remain a problem. A corporate respondent (C25) adds:

> It is important not to criminalize them but to advise them in order to improve recycling rates and techniques and in the long run the impact on human health as well as environment. They don't know the danger today, don't realize it, but also don't have the luxury to worry about the long term effects. There are no recycling facilities in Ghana, but wages are low and people can dismantle equipment very meticulously which you simply cannot afford in the EU.

NGOs should however be self-critical as well. Several NGOs or smaller-scale charity projects have been associated with illegal transports of e-waste. A government respondent (G22) explains:

> There are so many do-good initiatives in Europe that are actually doing wrong. Out-of-use and all those so-called charities that ask you to send your phone, it is for a so called good cause but so much disappears into the pockets of those that organize it. The question is why people, and mind you, major corporations and NGOs continue to be fooled by this. Even investment funds finance recyclers who don't necessarily practice what they preach.

The role of civil society actors thus seems to be in shaming illegal e-waste transports as well as in attempting to find the best governance approach attuned to the local context (cf. capacity building). Braithwaite (2008) referred to this as balancing the responsive regulatory pyramid with a strength-based pyramid.

Networked Governance Analysis of the E-Waste Flows

Same intentions and different realities in inter-agency cooperation

The analysis of the governance reality shows cooperation between actors. Each of the government actors that were analysed in this study made clear that their work on illegal transports of e-waste is only one part of the entire control mechanism. The first step of the governance reality is in the work of the environmental inspectorates and administration. Flemish inspectorates (export) will usually address corporations on their license by following the e-waste flow back to its source. The inspectorates negotiate about licenses of facilities. Of course, this inevitably relates back to the management systems – and self-regulation – of corporations. Similarly, the AEO system of customs gives corporations the opportunity to make sure a management system is in place which influences the degree of control. Neither of these however applies easily to the multitude of small-scale (often individual) shippers of UEEE/WEEE because they are difficult to trace. The federal inspectorate (transit) – which deals with 80 per cent of the e-waste shipments in Antwerp – moreover relies on other EU states to trace the transports back to the origin.

Depending on the features of the case one or another actor takes up a leading role. This can merely be a result of a practical reality, of the available expertise or can truly be out of concern for an integrated approach. The judiciary clearly takes a leading role in the approach to waste fraud in the Port of Antwerp. Customs takes a leading role in the risk analysis system. Inspectorates and administrations have the expertise on environmental issues. The primary role in the governance of illegal e-waste flows seems to be that of law enforcement rather than of the administrative level. Belgium has the advantage of having an environmental administration (OVAM) that takes up a role that other countries reserve for local administrations. The administrative/preventative aspects are developed into policy by the Flemish and Federal Administrations and are of course highly influenced by the European framework. The risk is that local authorities in Belgium are not fully engaged in the process (Braithwaite 2008).

Transparency and clear delineation of tasks and objectives is crucial to avoid government actors from fighting each other instead of crime (Sluis et al. 2012). The question is then whether these actors work with the same intentions in mind and the same realities at hand. Environmental inspectorates both clearly focus on illegal transports of e-waste for environmental reasons, but work within different realities. Whereas the regional inspectorates are in the position to address the topic earlier in the chain, the federal inspectorate only has the location of the port to work at.[85] OVAM is similarly oriented to environmental issues but focuses on initiatives earlier in the chain (licenses) as well as on policy. The customs' focus on illegal transports of e-waste is rather recent and struggles with balancing concerns for security and economy. Customs specializes in customs-related responsibilities, is at the front line in import and export of waste, has the technical means to control (scanning of containers and risk analysis) and has many 'eyes and ears'. Note however, that a system based on trust (potentially) does not match the approaches of other government actors. The question remains whether this system of trust in economic operators by customs and even the system of trust in compliance by the environmental administrations can be united with the strategies of judicial actors that work based on distrust.

The HMO's priority is with safety and compliance. E-waste is a rather recent concern and they have to maintain a balance with economic interests. HMO can now control for e-waste in second-hand vehicles and their increased resources are important. Customs as well as HMO relies, however, on the environmental inspectorates for the follow-up of the cases they find suspicious. Unless these agencies equally receive additional resources, the extra focus of customs and HMO risks becoming futile. Finally, the police and the judiciary are both clearly concerned with illegal transports of e-waste because they are environmental crimes and have a potential or alleged link to 'organized crime'. This only concerns the serious and extensive cases. The police expertise on strategic analysis could prove useful for all data on illegal e-waste trade.

85 The institutional reform of 2014 addressed this.

Although these actors are all part of the network or the chain that responds to these issues, their methods and everyday reality at work are different. One of the criticisms of corporations is that the implementation of the law seems to be valued higher than environmental concerns. Corporations experience an extra burden in terms of administration because of the fragmentation of agencies and perceive the staff resources invested in controls as inefficient. This efficiency of the network will get increasingly important, given the planned expansion of the Antwerp harbour and its goods flow.[86] The governance reality flows through different layers of authority and faces different objectives and means. Their cooperation could help in seeing the bigger picture of the governance reality and help overcome existing practical difficulties.

Starting cooperation between shipping lines and governments

Given the scale of e-waste transports and their illegal share, the transport sector can play an important role in governance. A first important step is raising awareness about illegal e-waste flows. Many company brochures and websites already mention sustainability, but it requires further translation into practice in both Belgium and Ghana. As witnessed during field visits and interviews, many port actors do not know what e-waste is and are very unaware of the potential harms. A civil society respondent (S20) suggests that 'information campaigns should contain practical advice directed not only at the managers of these companies but also at the actual goods handlers. This might not stop crafty criminals from shipping e-waste illegally, but might address "low hanging fruit"'. This will likely require a few major shipping lines to take the lead as is happening today, but it might be more difficult to involve smaller actors, like shipping agents, because, according to a corporate respondent (C5), 'these often haven neither the resources nor the management structure to seriously deal with this'. Corporations could become engaged based on economic as well as ethical motivations. As a testimony to the governance potential of shipping lines, the UK shipping lines are partners of the waste enforcement agencies. They provide them with information about their clients and in this way help to keep their business clean and help to trace waste back to its origin. It is however not possible to copy-paste this in Antwerp, according to a government respondent (G25), because '90 per cent of their shipments originate in the UK'. Stimulated by Dutch inspectorates, a seminar was organized by IMPEL-TFS to look at options for future cooperation with shipping lines. A similar thing is happening in countries of destination where shipping lines are increasingly providing the authorities with information to facilitate controls or even warn their clients in case of suspicions.

86 This expansion is part of the judicial district of Dendermonde (as opposed to the Antwerp district) and therefore a different department of the federal judicial police, which means police investigators and magistrates might be located in Ghent, the judicial district that since recently houses the functional magistrate.

The challenge of (better) information exchange

Information exchange between actors is crucial for successful cooperation in governance (Holley et al. 2012). Government agencies are faced with the challenge of better exchange, because the agencies gather information from different perspectives and on the basis of different objectives. Information exchange between private actors and government agencies is even more complex. Information-led investigations are a core issue for policing illegal transports of e-waste. Strategic analysis might allow bringing together data that is currently not always connected. The current systems are capable of detecting and sanctioning individual perpetrators of waste legislation though these efforts appear insufficient to tackle the repeat offenders. The information-led policing strategy is also applied by environmental inspectorates, particularly the regional ones, because they follow the goods in the supply chain and go in search of the source.[87] Currently, different databases and systems for information exchange are in use, but the respondents complained that these systems do not always work both ways. Administrative information does flow toward police or judicial actors, but the former do not always get feedback. Different agencies currently gather data, often with limited resources, but databases are not always interconnected. The coordination and communication platform in the Port of Antwerp is an important trigger for this, but by extension this requires the analysis of data across national borders. 'Cooperation between countries is essential to detect the scale of the networks. Often the same people are involved in UK, Belgium, Germany as well as Ghana', as a government respondent (G29) explained. Not all EU countries however allow for the exchange of administrative information. Each authority has to go through the respective national channels to get access to police files, customs files and so on (Ponsaers et al. 2008). Recently, Belgium, Netherlands and Hungary took the initiative to set up a network about environmental crime that can use the facilities of Europol (*Envicrimenet*).[88] Both soft and hard information will be gathered with the intention to coordinate actions and strategies based on the analysis. The major issue is using this intelligence, because it has been gathered for different objectives. Gathering all this information could take the governance system to a nodal level, covering different authority grounds (multi-disciplinary) and taking responsibility for the meta-perspective.

Similarly, an increase in information exchange could be useful for corporate actors. Privacy issues might pose a problem[89] and transport actors often do not know more than what is mentioned on the documents. Information exchange can make criteria that should raise suspicion with shipping lines and agents more

87 Similar approaches are used by the Netherlands ILENT (former VROM-inspectorate) 'Back to the source' ('*Terug naar de bron*') investigations.

88 This network is a follow-up of the *Augias* network, which focused on waste crimes and was established during the Belgian presidency of the EU.

89 Discussing the judicial possibilities of and limits to information exchange was not the intent of this study.

tangible. Examples of suspicious cargos that should ring a bell abound: clients offer to pay cash for 10 containers or provide a Hotmail address as contact details; the destination of the recycling is the ninth floor of an office building or a house in the city centre; shippers refuse to provide information on the destination. A government respondent (G15) adds: 'Companies can either consider this as business where you don't ask questions or they could be suspicious'. Respondents mentioned that some shipping lines already have informal 'black lists' that are fed with generic information from both corporate and government contacts such as descriptions of cargo and destinations. They make sure not to share personal information. A civil society respondent (S20) believed that '[a]lthough corporations and governments might be walking a thin privacy line in this matter, the risk of negative publicity gives them enough incentive. This information is however not shared lightly'. Once again concerns were raised about the one-sidedness of the communication. A concern for shipping lines was that despite the increasing information exchange, they did not get the impression a lot was done with it. A concern for recyclers and waste traders is the protection of data against competitors.[90]

The exceptions to the rule

Despite e-waste fraud being an issue of national and international importance, resources are limited as is political will (Griffiths and Jenks 2012). Compared to other international crimes such as drugs, the law enforcement resources invested in environmental crime are limited (Faure 2012; White 2011). Both in countries of origin and destination, there are a limited number of people involved. Despite their terrain knowledge and experience being crucial for the governance framework, they are bound by their limited resources. The following quote from a government respondent (G14) illustrates this: 'The problem is not that we don't know where the illicit traffic is, know where to find it or know how to check it. The problem is that we don't have the means to guarantee the follow-up, that's the bottleneck'. This refers to those environmental inspectors and police officers that are governing e-waste transports on a daily basis. It also refers to local police and inspectorates across the EU who might know where (informal) storage and handling facilities and practices occur and in this way can tackle the problem by starting at the root. Similarly, the shipping agents and lines that take initiatives on the issue of illegal transports of e-waste are valuable in the governance network. These exceptions to the rule are passionate about their job, but frustration looms. Taken to the extreme, this implies that the success of this entire networked governance depends on these 'exceptions' (sources of information). This goes against the requirements of effective environmental governance (Holley et al. 2012).

90 Business to business information exchange exists also, but only applies to a limited number of metals. 'Certain compositions are as accurate as a fingerprint. For other e-waste flows however, the situation is totally different because many actors are involved and in mixing waste, relabeling it, etc. modus operandi are multiple' (C16).

Harmonization of policy rather than implementation

The flows of goods – e-waste amongst them – are difficult to govern by national authorities (Brown 2010). Implementation is often problematic in governance, particularly in more complex arrangements (Holley et al. 2012). Supranational governance systems should not be met with limitless optimism, because they are often 'negotiated, rendered less efficient and even sabotaged by sovereignty games played by individual nation states' (Aas 2011, p. 333). The e-waste case illustrates that the translation from paper to practice entails many challenges. Electronics are a very dynamic topic, where new inventions become e-waste a few years later. The policy that defines what type of equipment is e-waste therefore needs to be fit to this dynamic governance reality. Currently, that is not the case as a government respondent (G24) illustrates: 'by the time CRTs will be considered e-waste by European law, the major share of CRTs – and thus the lead it contains – will already have been exported as second-hand goods and dismantled in unacceptable circumstances'. Every European country is supposed to do thorough checks of exports of e-waste, which would imply transit countries can trust their judgement. Government, corporate and civil society respondents however notice a North-South and West-East schism in Europe on how seriously inspections and transport controls are taken and the existing problems with e-waste transit in Antwerp testify to this. Both environmental inspectors and shipping agents responsible for sending back the units even come across authorities that doubt that the shipment originated in their country. This led different respondents to refer to the need for further harmonization of EU policy implementation to avoid displacements.

The continued harmonization on the level of implementation is politically very sensitive. Even if definitions and interpretations would be equal, Europe – let alone the global policy – is a long way from harmonization of implementation. Not all member states use complementary interventions besides the traditional environmental inspection and when controls become more severe in one country, illegal flows shift to another. A government respondent (G24) adds:

> If Europe would impose minimum requirements for inspections and controls, many countries would interpret that as a too much interference of Europe, especially if that would imply countries can call each other to order. As long as this remains as it is, informal networks of information and expertise exchange are the only means to narrow the implementation gap.

Another field lacking EU harmonization is sanctioning. Although the European waste legislation requires sanctions to be set, there are major differences. Fines differ with a factor 100 across the EU. Even within countries there are considerable differences in decision-making (Sander and Schilling 2010). It would be beneficial to organize the controls on an EU level for more unity, but this is a politically very sensitive topic. Besides the various initiatives for international networking, the responsible authorities cooperate bilaterally with their neighbouring countries as well as with countries of destination such as Ghana, but given the limited staff and resources this can prove difficult. Different international guidelines and soft measures exist and are stimulated by networks such INECE,[91] IMPEL-TFS,[92] Secretariat of the Basel Convention,[93] the WCO[94] and the StEP-initiative.[95] These initiatives organize training sessions in countries of destination and fund capacity-building projects. Despite their realizations, a challenge to these international networking initiatives is their voluntary character. Unambiguous measures (for example inspections and controls) are more difficult to agree on.

Conclusion

An assessment of the scope of the illegal trade in e-waste in Europe and in the Belgian research setting of the Port of Antwerp was followed by a discussion of the victimization associated with the illegal trade in e-waste. Then the chapter focused on the social organization and emergence of illegal transports of electronic waste and on its governance. The next chapter makes a similar analysis for the illegal trade in tropical timber. After this second case study, a comparative analysis follows, which starts out with a summary of the findings from both cases.

---

91 INECE stimulates training and exchange of expertise to increase the interception of vessels carrying e-waste.

92 IMPEL originated in administrations (inspectorates) and later involved police and judiciary. IMPEL-TFS plays an active role in standardizing port control practices for UEEE/WEEE and is involved in training and workshops in countries of destination.

93 The Basel Convention has a multi-stakeholder working group, Partnership for Action on Computing Equipment (PACE), that focuses on criteria for reuse of personal computers and aims to draft further regulation of export and to 'tackle the environmentally sound management, refurbishment, recycling and disposal of used and end-of-life computing equipment' (Basel Convention Secretariat 2011). The Basel Secretariat invests in capacity building and coordinating projects in countries of destination (for example e-waste for Africa).

94 The World Customs Organization's network supports and enhances the fights against transnational organized crime, amongst which hazardous waste and ozone-depleting substances (Otterson and Meiser 2009). WCO's operation Demeter focused on illegal hazardous waste to increase information exchange between customs administrations (World Customs Organization 2009).

95 Governments, corporations, NGOs and researchers jointly operate in the StEP initiative of the United Nations University. This is a platform for discussions which provides advice for policy-making. The sector itself has a major role to play in continuing to facilitate this network.

Chapter 6
Illegal Trade in Tropical Timber

Introduction

This chapter discusses the results of the case study into illegal transports of tropical timber.[1] The research setting is the Port of Antwerp (Belgium) but attention is paid to elements that explain the social organization and that impact the governance reality throughout the flows from locations of origin over transit to destination. The focus is on tropical timber and on the trade between Europe and Africa in particular.[2]

The structure of this chapter is as follows. First, the concepts of illegal logging and illegal timber are discussed. Second, the victimization related to the illegal trade in tropical timber is discussed. This pays attention to environmental, social as well as economic arguments that are at the basis of illegality discussions about timber. Third, the global and European scale of illegal transports of timber is examined, together with the inherent data challenges. Fourth, this chapter analysed the social organization and emergence of the illegal transports of tropical timber (Bisschop 2012). This sheds light on the legal-illegal interfaces in the places of origin, transit and destination of the tropical timber flows connected to this European setting. A fifth part discusses the governance reality of illegal transports of tropical timber (Bisschop 2013). The analysis provides insights into the facilitating and hindering factors for governance arrangements throughout the tropical timber flows, for actors individually and in their interaction.

Illegal Logging and Illegal Timber

Illegal logging and illegal timber are terms often used in policy-making to refer to the broad problem of the existence of illegal forest activities, which go beyond the

---

1 This chapter is based on the following two publications, which were used with permission of the publishers. Bisschop, L. (2012): Out of the woods: the illegal trade in tropical timber and a European trade hub, *Global Crime*, 13(3), 191–212; and Bisschop, L. (2013). Governance throughout the flows. Case study research on the illegal tropical timber trade. In P. Saitta, J. Shapland and A. Verhage (eds), *Getting by or Getting Rich? The formal, informal and illegal economy in a globalized world* (pp. 167–99). The Hague: Eleven.

2 This research studied the illegal tropical timber trade between Africa and Europe, and Belgium in particular. This chapter makes no claims for generalization of the findings to other regions and timber flows.

mere illegality of logging. Illegal forest activities can occur at all phases of forest management and the forest goods production chain, from planning over harvesting and transport of raw material and finished products to financial management. Harvesting can be illegal when it happens in excess of concessions, outside concession boundaries or inside nature reserves, but also when unlawful harvesting techniques are used or when protected species are logged (REM 2009). Harvesting is said to be related to corrupt or fraudulent activities to acquire forest concessions or establish rights to land (Tacconi 2007a).Transport is illegal when excise duties are not paid, when there is no authorization for the transport due to reasons of quota, bio-safety, tariffs or trade bans, but transport is equally illegal when forged certificates are used, species are misclassified or deliberately undervalued or when border authorities are corrupted.[3] Even apparently legal forest products, in fact, may have been fraudulently 'legalized' at some point along the production chain: either 'at the stump', in transport by using the same permit multiple times, by re-importing the timber[4] or in processing.

There is thus a difference between illegal logging and illegal trade. Illegal trade refers to the commercial activity, but a major share of the illegally logged wood never enters the international market and is used for domestic energy supplies, although this is generally not part of the international discourse on illegal logging and trade. For the sake of clarity, this study refers to illegal transports of timber and illegal timber as forestry products which were extracted from forests (or plantations) and subsequently processed and traded in breach of the letter or the intent of national law where a clear commercial interest is at stake.[5] This study focuses on tropical timber and on the trade between Europe and Africa in particular.[6] Belgium is an important destination for many countries in West Africa and the Congo Basin and these countries of origin have the biggest trade share in the Port of Antwerp (see below). Several corporate respondents, as well as those from civil society and government, moreover mentioned the particular connection of Belgium with this region and the suspected importance of illegal trade.

---

3 For the EU, imports can breach CITES, EU VPA or Forest Law Enforcement Governance and Trade (FLEGT), EU Timber Regulation, UN Convention against Corruption, on Organised Crime, on Organised Transnational Crime and so on.

4 For example, timber that is illegally logged in Honduras is then illegally exported to Nicaragua and later on legally imported as 'Nicaraguan' timber into Honduras (Wells et al. 2007).

5 Adopted from the definition provided in http://www.globaltimber.org.uk (accessed 10 June 2011).

6 The tropical forest regions of the world – South America, South East Asia and Africa – each have their particular social organization and way of working. This research studied the illegal tropical timber trade between Africa and Europe, and Belgium in particular. This article makes no claims for generalization of the findings towards the other regions and timber flows.

Illegal Logging and its Victims

Illegal logging has been acknowledged as a serious issue since the 1992 Rio Earth Summit[7] and concerns raised by non-governmental organizations (NGOs) have contributed to its rise as a policy issue (Tacconi 2007). One of the rare and binding international agreements on forest management is the International Tropical Timber Agreement (ITTA).[8] The ITTA created the International Tropical Timber Organization (ITTO), but is criticized for its primary aim to promote trade. This stands in contrast to the broader focus of multilateral environmental agreements (Flejzor 2005). The ITTO's focus on sustainable forest management and decreasing deforestation is only secondary to the focus on tropical timber as a commodity (Tarasofsky 1999). The ITTA is also criticized due to a lack of mechanisms to guarantee follow-through of their policies, which rarely result in actual implementation and monitoring. Disillusioned over the ITTO's performance to promote tropical forest conservation, the World Wildlife Fund (WWF) negotiated a labelling policy outside of governments in partnership with NGOs and timber traders (Humphreys 2013). The Forest Stewardship Council (FSC) is to date the only genuine multi-stakeholder third-party certification initiative.[9] Several NGOs followed in withdrawing support for country schemes in favour of voluntary non-governmental approaches to promote the sustainable management and conservation of tropical forests.

Despite the above-mentioned initiatives, there is no widely accepted and implemented international environmental regulation that focuses on timber in particular. The Convention on the International Trade in Endangered Species of Fauna and Flora (CITES) is the only international legal basis, regulating import, export and re-export of some timber species through a permit system to avoid endangering the species' survival. Regional regulations do exist that prohibit imports of illegal timber and require importers' due diligence. The United States has the Lacey Act and Australia has the Illegal Logging Prohibition Act which prohibits imports of illegal timber. Since March 2013, the EU has the European Timber Regulation, which prohibits the placing on the EU market of illegally harvested timber and products derived from such timber and obliges operators who place timber and timber products on the market to do their due diligence. This is a successor to the Forest Law Enforcement, Governance and Trade (FLEGT) Action Plan of the EU with the Voluntary Partnership Agreements (VPAs).

---

7 Rio Declaration on Environment and Development, adopted at the UNCED in Rio de Janeiro, Brazil, 13–14 June 1992.

8 The International Tropical Timber Agreement was originally adopted in 1983 under the auspices of the United National Conference on Trade and Development (UNCTAD) and was updated in 1994 and 2006.

9 This is discussed more extensively under *NGO Pressure and Consumer Awareness* in this chapter.

Despite this lack of international legislation, arguments for the criminalization of illegal logging can be made on ecological, economic and social grounds. Ecologically, the trade in illegal timber contributes to deforestation (FAO 2010), which in its turn has an impact on the regions' ecosystems and their fauna and flora biodiversity (Braat and ten Brinks 2008). Biodiversity loss is in turn linked to general ecological stability (Brook et al. 2013; Cardinale et al. 2012). Forests, moreover, influence the Earth's climate regulation (Houghton 2003; Peskett, Brown and Luttrell, 2006) and illegal timber extraction has an impact on climate change, even though the carbon remains in the logs when processed (Houghton 2003; Peskett, Brown and Luttrell 2006; UNEP 2011b). Where illegal logging activities allow trees to regenerate in logged areas, these ecological arguments do not apply in a straightforward way (Tacconi 2007a). This was illustrated as follows by a corporate respondent (C9):

> Selective cutting is not a problem in Africa because the heterogeneous forest takes care of the production on its own. But if you cut it blank, then the area is likely to be used for farming and by exploiting this barren soil it will be a desert for 400 years and might never re-grow.

This immediately brings us to the social impact, which occurs on different fronts.[10] Illegal logging is linked to armed conflicts and exploitation and can indirectly contribute to the occurrence of other crimes such as trade in endangered species, corruption, money laundering and organized crime (Boekhout van Solinge 2008; TRACER 2011; Hirschberger 2008). Illegal logging activities contribute to the occurrence of erosion, forest fires, flooding and landslides. Deforestation impacts the quality of soil and water. This indirectly affects the livelihood and culture of forest-dependent communities (Celik 2008; Miller, Taylor and Wright 2006). NGOs and forest activists have also published stories of destruction of communities and human rights violations that come with illegal logging (Urrunaga et al. 2012). Illegal logging also challenges law and order because of its link to corruption (Smith et al. 2007). A report by the UN and Interpol for instance estimated that global terror groups like al-Shabaab rely on charcoal and illegal logging as a finance for their activities, besides the ivory trade worth about 400 million US$ per year (Interpol 2014). Despite the negative social consequences of illegal logging and trade, alternative land use can have a positive impact and it can increase community cohesion (Tacconi 2007b).

---

10 Regulation of the European Parliament and of the Council laying down the obligations of operators who place timber and timber products on the market adopted on 20 October 2010 and published in the Official Journal on 12 November 2010 (entry into force on 3 March 2013).

On an economic level, governments lose revenue through the non-payment of taxes, in amounts estimated cumulatively to run into billions of US dollars yearly,[11] potentially hindering economic prosperity since the lost revenue is not spent on poverty reduction, health care or education (Haken 2011; Magrath, Younger and Phan 2009; Seneca Creek and International Wood Resources 2004; WWF et al. 2009). Timber prices on the global market are depressed by 7–16 per cent on average due to the influence of illegal timber, which increases the competitiveness of the timber industry and allows consumers to benefit from lower prices. However, legal[12] forestry has difficulty competing with the unfair pricing of illegal sources. The distorted global pricing of timber due to illegal logging causes an estimated loss of about US$15 billion yearly for the legal timber industry in Canada, the United States, EU and New Zealand, whereas legal producers of timber products in high-risk countries[13] are US$31 billion worse off (WWF 2008).

As illustrated above, sometimes the negative impact is challenged by positive consequences of the illegal logging and timber trade, such as alternative land use or less administrative hassle. This is likely to be part of the reason why illegal logging persists despite the declared commitment of many governments and international organizations to combat it. Illegal trade in fauna and flora, which includes illegal timber is, however, recognized as a transnational environmental crime (White 2011). These discussions on transnational environmental crime involve a multitude of issues of different scale and complexity reflecting the various environmental challenges the world faces today.

Assessing Illegal Timber Transports: Global, European and Belgian Best Guesstimates

Data Challenges

Similar to other types of environmental crime, illegal transports of tropical timber present challenges for data gathering and analysis (Gibbs and Simpson 2009). There are considerable differences in estimates of (il)legal logging and trade. National customs organizations have their own data on legally imported or exported goods. Suppliers, transporters and government administrations in countries of origin and destination work in separate systems and often differently identify and

---

11 The international trade in illegal timber products was worth US$8.5 billion in 2008 (UNEP 2011b).

12 Legal and sustainable forestry are not synonymous. Sustainable timber takes into account the ecological, economic and social development in the long turn, whereas legal merely means the timber comes from legal sources.

13 High-risk countries are those where wood products have a high probability of coming from illegal sources (between 20 per cent and 90 per cent of timber in these countries comes from illegal sources) (for example China, Russia, Indonesia and Malaysia).

report the transported forest products. Each of those actors claim they report the true export volumes, resulting in discrepancies and facilitation of smuggling.[14] A civil society respondent (S3) adds that, '[m]any countries do not have a reporting system so you end up with very nation-specific data which is hard to extrapolate or compare'. The trade classification allows differentiation between logs, sawn wood, plywood, mouldings, joinery and ornaments,[15] but does not specify which kind of timber it concerns, nor whether it is a CITES species. Moreover, port statistics often report the country of loading as the country of origin of the timber (cf. Antwerp statistics). Data about the available forest resources could serve as a baseline measurement for timber trade, but a government respondent (G26) warned that '[a]lthough initiatives have been set up to map the forest areas with satellite images, other data is guesswork'. Only limited information is provided about commodities in transit, which is particularly relevant for Antwerp as a transit hub. There are also discrepancies in import and export statistics of logs. These can partially be explained by illegal forest production, which is declared incorrectly or not at all, but also by the commercial reduction of volume.[16] In addition, data on illegal trade in timber are usually collected for breaches of CITES,[17] but data on other illegal timber rely on estimates. Interpol reports that ramin, mahogany, African teak and Brazilian rosewood are most often illegally logged and traded timber species (Magrath, Younger and Phan 2009). These are, however, all subject to CITES restrictions, which might explain the law enforcement focus on them. According to a government respondent (G8) interviewed for this study, even the CITES data are 'not complete because if you have 100 parties or members, you will be lucky if you have the reports of 50 or maybe 60. Even those countries who report their trade, do not report 100%'. Available statistics are therefore not a true reflection of the illegal trade but of the law enforcement efforts. Furthermore, data are often used to support the argument of a particular stakeholder and as such the data of one are likely to contradict the data of another stakeholder. Comparing statistics is moreover very difficult due to the different definitions of illegality and legality in timber trade.

---

14 There are, for instance, major differences between the timber trade data published by Eurostat and the timber trade statistics of a number of the EU's major trading partners (European Forest Institute).

15 Given the different measuring units, round wood equivalent (RWE) is often used as a standard unit to compare the timber trade of different countries.

16 Logs or other unfinished forest products will be reduced in volume once the production is finished and therefore the export of logs and finished products can differ in volume (Landro and Lo 2007).

17 The CITES seizures for the 27 EU member states and a few neighbouring countries are monitored with the EU TWIX (Trade in Wildlife Information eXchange) database which was developed and piloted in Belgium. This system is meant to foster cooperation through depersonalized information exchange. When police, customs, inspectorates or administrations come across illegal international trade, they will contact or warn each other about new means of forging documents, of concealing CITES loads and so on.

With the above data challenges in mind, it should be understandable that data on illegal transports of tropical timber globally, on a European level or within the research setting of this study, equal best guesstimates (Chen 2006; CIE, 2010; Lawson and MacFaul 2010; Tacconi 2007). The data used here are for illustration purposes and should not be seen as incontestable figures. These data, however, provide a general idea about the scope and the directions of the transports. The current situation with data gathering and analysis thus has room for improvement. It would be especially interesting if relevant trade and licensing information were to be made public and transparent, but according to the respondents of this study transparency about timber is likely to meet the sensitive issue of national sovereignty.

Global and European Guesstimates

The regions of origin for tropical timber are the Amazon and Congo basins and South East Asia. These are the regions where tropical trees flourish and where these natural resources are located. Despite some of the known problems in these regions (for example unstable political regimes, corruption), the extraction of the natural resources is inextricably linked to these countries. The locations of destination of global timber flows are the European Union (EU), the United States, Japan and China, which are also the biggest consumers of forest products. Different studies have tried to approximate the global scale of illegal timber, but assessments vary significantly. The Seneca Creek study of 2004, regarded as one of the most solid assessments of illegal timber logging and trade, concludes that 5–10 per cent of global industrial wood production is illegal, with higher percentages for developing countries and lower for developed regions of the world. Illegal logging estimates are very different depending on the regions under study: the scale of illegal logging is assessed to be 80 per cent of total production for Brazil, 70–100 per cent for Russia, 66 per cent for Indonesia and many other high-risk countries are in the same range (Ottisch et al. 2005; Toyne, O'Brien, & Nelson, 2002; WWF 2008). For Ghana, illegal logging represents 65 per cent of total consumption in 2006 (Lawson and MacFaul 2010).

Interpol and the World Bank (2009) estimate the global share of illegal timber equals between 20 per cent and 50 per cent of all timber products. According to the Organisation for Economic Co-operation and Development (OECD), around 6 per cent of the total trade in primary wood products is illegal, but this figure does not account for the products that are laundered (Contreras-Hermosilla, Doornbosch and Lodge 2007). The total trade in the forest industry equals about 1 per cent of the world's gross domestic product (GDP) and the suspicious volume of round wood entering international trade is about 1 per cent of global forestry, which would mean that the value of illegal wood on the global trade market for 2009 is approximately US$7 billion (Haken 2011; Contreras-Hermosilla, Doornbosch and

Lodge 2007).[18] According to the World Wildlife Fund (WWF 2008), the illegal share of the global industrial wood sector is 20–40 per cent, equalling a volume at least as big as the volume of certified forests.

Estimates of illegal timber have also been based on import and export data, such as for instance those provided by the ITTO. When exporting countries register less timber as legally exported than an importing country registers, this can be an indication of illegal timber trade. Also other timber trade (coniferous forest products, pallet and secondary processed wood) showed data discrepancies, but for tropical timber trade the data discrepancies were in many cases very large and significant. Studies by the ITTO into these trade data discrepancies found that illegal timber trade (including tax avoidance) was a possible cause next to a diversity of other causes such as data entry errors, misclassifications, mixed product shipments, inconsistent units of measures and conversions and trans-shipments (for example Hong Kong, Singapore and so on) (Goetzl 2005).

One of the issues that is difficult to assess given data reliability issues is the trend in illegal logging. A 2010 study[19] (Lawson and MacFaul 2010) finds illegal logging to have decreased by approximately 22 per cent since 2002 as a consequence of the improved policies. Imports of illegal timber have decreased by 30 per cent since their peak in 2004, and especially in the last five years, in seven consumer[20] and processing[21] countries studied. The NGO respondents in this study (for example S7, S8), however, warned that this seemingly decreasing trend in illegal logging can be explained because many of the concessions are granted despite existing moratoria – legalizing illegal logging – and have a doubtful legal status (REM 2009). Moreover, some trade might have shifted to less sensitive markets where information about imports is lacking.

Estimates for the EU, a major worldwide importer and consumer of timber and wood products such as furniture or paper, seem to be more consistent. Together with China, the EU accounts for most of the wood-based products exported out of West Africa as well as the Congo Basin.[22] In 2006, approximately 428 million m^3 of timber were logged in the EU and 163 million m^3 of raw wood was imported into the EU (WWF 2008). Many of these goods (451 million m^3 per annum)

18 Haken (2011) explains that the 2004 Seneca Creek report spoke of $4.9 billion, but this is explained by the lower GDP at that date.

19 The 12 countries studied represent 20 per cent of illegal timber production and 50 per cent of illegal wood trade. For Cameroon it has fallen 54 per cent, for Indonesia 75 per cent and for Brazilian Amazon between 50 per cent and 75 per cent. The illegal share in logging is still estimated to be 35–72 per cent for Brazilian Amazon, 22–35 per cent for Cameroon, 59–65 per cent in Ghana and 14–25 per cent in Malaysia.

20 The United Kingdom, the Netherlands, France, the United States and Japan.

21 China and Vietnam.

22 Based on the European Forestry Institute Trade Statistics for EU 27: http://www.efi.int/portal/policy_advice/flegt/trade_statistics (accessed 3 April 2012). This relates to analyses of Cameroon, Central African Republic, Republic of Congo (Brazzaville), Democratic Republic of the Congo, Equatorial Guinea and Gabon.

are internally traded making it very difficult to track the European wood flows. A 2008 report commissioned by the European Commission estimates the 2005 EU imports of illegal products from countries with a high-risk of illegal logging to be between 12 and 15 million m^3 (European Commission 2008). These figures as such are intangible, but compared with the total imports of wood-based products into the EU this ranges between 16 per cent and 19 per cent, or between 22 per cent and 28 per cent for imports from high-risk countries. NGOs estimate 16–21 per cent of the EU wood imports to be illegal (WWF et al. 2009).

(Illegal) Timber on the Belgian Market

Having provided a frame of reference with the global and European data, this chapter turns to the Belgian market. Belgium is the fourth[23] biggest importer of wood products in the EU and the sixth biggest exporter, with the Port of Antwerp being responsible for the major share of this trade. In 2011, Belgium imported 9.9 million m^3 (RWE[24]) of solid timber products from inside the EU and 3.4 million m^3 from outside the EU (Oliver 2012). Tropical hardwood comes mainly from Cameroon, Malaysia, Brazil and Indonesia. Imports from Cameroon increased between 2007 and 2011, at the expense of Brazil. According to the Port of Antwerp authority, 182,325 tonnes of wood was unloaded in 2010 and 478,080 tonnes was loaded, with Cameroon,[25] Ivory Coast, Indonesia, Brazil, Finland and DR Congo as the main countries of origin. These data refer to non-containerized cargo. There is no data available on the share of illegal timber trade in Belgium.

There was disagreement between the respondents about the importance of the timber trade in Antwerp. According to a corporate respondent (C2), 'Between 1990 and 1995 about 1 million tonnes of timber was imported, mostly in logs, but those years are long gone'. The timber trade in the Port of Antwerp is certainly less visible than it used to be. Especially in the older docks of the port, there used to be stacks of round wood, whereas now most of the wood is processed and containerized. This industry has changed because the timber is processed in the countries of origin or in processing countries like China (see below). Some of the corporate respondents said Antwerp and Rotterdam had seen the timber trade decrease in favour of Amsterdam and Flushing (Vlissingen). The timber importers who were interviewed, however, said Antwerp remained their major port of import. Both the NGO and governmental respondents confirmed Vlissingen and

23 This refers to commodity code 44. It is fourth after Germany, France and the Netherlands.

24 'RWE volume is a measure of the volume of logs (roundwood) used in the manufacture of wood-based products (including wood pulp, paper, wooden furniture, joinery and plywood)'. Available at: http://www.globaltimber.org.uk/rwevolume.htm [last consulted 30 June 2014].

25 Note that timber declared in Belgium as from Cameroon might actually derive from the Central African Republic or the Republic of Congo.

Amsterdam are relatively large timber ports, but the absolute quantities of timber transports in Rotterdam or Antwerp are still larger.

The question remains of course what the scale of illegal or suspicious flows of timber in Antwerp is. Neither the corporate respondents nor the government officials could provide data on the balance of legal versus illegal timber in Antwerp. A quote from a corporate respondent (C2) illustrates this: 'We have no idea of the current major flows of timber and neither do we know where the problems are. Officially all wood that enters the Port of Antwerp can only be legal. Illegal wood is supposed to be blocked by customs and import is prohibited'.

All breaches of CITES are registered by customs, but no cases were reported from 2007 until 2011. Given the amount of timber that passes through the Port of Antwerp, this is likely to be a reflection of a lack of law enforcement efforts rather than a lack of illegality in the timber trade. In comparison, in Rotterdam, there have been several cases in the last few years where illegal timber (CITES species)[26] was confiscated by customs and are currently the subject of prosecutions. There is no doubt about the existence of illegal timber shipments in Antwerp, given that other countries have reported seizures that had Antwerp as an earlier destination, but the amount and scale is unknown. It thus proved difficult to find conclusive data to assess the illegal share of timber trade. Both the share of illegal trade and the origin vary depending on the kind of forest product, as illustrated by a forest researcher (S7):

> Belgium imports sawn wood from high risk countries in the Congo Basin (primarily Cameroon) and Russia. It imports substantial volumes of plywood from high risk countries Brazil, China and Indonesia. Belgium imports moulding and joinery[27] from high risk countries China and Brazil, Indonesia and Malaysia. Most of this will be derive from PEFC-certified forest but without chain of custody.

Perceptions of corruption are sometimes used as indicators to assess the risk of illegal timber trade. About 87 per cent of wood imported into Belgium from outside of the EU comes from countries with high perceived levels of corruption (for example China, Russia, Latin America, Africa). The risk for timber imports from Africa is partially mitigated because of the increased negotiation and implementation of FLEGT VPAs or other legality verification systems (Oliver 2012).

---

26 CITES notifications reveal the four species mostly traded in Belgium are Afrormosia (*Pericopsis elata*) from Central and West Africa; Ramin (*Gonystylus* spp.) from Asia; Mahogany (*Swietenia macrophylla*) from Central and South America; and African cherry (*Prunus africana*) from Africa and Madagascar. CITES MA België, 'Handel in CITES-hout', in *Vorming Handel in CITES Hout* (Brussels: FOD Volksgezondheid, Veiligheid van de Voedselketen en Leefmilieu, 2010); and CITES Trade Database: http://www.unep-wcmc-apps.org/citestrade/ (accessed 3 April 2012).

27 The volume of these products is likely to be about half that of their RWE volume.

Social Organization of the Illegal Timber Trade

This section aims to gain insights into the social organization of the illegal timber trade that has a connection to the Port of Antwerp. The following explains how actors in countries of origin, transit and destination play a role in illegal transports of tropical timber. For each of these, this study analyses whether the legal-illegal interface is antithetical or symbiotic (Passas 2002).[28] This analysis will make clear how a variety of actors and legal-illegal interfaces shape the illegal timber trade (Bruinsma 2009; Casson and Obidzinski 2007; FAO 2010; Seneca Creek 2004; Tacconi 2007; Wells et al. 2007).

Countries of Origin

In countries of origin, informal workers are the first type of actors who are involved in illegal logging and can feed into the illegal timber trade. Although limited logging for personal use is generally allowed, export of this timber is prohibited. This informal production, often referred to as artisanal 'chainsaw' logging, however, equals an important share of the volume of exports out of tropical countries. Forest communities often rely on the illegal timber trade as a sole and secure source of (short-term) income and '[o]ften perceive harvesting neither as a criminal nor a harmful activity', as an NGO respondent (S9) added.

The owners of timber concessions are the second type of actor who is involved. Many of them work within the legal requirements of their permits. However, some are known to cross the boundaries of their concessions or disregard the tree-logging specifications set by forest authorities to allow the forest to regenerate. For Ghana, illegal logging represents 65 per cent of total consumption in 2006, with an estimated 26 per cent of that feeding into the formal timber industry (Lawson and MacFaul 2010). European timber importers indirectly play a role in this, according to a corporate respondent (C10): 'Whereas many European importers used to be owners of African concessions, many of those were sold (primarily to Asian corporations) and nobody knows what happens within these con- cessions anymore'. One *modus operandi* of these large forestry companies is the use of small permits to launder timber from other sources and avoid the payment of taxes (REM 2009). These permits are meant for those people who do not have the financial means to manage large concessions. However, according to an NGO respondent (S6) '[t]hose "tres petits titres" have become a major backdoor since it represents at least 10,000 m^3 of export each year, since the timber is often sold to major concessionaries'. Small-scale concessions are vulnerable to economic capture by powerful (illegal) timber traders because they have difficulties complying with regulations. Another NGO respondent (S9) added: 'the inconsistent and overly

28 An elaborate explanation of the theory on legal-illegal interfaces can be found in Chapter 3.

complex regulatory framework of these natural resource rich regions renders legal forest production uneconomic for small-scale producers'.

Different ways of working guarantee the success of the illegal supply chain. The transport of timber can be accompanied by false documents or fraudulent declarations. CITES permits, FSC labels and other transport documents can be forged or used to disguise the illegal trade in timber. This was confirmed by the government, corporate and civil society respondents who came across these in their work. Illegal timber is also rather easily mixed with legitimate distribution to avoid it from being detected.

Timber processors in countries of origin are therefore another actor who can be involved in illegal timber. The illegal nature of the wood can more easily be concealed in processed goods, which constituted more than half of the illegal wood products traded in 2008, compared with just 15 per cent in 2002 (Lawson and MacFaul 2010). The limited bulk cargo shipments that do occur – used for log transports – cause suspicion because the ships change owner, flag, crew, captain and name, making control difficult (Landro and Lo 2007).

The decrease in round wood transports can be explained not only by the processing being a concealing technique for illegal timber. There are other factors at play: wood is increasingly sawn in countries of origin, because many countries prohibit the export of logs. Countries in West Africa, for example, are increasingly stimulating their forest industry to deliver processed goods and this trend is therefore likely to continue, as a corporate respondent (C9) explained: 'Whereas before sawn wood was processed into windows and doors in the EU, this now happens before import, since it is a lot cheaper to process it there rather than here. Moreover, if the wood is sawn first, it fills a container more easily'.

Illegal timber involves other corporate actors as well, and namely those who work in the extraction of other natural resources such as gold or other precious metals. One of the government respondents (G29) illustrated this for the case of Ghana. 'The majority of this gold mining is known to lack the necessary permits and licenses, and has both a bad environmental and human rights reputation. The timber is logged and traded illegally'. He explained how, in the search for gold in many regions of Ghana, the entire surface layer of the ground is removed. Moreover, the gold is extracted using mercury, which degrades the quality of the soil even further (Rothe and Friedrichs 2015). The trees that grew on the soil are sold, sometimes without permission, but the forest has no chance of growing back.

Government authorities in countries of origin are another actor that contribute to illegal timber. The controls in regions of origin are often limited due to the unwillingness or inability of lower levels of government to enforce the law, particularly when there are conflicts with central governments. Central authorities are often perceived to be biased against rural communities, criminalizing local forest users who are denied secure resource rights (Tacconi 2007b). These states often do not have accurate assessments about the available resources, let alone about what has disappeared. Their regulatory framework is often weak, which decreases the likelihood of illegal logging being detected.[29] Moreover, governments in countries of origin have been found to be corruptly involved in granting permits, controlling transport of timber or inspecting forest enterprises (Haken 2011; Smith et al. 2007). Once again, the case of Ghana (see above) illustrates this, as the following quote from an NGO respondent (S26) makes clear: 'States act as accomplices because they would rather see revenue of the gold mining than act upon the environmental harm. This issue of preservation of the forest or even sustainable exploitation of the forest is balanced with the importance of mining the gold'.

In a way, the government authorities thus contribute to the illegal timber trade. In interviews, NGOs and independent illegal timber experts explained their concern that CEOs of (international) enterprises, politicians and government and law enforcement officials facilitate the illegal trade in these forest products. Similarly, the involvement of the military has been mentioned. It is estimated that about US$7.3 billion is annually invested in corruption money for illegal logging (Smith et al. 2007; Duffy 2007). An NGO respondent added: 'One hardly ever wonders how embedded corruption is in forest practices. There is corruption from the chief of a small village to the highest level of administration responsible for granting concession rights'.

Finally, there is the potential involvement of organized crime (Magrath, Younger and Phan 2009; WWF 2008). This was confirmed by one of our government respondents who referred to the involvement of organized crime in Central and South America given the use of business structures, violence[30] and intimidation. None of the other respondents, however, mentioned the involvement of organized crime syndicates in illegal transports of African timber.

The interfaces in countries of origin connect legal, illegal and informal actors (Passas 2003). Informal loggers compete in the same forests as legal and illegal actors. This implies an antagonistic interface and might even be aimed to extort (parasitical interface) or destroy (predatory interface) other actors. There is another legal-illegal interface that presents itself. The raw materials that were extracted by informal actors feed into the illegal production. This constitutes an interface of reciprocity or collaboration between illegal and informal actors (symbiotic interfaces). Some legal timber processors get their timber supplies from illegal actors. In this interface, legal actors might be facilitating and maybe even initiating crime, but the line is difficult to draw. The interface is then one of cooperation or reciprocity, but might well be one of co-optation if there is an uneven power relation (symbiotic interface). These illegal timber actors, of course, compete with legal actors in countries of origin, constituting at least an antagonistic and most likely an injurious interface. Neither parasitical nor predatory interfaces

29 Note that the same can be said about many destination countries as well (see further).

30 An example of this violence is the murder of Joao Claudio Ribeiro da Silva and his wife, Maria do Espirito Santo, who were found murdered on a nature reserve near Maraba in Para State, Brazil.

were found in this research. Finally, governments that tolerate or facilitate the illegal timber trade are competing with the legal actors (antagonistic interface) and meanwhile support illegal actors or are financially supported by them through corruption (symbiotic interface).

Countries of Transit

The trade routes are multiple in the globalized world and shipping itineraries allow for flexible trade chains. A large amount of timber is exported to a third country before reaching its final destination. There are known trade routes and usual suspects in the illegal trade of tropical timber in terms of countries of origin, transit and destination, as explained earlier. Timber smugglers are, however, very inventive in the trade routes they use, as a government official (G12) explained:

> If we think protected illegal Afrormosia comes straight from West Africa to the EU, we are naive. The seller and buyer also know that we know it comes from West Africa. Therefore it gets sent to Brazil, stays there for a few years, an edge is machined into it and then it is shipped to Europe. They know our alarms don't go off if this type of wood comes from Brazil.

The other way around, ships from Brazil might go to Africa first before travelling to the European ports. In this way, illegal timber traders aim to catch governments off guard. In the same way, in the Congo Basin many timber transports cross national borders: of the timber handled in Cameroon ports, close to half originates in the Republic of Congo-Brazzaville, the Central African Republic or Gabon (Ducenne 2008). Similarly, Singapore is often used as a transit port for timber transports. In fact, one of the government respondents (G13) said Singapore has a reputation for illegal or at least suspicious timber: '[I]t is basically a free port … they don't care so much about the origin of the wood. If the documentation shows that it's a legal export, although documents have been laundered, it's legal in Singapore and then it goes to any other third countries as legal timber'. The use of transit countries is a *modus operandi* for illegal timber within the EU as well. Another government respondent (G12) talked about a case where illegal timber species were spread out over five different interconnected EU locations. As a government actor (G26) explained, the timber industry is influence by global dynamics: 'Timber follows many trade flows in processing before it reaches the retailers and consumers. Major actors in the timber business in Asia – China and India – do not exercise the necessary due diligence for their supplies. Once processed, nobody is able to check the goods'.

Containerization has facilitated the rapid growth of international trade in recent decades, including the trade in illegal timber, because the anonymity of containers offers particular advantages for organizations wishing to transport illicit commodities (Griffiths and Jenks 2012; Levinson 2006; UNODC 2011).

The respondents in this study noted a change in the orientation of the European timber flows with less direct timber imports from the countries of origin and more imports of wood products processed in China. China's internal market demands a lot of timber, and it has a large export of wood products to the EU, the United States and Japan.[31] Although imports of illegal wood into China seem to have decreased, probably due to the global economic slowdown, it is still in the range of 20 million m³ and China is the most important market for East Asian and African tropical timber. Given that China exports a lot of processed timber goods, it is alleged to be a transit country for illegal timber. A corporate respondent (C6) explains that '[t]he problem is with African timber that goes to China first and then reaches the EU as finished products (furniture, plywood, doors, floors). It is necessary to make that transparent, since the direct supply from Africa to EU is limited compared to those going over [to] China'. It is suspected that the majority of global trade in illegal timber is transported to China and often implicitly exported from China – implicitly because these exports usually have a legalized label. Comparisons of China's import and export statistics – allowing for domestic logging and consumption of wood – reveal mismatches.[32] According to a Belgian timber importer (C10), the European timber sector contributes to this because its quality standards are so high that the profit for timber concessions is lower: 'It is often easier for timber producers to sell to other actors (e.g. China) who are fine with somewhat lower timber quality'.

There are other corporate actors that play a role, for example the shipping companies, which might not check the legality of the timber because they do not perceive it as their responsibility (REM 2009). The shipping line that was consulted for this study explained that this topic is of increasing concern to them, although there is not a strict liability because they do not know what is inside the containers. Similarly, the shipping agents and terminal operators have a role to play. Shipping agents usually do not engage themselves with the content of the transports and merely arrange the paperwork. Through this activity, however, they facilitate illegal transports. Shipping agents and lines are both engaged in the transport of illegal timber, whether knowingly or unknowingly. Likewise, banks can play a role in global trade and therefore in timber trade as well. Through the transfers of money and in providing financial credit, banks have access to all the relevant documents. Through money-laundering laws, banks could theoretically be held accountable for the legitimacy of the transactions and in this way financing for illegal logging might be tackled. Insurance companies also theoretically have access to a lot of the same information, because owners who claim compensation for lost goods must provide a certificate of origin, product specification, nomenclature and commercial

31 Domestic consumption is thought to have been about 202 million m³ in 2007 and is likely to increase to 460 million m³ in 2020. In 2009, China exported US$7.5 billion to the EU, US$5.1 billion to the EU and US$3 billion to Japan (Xiufang and Canby 2011).

32 Clarifying illustrations of this trade, with explanations, are available at http://illegaltimber.uk.org (accessed 3 April 2012).

invoice. In practice, however, neither banks nor insurance companies are liable for the legality of the cargo and therefore do not need to check the documentation (Landro and Lo 2007). The financial proceeds of the illegal timber trade might thus be widespread, illustrating the legal-illegal interfaces.

As for the legal-illegal interfaces in countries of transit, it is difficult to assess to what extent each of the actors knowingly participates in the illegal timber trade. The findings indicate that some actors do participate deliberately, given the trade route disguises and document fraud. Shipping lines, shipping agents and terminal operators – and by extension banks and insurance firms – have illegal timber traders as clients, whether the timber cargoes are in containers or as round wood. This fits a symbiotic type of legal-illegal interface because legal actors work for illegal actors, but it is unclear to what extent the former knowingly collaborate. In case they do not know, this interface is one of synergy. In case they do know, this interface is either one of collaboration if there are long-term links or one of reciprocity for shorter term but still mutual benefits. Many of the transit actors can therefore at least be accused of a lack of due diligence, a denial of responsibility and even of culpable negligence. Those that facilitate the illegal timber trade are in an antithetical relationship with the legal market.

Countries of Destination

In countries of destination, the principle actors are timber importers and consumers. It is difficult to get an idea of who is involved in timber trade, since timber traders and intermediaries are instrumental in facilitating supply chains. The timber importers are a first actor in countries of destination who might be contributing to the illegal timber trade. According to several government respondents, timber companies used to deny the problem of illegal timber existed. This was exemplified in this research by the responses of tropical timber importers who suggested that there is no illegal timber in their forest activities. Other timber importers, however, acknowledge the existence of illegal trading in their sector. These importers explained that illegal timber is destructive for the long-term survival of their business, but warned that not all importers are concerned with long-term outcomes (Miller, Taylor and White 2006). Government officials clarified that the major timber importers pose little threat because they would not risk their reputation. They believe, however, that major timber importers might be more involved in trading in illegal timber than in illegally trading CITES regulated timber. However, the scale of the illegal trade does assume some degree of organization, like the following quote from a government respondent (G13) explains: '[I]f you take into consideration the complexity of arranging 20 or 40 containers in a single shipment, you have to have several persons working together, it is not the actions of single individuals. It must be corporate'.

The traders, brokers and intermediaries are thought to be the 'biggest crooks'. According to the corporate respondents, timber importers used to have closer connections with the timber-producing countries. Many (international) corporations still have concessions in these tropical regions, but they increasingly go to existing concessions to buy the timber they need. Moreover, some of the European timber importers sold their African concessions, mainly to Asian corporations. By setting high-quality standards for the products – consumers do not want timber with uneven timber grain – European timber importers drive the processing away. A corporate respondent (C6) added: 'I've witnessed a Belgian corporation in West Africa who wanted to buy timber. They required high quality wood, with certain diameters and length. There was an Asian competitor who would simply buy all of their wood, disregarding quality standards'.[33]

Timber processors are other actors who are involved in countries of destination. The processing, however, differs greatly for each type of wood, ranging from flooring over paper to antique furniture restorers, ship builders and musical instrument makers. Other processors use timber in construction and also there a market exists for illegal timber.

Besides the timber importers and processors, consumers also play a role. There is a high demand for timber, especially for cheap timber. Due to the increasing world population, the demand for industrial wood is likely to increase. Consumers refer to corporate and government consumers, but also individual consumers. Admittedly, it is often difficult for an individual consumer to know where timber originated or whether it is from legal or sustainable sources. In many European stores, there is for instance FSC timber on the market, but consumers often still go with a cheaper alternative. Although many consumers still buy the cheapest timber, consumers in more affluent regions of the world are increasingly conscious about the sustainability of their timber purchases. According to a corporate respondent (C6), this, in turn, has 'created pressure on the timber market [...] and as a consequence timber producers or brokers are tempted to commit FSC labelling fraud'. Illegal timber trade exists due to markets that are not environmentally sensitive, that demand timber products without considering whether the timber was harvested illegally. Essentially, this is driven by the financial benefits it generates.

Of major influence is the regulatory framework in countries of destination to tackle illegal timber trade and its ineffectiveness. By not considering timber as a priority, governments in countries of destination are another actor that indirectly shapes the illegal timber trade. Certificate fraud does not only happen in developing countries but also happens in the EU. Trade prohibitions or documentation requirements are often not necessary for processed CITES goods, a potential *modus operandi* for illegal timber trade. Sometimes timber transports are declared under higher import taxes which protect them from being detected in standard risk assessments. A discussion of each of these governance weaknesses follows later in this chapter.

In reference to the legal-illegal interfaces in tropical timber flows, consumers contribute to the illegal trade in tropical timber, since they buy it for low prices.

---

33 In reference to the legal-illegal interfaces this indicates an antithetical relation, see below.

These consumers can be individuals as well as governmental or business organizations. Consumers therefore have a symbiotic relationship with illegal actors since they profit from them. It is unclear, however, to what extent this is motivated by a search for cheaper purchases and a lack of awareness about the harmfulness of illegal timber or, on the contrary, by an intentional choice for illegal timber. Alternatively, consumers might simply not be provided a choice for legal or sustainable timber. As made clear in the above example about Asian and European importers, the illegal actors sometimes compete with legal actors in the same market, constituting an antagonistic interface. This is clearly present for the illegal timber trade, because they compete with the legal market. This might well be perceived as injurious, since illegal actors harm the legal market by offering prices the legal industry cannot compete with. This case study did not come across the other two antagonistic interfaces where illegal actors extort legal actors while keeping them viable (parasitical) or where illegal actors aim to destroy the legal business (predatory). Besides these antagonistic interfaces, in many cases legal and illegal actors interact symbiotically in the illegal timber trade. This happens when legal actors hire an illegal actor to do the dirty work for them (outsourcing), which is present in cases where legal timber importers get their timber from illegal suppliers. Given that importers and forest concessions often have long-standing relationships, this might be an interface of collaboration and both might benefit from the conscious involvement in illegality (reciprocity). The power relation between these legal and illegal actors can be uneven, despite the benefits generated for both of them (co-optation interface). Sometimes the importers are unaware about the illegality (for example due to forged certificates), in which case a synergy interface is present.

Governance of the Illegal Tropical Timber Trade

Governance frameworks have been subject to analysis in theory and research, but environmental crime flows, and the illegal tropical timber trade in particular, are at an interesting crossroad of influences (van Koppen 2006). Throughout the departure, transit and destination locations, different actors potentially have a governance responsibility. Governments have a role to play in drafting policy initiatives and legislation as well as in the implementation of it. These government institutions however face numerous challenges in dealing with this topic. Despite the harmful impact, the illegal logging and trade in tropical timber has not been subject to a global convention or universal social reaction to it (Tacconi 2007b). Non-state actors have therefore taken up responsibilities traditionally reserved for the nation state (Loader and Sparks 2002). These actors can be legal entities such as (multinational) corporations or non-governmental organizations. Corporations in the timber industry may be concerned with the social implications of their operations. NGOs can play a role in policy-making, awareness raising and maybe even in monitoring logging and trade activities.

Together governments, business, civil society and international organizations therefore have the potential to shape the governance and regulation of the tropical timber trade, but it is not always clear what governance framework this resulted in. This study therefore analyses what actors are involved in these governance arrangements and provides insights into the facilitating and hindering factors for these actors individually and in interaction. As explained earlier in this book, the frame of analysis used is a nodal-networked analysis and the analysis relates back to the models of the responsive regulatory pyramid and networked governance (Braithwaite 2008; Holley, Gunningham and Shearing 2012; Shearing and Johnston 2010). First, the governmental, corporate and civil society governance actors are analysed individually.[34] Second, the networked governance analysis discusses their interaction, which includes an analysis of the multi-stakeholder initiative, the FSC.

Government Initiatives in Countries of Origin and Processing

Governments in countries of origin[35] need to grant certificates for forest exploitation, certificates of origin and certificates for trade in CITES species. These departments are often very limited in resources and staff, which is perceived by traders as having an adverse effect on trade. Some countries of origin have the necessary expertise and professionalism to deal with this, as mentioned by government respondent 13: 'Many countries of origin realize timber is big bucks and do not want their natural resources to be exploited by criminals'. Others have invested significant staff and resources, but have not set the right priorities nor worked together to reach better results. Much of the legislation in countries of origin about property rights, licensing and logging terms is, however, difficult to enforce for reasons of lack of resources, contradictions between laws and challenges to their legitimacy by indigenous groups (Tacconi 2007b). A Ghanaian government respondent (G26) for example explained that they intend to eliminate illegal logging in their country and aim for sustainable forestry for this and future generations. They signed the Voluntary Partnership Agreement (VPA)[36] with the EU because it will allow access to the European market. Although there is no

34 In the scope of this study, it is impossible to discuss all governance characteristics of these actors. Therefore, this is focused on those elements relevant to the tropical timber case.

35 This analysis uses information and quotations regarding Ghana, Cameroon and the Democratic Republic of Congo. Whenever necessary, the text mentions to which country the quote refers. This is important because each country has its own characteristics and findings cannot be generalized.

36 The EU has tried to impose stricter controls on countries of origin of tropical timber through a licensing system based on the Voluntary Partnership Agreements (VPAs), negotiated with exporter countries under the Forest Law Enforcement, Governance and Trade (FLEGT) Action Plan (UNEP, 2011b).

VPA timber on the market as yet, they see this as an important instrument. Ghana is also one of the few African countries that has conducted an official review of illegal logging. Despite being a quite progressive country in the region, it is also faced with challenges in implementation. The police for instance assist the forestry commission in prosecution, but this does not result in appropriate and deterrent fines. One critique is that the judiciary is often not able to assess the true value of the resources that were illegally obtained and traded. Strong penalties exist, but are rarely ever applied with fines being typically around 5 to 6 per cent of the value of the seized timber (Lawson and MacFaul 2010). Despite improvements in enforcement efforts, prosecution remains difficult. The same is true for other countries, where 'the likelihood of being both convicted and actually obliged to suffer a penalty is generally too low to serve as a disincentive – particularly when compared with the option of corrupting the legal process'.[37]

Many forest-producing countries simply do not have the resources to inspect timber trade or to monitor logging. A Ghanaian government respondent explained they were in the process of mapping them. This need for improvement in information systems has already been stressed in previous research (Seneca Creek and International Wood Resources 2004). Talking about the Democratic Republic of Congo, an NGO respondent (S6) said: 'In a country where nothing works, where a forest inspector does not have a jeep or plane to control 100,000 hectares of forest, legality means they got the right papers, but how they got those, that's a totally different thing'. Another NGO respondent (S5) added that '[g]overnments do not develop valid control systems and the controllers that do work there have no means or capabilities to do so'. Ports of exports often do not know whether the timber originated in their country, because they cannot check the sealed containers. These offer the advantage of better protection against damage and allow for more flexibility in transport, but are also a means to disguise illegal trade (Levinson 2006). Cameroon for instance faces a real challenge because it transits a lot of dubious timber from neighbour countries, despite its commitment in the VPA. Involving transit countries is thus crucial for the prevention of illegal timber trade. In June 2014, Kenya, Tanzania and Uganda – together with Interpol, UNDP, FAO, UNEP and UNODC – decided to curb illegal logging and timber trade within the East Africa region while at the same time committing to prevent the continued transit of illegally obtained timber from the Congo Basin through their ports.[38]

In order to support processing in countries of origin and create added value, many African countries no longer allow logs to be exported. Despite these good intentions, the local processing infrastructure is not always sufficient, resulting in many *ad hoc* initiatives that have difficulty accessing the export market and

---

37 Available at: http://www.globaltimber.org.uk/IllegalTimber.htm [last consulted 16 May 2012].

38 Available at: http://www.unep.org/newscentre/default.aspx?DocumentID=2791&ArticleID=10913 [last consulted 1 July 2014].

let a lot of timber go to waste. Nevertheless, this ban on log exports is generally respected towards the EU, but not toward China. In turn, the EU indirectly imports timber from African countries after processing in China without checking their legality. By setting stricter standards for imports of processed timber from China, the EU could therefore influence forest governance in regions of origin. This might counter some of the (allegedly increasing) illegality of China's timber industry. Transit and processing countries thus play an important role in countenancing the existence of illegality.

As a consequence, consumer countries often (rightfully) question the certificates of origin. However, it is a politically sensitive issue for government officials to question the legality of timber transports, which requires hard evidence. An NGO respondent (S7) asked: 'Who dares to challenge a legal label when it comes from China? Their role is so dominant that neglecting these supplies might jeopardize the reputation of timber in general'. Moreover, the EU also needs to address the governance system within some of its own member states. A corporate respondent (C29) claimed that '[s]ome EU countries are chopping down everything'.

Countries of origin often cannot (yet) adequately assess the remaining forest resources. Increasing enforcement capacity in forests, processing facilities and harbours will solve part of the problem. Both positive and negative incentives are however needed to address illegal logging and trade. A trade ban for instance is likely to take away all value from the forest and therefore might lead to its destruction to convert it to other uses. Countries with a high risk of producing illegal timber, therefore, need policy changes that go beyond the mere topic of forestry and address basic development issues such as education, health care and investments in natural resources, so-called capacity building. This implies the need to differentiate the approach between regions and countries of origin because each has its own particularities.

Government Initiatives in Countries of Destination

It is unrealistic to think that countries of origin can detect all of the illegal timber trade, as illustrated above. By not considering timber as a priority, governments in countries of destination are another set of actors that indirectly shapes the illegal timber trade. This section discusses what is happening in relation to governments in countries of destination, for example by setting up border controls to prohibit illegal imports from entering. The following concentrates upon the research setting of this study: Belgium.

A lot of policy, much less implementation

Despite the manifold private and public initiatives governing the timber trade, there is no international convention to combat illegal logging effectively (Chen 2006). There is only limited criminalization, which explains why it is not a priority for the criminal justice system. CITES is the one exception that does allow the regulation of trade, but it only applies to a limited number of timber species and does not address domestic consumption. Even within CITES, effectiveness cannot be guaranteed given weak permit monitoring, diverse interpretations of round wood vs. processed timber and the lack of judicial follow-up. Combating the illegal timber trade through judicial means has led to falling back on the legal frameworks of individual nation states. Timber-consuming countries, such as Belgium, often lack national legislation to criminalize transports of illegal timber (going beyond CITES-species). As an importing country, it can prosecute but needs to prove that the imported goods violated the laws of the country of origin. To determine the legal status of the timber, law enforcement agencies thus rely on the numerous national and local laws in timber producing countries.

Intergovernmental initiatives on timber have been difficult to achieve because they would go against trade conventions, despite successes on other environmental topics (for example Montreal Protocol) (Bartley 2007; Meidinger 2002). In the absence of a legal framework for timber, the EU has tried to impose stricter controls on countries of origin through a licensing system based on the Voluntary Partnership Agreements (VPAs), negotiated with exporter countries under the FLEGT Action Plan (UNEP 2011a). The strength of these initiatives is that they involve all necessary stakeholders along the supply chain. They involve government actors on policy development as well as at the implementation level such as the judiciary, police and customs. The private sector is included, as are NGOs and local communities. A major problem, however, is that there are currently hardly any results in the field, as the following quote from a corporate respondent (C9) illustrates: 'There is not a single FLEGT log in our premises right now and it's been operational 3–5 years. They set the objective to have it available by the end of 2012, but the administrations know it is not doable'. Another corporate respondent (C10) warned for unfair procedures: 'It seems to be so much easier to tell a country like Gabon or Cameroon what it should do than telling this to China, Canada or even to EU countries'.

In March 2013, the EU Timber Regulation (EUTR) entered into force, prohibiting the placing on the EU market of illegally harvested timber and products derived from such timber and obliging operators who place timber and timber products on the market to do their due diligence. At the time of the interviews, this had not been implemented yet and the time of writing this book, it was still unclear how the EUTR would be implemented despite responsible authorities being appointed. A 2014 report by Chatham House and CIFOR also pointed towards uncertainties and inconsistencies with EUTR implementation (Saunders and Reeve 2014). Several respondents expressed worries about the direction the EU chose. The EUTR seems to have been limited to a legality check and to traders doing everything they can to guarantee legality (due diligence) (European Commission 2011). This is to the disappointment of environmental NGOs, because, seen from a perspective of environmental harm, legal logging might be equally harmful (Green, Ward and McConnachie 2007). A few of the corporate respondents agreed that the focus on legality is to a certain extent a missed opportunity, with one (C10) explaining that '[b]ecause it became a mere legality check, the timber sector is unlikely to pay for monitoring and certification of the entire supply chain. Many corporations will simply wait for controls to occur, since that happens once every 10 years'. A government respondent (G13) warned about the risk of this regulation becoming a mere paper tiger, since '[a] lot depends on the political willingness and commitment of enforcement agencies as well as the timber industry'. Moreover, the EUTR maintains the reliance on national legislation and certification in countries of origin. A corporate respondent (C7) added: 'many countries will make sure to provide the necessary documentation to prove the legality of the timber and that is all the EUTR will control for, regardless of the environmental value'. Another corporate respondent (C29) added that would be good for the EUTR to go beyond a mere paperwork check, because 'not a single shipment today does not have paperwork that is or looks legal, but how that will be checked is the question'. The EU is facilitating consultation and cooperation amongst the individual member states, but much of the implementation is still unclear. Six months before the entry into force, none of the respondents knew which institution would be responsible for its enforcement. A corporate respondent (C10) warned that '[c]onsultants are waiting to get involved, to start earning money. They will be best off, certainly better than the forest owners and workers in the countries of origin'. This same importer (C10) was also worried about the judicial implications of the EUTR: 'It makes seizures possible and while proof is gathered the shipment can be blocked. Given the speed of our judicial system, importers are likely to see their shipments blocked for years'.

Despite the private initiatives to govern forest activities (see below), a part of the illegal timber governance hence falls back on government actors and on command and control. This system is, however, not fit to deal with legal, illegal and sustainable timber, as each of the respondents agreed. CITES is regarded as the best system, seen as a very successful convention. It however requires transposing into national policy, which does not seem to have occurred in many countries. It also results in a lot of administrative pressure for corporations and for governments. As was evident from the discussion of the Belgian case, controls on CITES are very limited due to lack of prioritization and resources for preventing and controlling the illegal timber trade. Even in the Netherlands, which has more means for CITES and timber control than many other countries, the results are limited. Government respondents explained that the governance system is too immature to deal with illegal timber trade:

> Timber is often considered an environmental issue and of course it is. However, if you want to deal with illegal timber trade as an environmental crime, this requires the assistance of policing authorities in multidisciplinary teams. As long as the illegal timber trade is only a priority for environmental policy and not for policing, judicial follow up is inexistent. (G1)

> It's not police or customs that are dealing with wildlife crime, nature or environmental crime, it's governmental agencies, such as wildlife inspectorates and for some countries even those agencies do not focus on it. That's the status quo. (G13).

Governmental as well as NGO respondents in Ghana moreover mentioned that international policies often do not take the local situation into account and fail to consider the practicalities of local implementation. The following quote from a government respondent (G26) illustrates this: 'By and large environmental treaties involve all essential aspects. The implementation is however a different issue than designing the law. Many things are very nicely written but there is hardly enough incentive to ensure it is happening in practice'.

Lack of concern for timber issues

'Nobody in Belgium seems to be concerned about timber', was the reaction of an international timber expert (S4) when asked about the governance of illegal timber trade. The following explains that this respondent might indeed have been right about the lack of attention, despite some intentions. As a country of destination, Belgium is faced with a clear lack of resources for implementing timber policies. The administrative responsibility is with the Federal Public Service for Health, Food Chain Safety and Environment, where the CITES authority[39] is located. Since March 2013, the same federal service also harbours the EUTR authority. This service has primarily focused on CITES issues, with lesser priority given to other legislation. Indirectly, this administration comes across information about illegal transports of CITES species, but this has limited relevance for processed timber or non-CITES timber. Moreover, many countries, even in the EU, were thought to be giving CITES certificates without checking the credits of those that ask for them. An NGO respondent warned that 'the system relies on trusting other parties, but can we? They grant the export permit so we grant the import permit without hesitation?'.

In a similar way to the administration, the border agency (customs) primarily focused on CITES breaches. This form of enforcement was, however, very limited. There have not been any reported cases of illegal imports of timber from 2007 until 2011. As was explained earlier, this is likely to be a reflection of a lack of control rather than it being the result of a lack of illegality in the timber trade. Non-CITES illegal timber was not a focus for customs because of the lack of relevant

39 The CITES authority consists of three institutions: the scientific committee provides advice about imports into the EU; the enforcement committee deals with everything related to control and implementation; and the CITES Management Authority chairs this meeting. The other members are the environmental police, the regional administrations that deal with fauna and flora protection (for example birds of prey are more highly protected in the EU than internationally), federal agency for food safety (responsible for sanitary controls) and customs.

legislation. In practice, controls on illegal timber trade in Antwerp were virtually non-existent. The investigative service of customs was interested in the topic, but despite their good intentions it was felt to be still in its infancy. Customs was faced with a lack of resources and expertise about timber species for efficient follow-up. Some countries have specialized customs teams that solely deal with CITES issues and even with illegal timber in general, but that was the exception rather than the rule (for example the Netherlands). Moreover, the focus on environmental issues seemed very dependent on the individual commitment of those involved. When customs came across timber in the Port of Antwerp, this usually happened as being related to drug searches or checks for tariffs and not out of concern for CITES or illegal timber as such.[40] In 2011, there was a timber enforcement action by customs – *Woodpecker* – but this did not result in seizures. According to a government respondent (G13) this is 'too ad hoc to be effective. It seems to be a matter of 'let's go to the harbour, get some samples and analyse those'. That's just a drop on a hot plate'. That particular action did manage to gather information about the timber trade in Antwerp and raise awareness about a new topic. Some participants (G8 and G11) were disappointed and remained sceptical about the results – no illegal timber was found – which they feared was partially a result of a lack of knowledge.

There is an enormous volume of trade and a limited number of customs officers to deal with all types of commodities. At the time of the research, less than 1 per cent of shipments were controlled and even a marginal increase would require a significant increase in staff. Most customs controls were therefore paper controls and happened by using a risk analysis system. The risk analysis was based on the transport documents, which should explain who is shipping the timber and where it originates, but often this information was incorrect. A lot of economic operators, including timber importers and shipping corporations, have been granted an Automatic Economic Operator (AEO) certificate,[41] which means only random controls happen. The AEO certificate's aim is to stimulate self-regulation by rewarding proper behaviour with quicker processing. In practice, a large amount of illegal traffic was part of AEO and went through the green lanes, which had

40 Most seizures of CITES species happen at Brussels airport, which does not concern timber.

41 Holders of the AEO certificates obtain certain advantages such as quicker and simplified customs procedures, less physical verification and less other controls. In the case of controls, AEO certified companies had priority and could ask for a physical check of the goods at a particular location. In order to receive AEO certification, companies needed to have a good customs track record, trade and transport administration that allowed for sound customs controls, financial solvency and sound safety provisions. A system audit was required (by means of a self-assessment) before AEO was granted. AEO certification can be granted by all EU member states and a granted AEO certification applies throughout the entire EU. There was follow-up through self-assessments and there were still limited random controls. AEO – Wat. Douane & Accijnzen. Available at: http://fiscus.fgov.be/interfdanl/nl/aeo/wat.htm [last consulted on 8 February 2012].

only random checks. NGO respondents mentioned that this system was used for timber fraud. Moreover, as a commodity, timber is subject to import duties, but on the other hand there is a risk of illegal timber. Combining both objectives was seen as difficult, according to a government respondent (G12): 'Every time, I control, I can find something, but governments do not like that happening. There is simply no follow-up on these cases. Entire projects, focusing on timber, risk becoming useless'. Sometimes these transports are even declared under higher import taxes which avoid them from being detected in standard risk assessments.

An NGO respondent (S4) expressed concern about the lack of awareness and knowledge about timber and believed this to be a clear challenge for enforcement: 'Governments would be very happy to conclude there is no illegal trade because there are no seizures. That is a mere 'What the eye does not see, does not exist'-approach. The willingness to do something about it is often missing and that is obvious based on the resources invested'. Controllers need to be knowledgeable because fraud is hard to detect and prove. Initiatives had been taken to make customs officers more aware of the CITES issues and the timber trade. Their training happened through this same enforcement action, but the follow-up was unclear.

A lack of knowledge was a problem for environmental inspectors as well. It was difficult for them to know what type of timber was being presented and to check whether the documents were genuine. An NGO respondent (S5) agreed in saying that '[p]eople knowledgeable enough to do this are very few. This requires taking samples and doing microscopic research in a lab. That hardly ever happens and mostly only occurs when there is NGO pressure'. When samples are analysed, the issue of the cost surfaces as well.[42]

Corporate actors explained that they only experienced CITES controls on documents. Other controls were by private organizations in view of the FSC chain of custody certification. They said they would not mind increased controls as long as they would not hinder trade and would be flexible. Both corporate and government actors warned that enforcers tended to target the usual suspects, leaving some importers entirely uncontrolled.

Not a police or a judicial priority

In theory, both the police and the judiciary have a role to play when illegal timber is discovered. Given the limited amount of controls, it should come as no surprise that the judicial follow-up in Belgium was found to be limited. For the police, timber was not a priority, except for CITES species. However, even then, the police acted only reactively.[43] Practically this implied an investigation

42 Once continued technological innovation results in worldwide databases to compare these samples, the costs should decrease.

43 Their priorities are listed in the National Security Plan, which is drafted every four years. The current plan (2012–15) lists waste fraud as a priority, which means proactive investigations happen. Waste fraud is the only environmental topic mentioned.

could only be initiated when information was brought in and the police limited their activities to information gathering to better understand the phenomenon and the limitations of the legislation. A government respondent (G1) explained that '[t]he priorities of the Belgian police largely reflect the security issues that concern the EU, limiting itself to terrorism and drugs, but the environment is generally not part of this. Timber is even less of a priority than CITES animals'. Police officers were aware that there might be networks of organized crime behind the trade, but said they had insufficient means to follow up on this. A newly established network for information exchange *Envicrimenet* will, however, focus on severe environmental crimes[44] (with the support of *Europol*) and wildlife crime is one of the topics for this network. This should result in better assessments of the risks and a better focus for law enforcement efforts. Similar to customs officers, the police felt they needed a lot of expertise to control for this type of crime. A government respondent (G8) added that '[t]here are not many people that are able and willing to determine the species and the origin with legal certainty. That of course explains why the police reports are never filed. And even if a report was filed, who has the expertise to follow this up?'

When a timber load does not have the necessary CITES certificates, the case is clear. When it concerns non-CITES timber, the case is less straightforward. Within the pre-EUTR legal framework, investigators needed to fall back on the local legislation of the countries of origin and needed their cooperation. A government respondent (G13) added that 'you can circumvent this by addressing the issues of document or labelling fraud (e.g. with FSC labels), but the success rate is low'. Moreover, police officers found that these cases were not a priority for prosecutors. Prosecutors hardly ever managed to put a case before the court, even in the Netherlands where a functional magistrate is responsible for it. It was very difficult to prove cases in court and judges are found to be hesitant to sanction, similar to other environmental topics (Faure and Heine 2005; Faure 2012). Both police and judicial authorities explained that they realized the importance of addressing illegal timber trade, given the huge profits made. They drew the line on the effort because of practical issues.

Corporate Self-Regulation

Corporate actors have also taken initiatives to govern the illegal timber trade. Corporations may be concerned with their reputation and see self-regulation, particularly certification, as a way to distinguish themselves from the bad apples in their sector and a way to avoid these bad apples from free-riding on the image of the sector. Moreover, self-regulation can be a way for corporations to inform consumers about their responsible business which in addition can provide them

44 This means they are organized, linked to a corporate environment, involve high profits, are international, involve repeat offenders which engage in other criminal behaviour and have an impact on the environment as well as citizens' health.

with a competitive advantage over firms that do not uphold these high standards. Firms can also anticipate rules being strengthened or try to ward off more intrusive government standards by means of self-regulation (Gunningham, Kagan and Thornton 2003). Besides these market-based incentives to become involved in self-regulation, this can be guided by broader political and social developments, as was the case for FSC (see below) (Bartley 2007). The following discusses self-regulation in countries of origin, in processing, by importers and by the transport sector.

Self-regulation in countries of origin

Timber exporting countries are increasingly concerned with self-regulation in order to guarantee the legality of their timber and have continued access to the European market. The Ghanaian forestry sector aims for continued self-regulation of their industry, and they are supported in this by their government. It is however difficult to monitor this for the forests in West and Central Africa and certification is difficult to achieve (see below). Responsible forest management is in place for several concessions, but many others are not involved in self-regulation. Not all corporate actors are concerned with long-term benefits of self-regulation and sustainable forest management. Several Ghanaian and Cameroonian respondents for instance warned about the Chinese timber exploitation in their countries, which was completely outside any of the governance systems. Remember, moreover, that deforestation is driven only partially by logging and timber exports, but also by mining, agriculture and energy needs (Marx and Cuypers 2010). Illegal timber therefore involves other corporate actors than those in forestry and these are not always accounted for in multi-stakeholder or self-regulation initiatives.

Self-regulation in processing

The timber industry often works with processors in third countries and changes owners several times before reaching retailers and consumers. This implies that the timber might have passed through many hands before arriving, for example at the Port in Antwerp, making legality more difficult to verify. Processing countries have not always taken measures to address the illegal sources of this timber (Lawson and MacFaul 2010). Particularly China is considered to be a hub for the trade in illegal timber, challenging the due diligence requirements in countries of destination such as the EU (Hewitt 2005).

Although Asian processors may care less about due diligence, they often provided better effectiveness in their production, because they developed techniques to use timber waste. By setting high-quality standards for their products on the assumption that consumers do not want timber with an uneven timber grain, Asian processors are often preferred over European timber importers as buyers of the raw timber. The following quote from a corporate respondent (C6) illustrates this: ‘I’ve witnessed a Belgian corporation in West Africa who wanted to buy timber. They required high quality wood, with certain diameters and length. There was an Asian competitor who would simply buy all of their wood, disregarding quality standards'. Despite their efforts to do the necessary due diligence to avoid buying illegal timber, European timber importers thus face a challenge of competing with other – less diligent – buyers. According to a corporate respondent (C10), structural changes to the European timber industry, such as in techniques to use timber waste, are needed to counteract this.

In search of better guarantees for imports of legal timber, many countries require traders to ensure that their imports comply with the legality verification criteria (Contreras-Hermosilla, Doornbosch and Lodge 2007). The importers interviewed for this study explained that illegal timber is destructive for the long-term survival of their business. The sustainability of their business was their core motivation to undertake due diligence in relation to their supplies. A clear economic incentive to promote self-regulation and timber tracking lies also in the deflation of global timber prices as a consequence of the illegal timber trade (Auld et al. 2010). To a large extent, the timber business relies on being able to trust overseas suppliers. This requires companies to have trustworthy contacts across the globe, as a corporate respondent (C9) explained: 'There are things happening in Africa that are dubious, but it is impossible to control everything. We know our suppliers very well, know which are suspicious and know when to ask for more proof'. This often requires importers to check the timber and the documents on site. The extent of direct interaction between importers and timber concessions, however, differs for each region and type of timber trade. A timber importer (C9) explained that the trade in round wood and processed timber with West Africa is usually checked on location to keep in good contact and provide advice on processing, whereas 'in South-America, local agents are necessary intermediaries, because it is impossible and dangerous to do business with producers directly'. This implies that timber importers have a less direct way of guaranteeing both the quality and the legality of the timber they buy.

Some corporations are aware of illegal logging concerns and were often involved in the labelling and certification initiatives and cooperated with forest owners in countries of origin to make them understand the importance of answering to the EU's requirements (in order to have access to the market). The importers that were interviewed said they wanted a clean timber trade, but acknowledged the sector had a problem. The following quote (C9) illustrates this: 'We know which forest concessions are doubtful and ask for certificates. Other importers are less 'due diligent' and import the timber despite the doubts about the legality. These have been doing this for years and we as competitors know'. Some importers are thus aware of the problems in their sector, whereas others do not have the necessary management system in place to check the legality of their supplies. Other importers declined the invitation to participate in this study, replying that their business has nothing to do with illegality.

Self-regulation and monitoring are an investment which mostly big players or corporations that focus on niche markets are able to commit (Gunningham, Kagan and Thornton 2003). Smaller actors can be connected to these multinationals through supply chain management and due diligence. This is happening with the timber trade by means of the FSC chain of custody certification and the (future) EUTR requirements where timber importers need to demonstrate the legal origin. The newly drafted legislation wants to increase transparency about timber flow. The proof they have is a document from the country of origin's government confirming the timber's legal origin. The EUTR however hints that these documents cannot be trusted. Importers worry about the implementation of this due diligence, as a corporate respondent (C7) explained: 'The burden of proof is turned around. We need to prove there is no crime associated with it. But all we have to fall back on is the country of origin'.

Self-regulation in transport

Besides the timber sector, there are other corporations that could play a role in the governance of these flows. The sector of international maritime transport and trade through ports is known for its somewhat non-transparent way of communication (Levinson 2006). It is indeed true that contacting shipping lines for this research was challenging. One major shipping line was, however, willing to talk and explained that the shipping line's involvement (or some shipping lines' involvement) was guided by both society's tendency to increasingly challenge shipping lines on legal and ethical issues and the fact that the 21st century is a hyper-transparent community. Shipping lines have noticed that their responsibility is increasingly becoming part of the legislative framework. They are worried about taking up a responsibility that is not theirs. They prefer to follow the legislative framework in terms of what they are allowed to ship. This concern, however, is also guided by the criticism from their stakeholders and by the corporate responsibility standards they adhere to. Both commercial and ethical considerations guide them to refuse certain shipments that are not strictly part of the legal framework. This involvement is in practice limited because they do not know what is inside containers and have no authority to open them. They rely on the trustworthiness of shippers and shipping agents.

NGO Pressure and Consumer Awareness

NGOs have an important role in raising awareness about the harmfulness of the illegal timber trade and in influencing governments, and corporations as well as consumers. Their position in raising awareness and advocacy was explained as followed by a Ghanaian government respondent (G26): 'They are watch dogs of the sector, but they should try and find a balance because sustainability is important but also requires the continued guarantee of livelihoods and needs to avoid cutting down the entire forest for farming because the forest harvesting is no longer allowed'.

They were supported in this by corporate actors who feared NGOs were not always correct in their assessments of what is ecologically best. One corporate actor (C9) provided an example of NGOs advocating for tropical timber trade bans, 'without realizing this would take away all remaining value of the forest, but meanwhile influencing policy makers and public opinion for years to come'. According to both civil society and corporate actors, NGOs increasingly take the entire spectrum of arguments into account and realize that the economic value of the forests is a very important constituent of their sustainability and that one-sided communication needs to be avoided. A remaining challenge for NGOs is in their rivalry, according to NGO respondent S4: 'We are sometimes on opposite sides on certain topics, but fish in the same pond'.

In Belgium, NGOs play a role in investigations, by pressuring governments to act. An NGO respondent (S7) explained: 'When we see enforcement agencies do not respond, we indeed go sit on the timber, chain ourselves to it, hang a banner to make a statement'. NGOs indeed regularly target suspicious shipments of timber, such as for instance a recent import by a Belgian corporation of timber from the Brazilian state Para.[45] This recent action aimed to test Belgian governments on their implementation of the EUTR. Another NGO respondent (S6) did add that their objective is sustainable forest management, which is why their campaigns sometimes target legal logging as well: 'A remote illegal logger in East-Cameroon has to cut selectively because he simply cannot get large transports to the port that is 1000km away. That's less destructive than a legal concession that is being clear cut'.

Finally, consumers can influence the illegal trade in timber, by making conscious choices for sustainable or certified timber. These third parties have an important role in pressuring processors to use legal timber. For instance, given that much of China's imports originate in developing countries with poor forest governance, the risk of reputational damage in the eyes of consumers in the EU might cause a change in market dynamics (Cerutti et al. 2011). Currently, this is visible in public procurement policies, but individual consumers seem to have a lesser effect. A corporate respondent (C10) provides an explanation for this: 'You cannot expect the individual consumer to take the responsibility because the price is what counts for Mr. Average. The biggest challenge is in providing information and thereby influencing the demand for timber'. Several respondents explained that this is a task best suited for joint action between governments, corporations and NGOs.

Networked Governance Analysis of Tropical Timber Flows

In the globalized timber trade, relying on command and control regulation or on self-regulation alone faces many challenges, as discussed above. To overcome these challenges, multi-stakeholder certification initiatives have been set up, and are described more fully below. Environmental issues have in fact been at the forefront of these networked governance arrangements (Holley and Gunningham 2011). A wider stakeholder participation is deemed to be able to achieve the

45 Available at: http://www.greenpeace.org/belgium/nl/nieuws-blogs/nieuws/Belgische-houthandelaar-verscheept-verdacht-Amazonehout-naar-Frankrijk/

necessary transformation of forest governance and the timber trade (UNEP 2011a). The following first discusses these multi-stakeholder initiatives and the particularly relevant case of the FSC. It then discusses other findings of this study about the interaction between actors in the governance of (illegal) tropical timber flow.

Multi-stakeholder initiatives

In non-state market driven (NSMD) governance systems, rule-making comes from corporate and third-party actors (Marx and Cuypers 2010). Standards are usually set by one actor, or by coordination between different actors, whilst another actor seeks to receive certification and a third party assesses whether they have complied with it. Multi-stakeholder initiatives have seen the light of day to tackle the problem of illegal logging and trade. Examples are certification mechanisms like the FSC or the Program for Endorsement of Forest Certification (PEFC) and policy programmes like the EU FLEGT. FSC is a multi-stakeholder certification initiative, which integrates social, economic and environmental criteria in the certification of forests and actors in the timber sector. PEFC also promotes sustainable forest management, but is based on national autonomy rather than the international controlled FSC. PEFC[46] was created by the European forest owners' associations to facilitate the mutual recognition of national schemes and to provide them a common eco-label.

The FSC is to date the only genuine multi-stakeholder third-party certification initiative (Cashore et al. 2005). It has taken up the challenge of integrating social, economic and environmental concerns and is considered effective because it is performance based (instead of system based) and operates on a global scale, while it still allows its criteria to be locally defined. Despite the absence of a legal basis for the FSC, many market actors see FSC criteria as legitimate (Black 2008). The FSC has stimulated improvements in other systems and spurred governments to improve regulation on a long neglected topic (Meidinger 2002). Labels such as that of the FSC engage both producers and consumers in the biodiversity debate and thus manage to bridge the distance between corporate, government and civil society actors in the global trade flow (van Koppen 2006).

Inspired by the example of the FSC, several of the stakeholders interviewed believed the best solution to tackle the illegal trade in timber is legal timber monitoring and certification by third parties. Corporations preferred an independent referee to be appointed to monitor and control the timber trade. Their concern was with the protection of their commercial secrets, which they deemed better protected with a private actor. Their preference was then regulated self-regulation by independent auditors, as the following quote from a corporate actor (C9) illustrates:

> We don't mind if those controls and that accreditation ask a lot of administrative information and do very thorough checks. That is our experience until now, that

46 Formerly called Pan-European Forest Certification (PEFC).

> these checks prior to accreditation are very thorough and correct and therefore we have a better trust in their capacity to control. If that agency is accredited by all parties, no one will doubt the credibility of their decision.

An advantage of the FSC is thus its monitoring by independent organizations. This even allows suspicious concessions of the most powerful families and their associates (including law enforcement authorities) in the countries/regions of origin to be audited.[47] Because certifiers are paid by the corporations, considerable importance is placed on empowering third parties to monitor this system. Similar to the certification that exists for sustainable timber, legal timber certification would then have to be located outside government institutions, but acknowledged by corporate, government and NGO actors alike.

The FSC system is faced with challenges within its actual governance, despite its good intentions. A first important challenge has been that the certification of forests is lagging behind, particularly in developing and tropical countries that are rich in natural resources. Most FSC forests are located in northern developed countries. The main reason is probably the high cost of certification and the limited incentive to invest in sustainable forest management due to the absence of good contacts with important export markets (Marx and Cuypers 2010). As a result, certified sustainable timber quantities are so low that their unit cost is very high. This makes it very uncompetitive and unattractive to forest owners. The FSC forests in Africa that do exist are mainly owned by European-based international companies exporting to the EU or have long cooperated with international initiatives like the Tropical Timber Action Plan which stimulates the forest certification of concessions. As one subject of this research (C29) noted: 'In my experience, certification mostly happens in forests that were already working OK before and therefore unlikely to be dealing in illegal timber'. The FSC's usefulness as a general forest governance tool was therefore seen as limited, but it can have an impact on the illegal trade in timber. Even this FSC certification, however, falls back on national legislation, because conforming to national standards is one of the criteria. A third challenge is that the system can easily develop into a monopoly system and needs continued monitoring of its own functioning (Meidinger 2002).[48] A corporate respondent (C7) added: 'The ideas behind FSC are good, but it developed into a direction that is not always environmentally effective. 90% of the costs go into chain of custody certification. The system risks becoming a means rather than a means to an end'. Furthermore, corporate actors perceived some of the sustainability labelling to be skewed because directly imported timber

47 Available at: http://www.globaltimber.org.uk/IllegalTimber.htm [last consulted 14 May 2012].

48 This is similar to developments in the Kimberley Process Certification Scheme (KPCS) which aims to prevent conflict diamonds entering the diamond market, but was criticized for failing to address problem cases (Grant and Taylor 2004). This led one of the partner NGOs (*Global Witness*) to leave the tripartite structure that monitors KPCS.

can have the FSC label, but products from recycled materials cannot. This led a corporate respondent (C7) to ask: 'Is recycling not sustainable? Government consumers buy FSC timber – within the public procurement policies – that might in fact not be the best choice for what they need it for'. Corporate respondents promoted a legal wood certificate, applicable on a bigger scale: 'This could reach 60% of the market, whereas FSC reaches 20% and would allow for easier targeting of the illegal timber by law enforcement' (C9). Key to the success of any of these measures is the guarantee of a level playing field and thus of avoiding opportunities to circumvent the certification scheme. This is where the need for a punitive escalation – when necessary – was put back on the table by a corporate respondent (C9): 'All timber that is not certified should be considered illegal and sanctioned appropriately'.

The interaction between NGOs, governments and corporations

Cooperation between government actors is crucial because each has particular expertise. The police are, for instance, best equipped to investigate a case with a view towards prosecution. The environmental administrations have the technical expertise. In theory, the prosecutor is responsible for gathering all the judicial information together and leading the prosecution. In practice, they are all challenged by the lack of legislation and the difficulties of determining the type of wood and its legal or illegal nature. It might help to have closer cooperation between countries of origin and destination because the former could help determine the legal origin of the timber and the validity of the documentation presented.

There is not only interaction between government agencies, but also with various other stakeholders. It was noted that NGOs influence Belgian enforcers' investigations of CITES shipments and sometimes provide them with evidence. NGO respondents, however, said that their experience with government respondents in countries of origin suggested that they were often bribed by importers to deliver the necessary documentation in order for the timber to be allowed to enter: 'That puts us with our back against the wall. Corrupt activities simply run as a thread through the timber story, from the smallest village office to the granting of concessions' (S7). In drawing attention to a shipment, NGOs and importers are of course often on opposing sides. NGOs might wish to deem the shipment illegal and ask the authorities for seizure of the timber. But in the opinion of corporate actors NGOs were just asking for attention. They also criticized the approach of NGOs who, according to them, tackle the usual suspects, the major actors in the business, whereas other importers, who are known to be suspicious, were not their target. Some corporate respondents suggested NGOs could cooperate with corporations in whistle-blowing systems. In such an interaction, corporations are sensitive to economic concerns and could therefore be guided by NGO criticism or consumer behaviour (Seneca Creek and International Wood Resources 2004). Several respondents, however, explained that consumers often do not care about more than the price. Therefore, they believed that NGOs have a bigger role to play in influencing consumer behaviour, such as, according to corporate respondent C10, advocating that 'the ecological footprint of timber is lower than that of aluminum and PVC'.

Governments and corporations interact as well. Government actors in Ghana considered the timber industry as important partners to create structural change in the industry. Moreover, contacts with local forest communities and transparency about policies were deemed indispensable to the success of any forest governance framework. On the one hand, government actors in Belgium saw the timber sector as important partners to stimulate development towards legal and sustainable timber supplies. On the other hand, importers perceived government controls to be oriented towards the usual suspects. Several would prefer more systematic inspection of all timber containers in the harbour rather than the targeting of particular importers. To this end, corporate respondents perceived that they were consulted by policymakers more often than in the past, which might result in more practical policies. Civil society respondents also supported them in this because corporations have a good view about the contextual challenges and could provide advice on how to work within those: 'If advice can never be achieved, you know nothing can ever change' (S4). Importers expressed their concern about the need for other actors than corporations to be involved in the governance process: 'Importers alone do not have enough influence on the governments of countries of origin. We should always be very cautious moreover, because producers will easily sell to someone else if you ask too many questions' (C9).

In interactions, actors can leverage each other into participation in governance. Weaker actors might even be able to enrol stronger ones when they have similar goals, even across transnational borders (Braithwaite 2008). This requires the nurturing of governance through sufficient funding and expertise. Most importantly, it requires transparency about and knowledge of the strengths and responsibilities of each stakeholder (Holley, Gunningham and Shearing 2012). This interaction between different stakeholders can be difficult as is evident from the FLEGT initiative. An NGO respondent (S6) explained that they were disappointed with the FLEGT system, because it did not uphold environmental goals such as land use policies: 'The result is legalization, better rules, transparency and monitoring, but fundamentally it is not changing the fact that too many concessions have been granted'. In addition, NGOs explained that the state revenue has not increased enough and too many conflicts remain. Corporate actors clarified that it has not resulted in the hoped for economic benefits. Being a result of negotiations amongst different stakeholders, it would appear logical that some partners were disappointed (Marx and Cuypers 2010). 'Maybe I was unrealistic in expecting this from FLEGT, maybe most stakeholders were not interested in solving the fundamental questions', an NGO respondent (S6) added. FSC seems to do better in coordinating the goals and practices of the various stakeholders, despite the remaining challenges.

Lack of data gathering and harmonization of standards
Communication and data exchange between different stakeholders in governance arrangements had already been found to result in more realistic assessments of what a governance framework could achieve, because it allows the different partners to gain better insights into each other's point of view (Holley, Gunningham and Shearing 2012). By being transparent and exchanging information, peer review within the governance framework is encouraged. What is happening in the governance of the illegal timber trade shows there is room for improvement on this issue. First of all, in order to assess the scale of illegal logging and trade, better data gathering and analysis are necessary. The existing data do not allow for accurate assessments about the (illegal) timber trade in Belgium, about the routes followed and about the actors involved.[49] This information can guide the governance approach and is a prerequisite for effective risk analysis. To this end, customs statistics might be a good start, but will require better standardization. The current import statistics only mention the port of export, which does not necessarily equal the actual country of origin.[50] Different actors claim they report the true export volumes, resulting in discrepancies and facilitation of smuggling.[51] Installing a harmonized system of reporting on timber trade would be a major improvement. Transparent information about timber imports could be encouraged from both traders and retailers (UNEP, 2011b). This could then be used proactively to determine where the potentially illegal timber trade is happening.

Databases of timber species are crucial to determine the origin of timber samples. Using GPS tracking, these imports can be traced back to their origin to an accuracy of 200–300 metres. Pilot projects run in Cameroon, Central-America and South East Asia have genetically mapped timber based on microsatellite markers. Samples of imported timber can then be compared to those data. The first condition to improve governance is to have these databases available. This requires a lot of time and effort, implying that the technique is not (yet) suitable to be applied on a large scale. Moreover, this technique is best used for pure wood, not processed goods, whereas the latter forms the majority of the trade. Samples still require a couple of days for determination and require significant expertise that is not always at hand. What is positive about this system is that it can unite different stakeholders in one project, despite their different objectives (Reingoud 2010). Several respondents thought that NGOs could play an important role in helping to map the forest resources. They could be joined by corporate efforts to

49 See also *Data Challenges* earlier in this chapter.

50 Similar observations were made by the European Forest Institute in the Forests Products Trade Database. http://www.efi.int/portal/virtual_library/databases/forest_products_trade_flow_database/ [last consulted 14 May 2012].

51 There are, for instance, major differences between the timber trade data published by Eurostat and the timber trade statistics of a number of the EU's major trading partners (European Forest Institute – http://www.efi.int/portal/virtual_library/databases/forest_products_trade_flow_database/ [last consulted 14 May 2012].

map their timber supplies. As this technology improves and the database contains more samples, the usefulness of it will increase and this might diminish the costs. However, this will only allow tracking the origin of timber, not the way the timber was harvested. Nevertheless, this more modest goal 'may help nurture and develop supply chain tracking systems, which would permit more stringent standards or more ambitious environmental or social objectives at a later time' (Auld et al. 2010, p. 24).

The lack of value of forests

In order for the governance of the timber trade to stand a chance, it is necessary to take into account the value of forests apart from their use for timber. The timber industry competes with other sectors working in forests – agriculture, mining and energy – that may not be equally interested in sustainability (UNEP 2011b). This could be countered by initiatives that value other qualities of forests such as carbon capture and storage in timber and wood products (UNEP 2011a). The countries dealt with in this study are typical wood exporters and therefore usually start from an assumption of continued timber export, with better forest management as a way to make their business more sustainable. Other countries such as India have, however, chosen to protect timber and promote sustainability, biodiversity, reduce climate change and provide jobs by transforming forests into eco-tourist areas (Karanth and Nepal 2012). Initiatives that value externalities stand a good chance of increasing the value of forests to the same level as sustainable forest use (Marx and Cuypers 2010). Governance initiatives therefore need to be very balanced and need to take into account these different arguments. This means that less measurable advantages should be taken into account and reward forest managers for that. In order to be successful this must provide enough benefits compared to unsustainable and illegal forestry. This requires the involvement of sectors outside forestry that might compete for the land use. Local stakeholders therefore need to be involved because they are currently often losing out against powerful outsiders but have the potential to be capable guardians of their forests (UNEP 2011b). In order to promote this, information is needed on what incentives – reputational, economic and regulatory – might influence markets towards environmentally sound and eventually competitive outcomes.

Chapter 7
Comparative Case Analysis

Introduction

The case studies provided insights into the reality of illegal transports of e-waste and tropical timber. In this chapter, the cases examining tropical timber and e-waste are analysed comparatively, pinpointing similarities and differences in their social organization (*research question 1*) and governance (*research question 2*). In a first part of this chapter, the cases are compared on their social organization. This starts out with a summary of the findings of these separate case studies, before putting the results into perspective by relating them to previous findings and theories about legal-illegal interfaces, push, pull and facilitating factors and the criminalization of transnational environmental crime. A second part of this chapter is a comparative analysis of the governance of the illegal trade in e-waste and tropical timber. This also starts out with a summary of the findings of the separate case studies before relating these findings to previous research on the governance of environmental, corporate and transnational crime.

Comparative Analysis of the Social Organization of Transnational Environmental Crime

Reference to illegal markets might immediately bring to mind pictures of organized crime syndicates on national or international levels. Illegal market activity does not necessarily refer to these mafia-like organizations, however, but to situations where business or government actions are on a thin line between legal and illegal (Passas 2003; Punch 1996; Kleemans and van de Bunt 2008). This study aimed to provide insights into the social organization of illegal transports of e-waste and tropical timber to achieve a more complete view of the network of actors involved in them, which in turn can progress theory on transnational environmental crime and guide policy-making (Huisman and Vande Walle 2010; van Duyne 1993). This study asked the question which legal and illegal actors are involved and whether their interaction is symbiotic or antithetical (Passas 2003). For both cases, we find a set of legal-illegal interfaces.

The causes of transnational and environmental crimes are often neglected or reduced to a mere focus on the profits or greed of a few bad apples instead of looking at potential systemic causes (Box 1983; Lynch et al. 2013). Although profit is a major etiological factor, this study illustrates how other push, pull and facilitating factors provide the necessary contextualization for these arguments.

It does so by paying attention to individual, organizational and societal levels of analysis and motivations and opportunities of actors in locations of origin, transit and destination of the trade in e-waste and tropical timber.

This section continues with a summary of the findings of the separate case studies, before putting the results into perspective by relating them to previous findings and theories about legal-illegal interfaces, push, pull and facilitating factors and the criminalization of transnational environmental crime.

Summary of Findings about the Illegal Trade in E-Waste

At the start of the flow, consumers sometimes sell their e-waste to actors who offer to treat it for (too) low prices. Whether this is due to a lack of awareness and due diligence or a conscious choice for cheaper illegal disposal, both cases constitute a legal-illegal interaction in which governments, as well as corporations and individual consumers, can be involved. Depending on the legal actors' awareness of the illegality, this interface is either one of synergy or outsourcing. This outsourcing particularly applies to the case of e-waste, because this allows the legal actor to externalize the harm.

Further down the flow, e-waste collection has various potential interfaces between legal and illegal. Waste tourists, and collection of waste for charity and via the internet, are illegal sources of e-waste that compete with the legal market (antagonistic interface). E-waste brokers are on an even more complex legal-illegal nexus. On the one hand, they have a role as legal intermediaries in transactions and therefore promote similar interests as the other actors in collection of e-waste. On the other hand, through waste storage and handling, these brokers function as intermediaries for illegal trade. Depending on whether this is a knowing or a long-term involvement in illegality, this is an interface of synergy, collaboration or reciprocity. Other legal actors in e-waste collection are scrap metal dealers and refurbishers. Some of those are, however, known to (intentionally) feed into illegal transports.

Besides these legal-illegal interfaces in e-waste collection, actors can be on a thin line between legal and illegal in the transport of e-waste. Shipping lines, terminal operators, expeditors and shipping agents all have e-waste smugglers as their clients. The involvement of the first two seems to be one where they can be accused of a lack of due diligence (synergy interface), whereas the last two sometimes play a more deliberate role in facilitating illegal transports of e-waste (collaboration or reciprocity interface).

At the end of the e-waste flows – in countries of destination – the line between legal and illegal may be even more difficult to draw. Informal collectors and dismantlers compete on the same market as formal actors and organized crime, and cooperate with legal actors by selling them the extracted secondary raw materials. This implies an antagonistic interface and might even be aimed at extortion (parasitical interface) or destruction (predatory interface) of other actors. Moreover, informal dismantlers and sellers of second-hand e-goods in countries like Ghana cooperate with both illegal (e-waste) and legal (used goods) transporters. Governments in countries of destination that tolerate the import of e-waste – against national or international regulation – are competing with the legal actors in countries of origin. These countries of destination thus witness interfaces of reciprocity or collaboration between legal, illegal and informal actors. These could be categorized as facilitating and maybe even initiating crime (Kramer, Michalowski and Kauzlarich 2002), but it is not all black and white: although the imports of e-waste are illegal, they provide many inhabitants with a stable source of income or access to the digital age. Moreover, informal dismantlers in some regions (for example Accra) are said to be improving both environmental and labour standards. In sum, legality and illegality is not clearly depicted when talking about these actors.

The analysis of the social organization of illegal transports of e-waste makes clear that the powerful are not necessarily knowingly involved in transnational crime or deliberately crossing the line from legal to illegal. There is, however, at least a lack of due diligence on the part of some actors. Take the example of government agencies and corporations in countries of origin that sell e-waste for prices which should ring alarm bells. A major part of the trade is in legal hands, but this legal character is easily stretched or shed and constantly in evolution. It is therefore difficult to give these transports of e-waste an unambiguous legal or illegal label since they are a result of a multitude of legal-illegal interfaces. Indeed, waste is part of the legal economy, but meanwhile prompts different kinds of illegalities (van Daele, Vander Beken and Dorn 2007). Recycling e-waste, especially in developing countries, can be on a thin line between environmental sustainability and disregard of environmental and labour standards. A shipment of good quality second-hand EEE to most non-OECD countries is legal[1] and a shipment of damaged or non-functioning goods is illegal. Whether an illegal e-waste shipment has value is in the eyes of the beholder and is responded to differently in both the Global North and South. In addition, the thin line between legal and illegal is apparent in the definition of what e-waste is and what constitutes used goods or recyclables. One corporate respondent (C13) illustrated that by remarking: 'What is listed as waste is often the cleanest thing that is shipped'. E-waste is a massive industry, with recycling, second-hand EEE, parts, fixing, refurbishing and so on; only a part of it is truly going to waste. The bottom line, however, is that these practices – regardless of whether the transports are legal or illegal – cause harm to humans and the environment, because there are no adequate e-waste recycling facilities in Ghana (or in West Africa). Legal transports of second-hand goods might thus have equally detrimental effects. Trade laws in this way allow the exploitation of nature for consumption and production processes and continue the externalization of harm and risk (Lynch and Stretesky 2003). These actions mostly remain off the political agenda, rendering them neither illegal nor criminal (Passas and Goodwin

1 A number of Asian countries (for example Vietnam) refuse the import of second-hand monitors and computers.

2004). Taking environmental harm as a frame of reference for the legal and illegal flows of e-waste – and by extension other transnational environmental crimes – could overcome the challenge of the thin line. Therefore, it is crucial to focus not only on the strict crimes of illegal waste transports – the breaches of international and national legislation – but also on those activities that are on a thin line between legal and illegal.

This study illustrates that e-waste is not only about the 'big fish', globalization and the corporate dimension, although the corporate and economic rationale remains crucial in understanding the illegal flows of e-waste. It is essential to analyse the economic dimension of the phenomenon on a global scale, since waste is not contained within one country or continent. The importance of transit for e-waste flows in Antwerp is a clear illustration of this, with just 20 per cent Belgian e-waste and the remaining 80 per cent inflows from abroad. This illustrates how the open and global market results in illegal cross-border mobility. However, push, pull and facilitating factors on other levels than economy also need to be taken into account. Producers, consumers, waste collectors, transporters and (informal) recyclers – actors big and small, legal and illegal, powerful and powerless – all have motives and opportunities that jointly influence (illegal) transports of e-waste. This study illustrates how a criminological analysis of illegal transports of e-waste inevitably encounters economic, cultural, political and social motives and opportunities that together determine the flows (Heiss et al. 2011; Michalowski 2009). This entanglement makes it difficult to draw a line between what is or should be illegal. The challenge lies in 'protecting vulnerable countries from unwanted hazardous waste imports, while not precluding the import of wastes considered valuable secondary raw materials to countries in a position to manage them in an environmentally sound manner' (Kummer Peiry 2010, p. 5).

The various actors involved in e-waste flows and their diverging motivations and opportunities require a governance framework that is equally diverse and flexible. Initiatives to heighten awareness about e-waste throughout the flows – from production and over-consumption to collection, transport and recycling – combined with national and international governmental control and self-regulation are necessary ingredients of this governance mix (Gibbs, McGarrell and Axelrod 2010; van Erp and Huisman 2010). Given the global dimensions of transnational environmental crime, limiting this to national policy is to no avail (Aas 2007). However, the local impact should not be neglected either because illegal transports of e-waste may result in harm to environmental and human health, but they might also have positive effects locally (for example secure livelihood, bridge digital divide). This implies that policy needs to take both the global and the local into account. Future studies should look at the exact implications of these characteristics for the governance framework of transnational environmental crime.

By analysing the case of illegal transports of e-waste in a European trade hub, this study responds to the call for more empirical knowledge about transnational environmental crime. The data revealed different legal-illegal interfaces throughout the e-waste flows. Governments and corporations as well as individual consumers can contribute to illegal transports of e-waste. Actors in e-waste collection were shown to be on a legal-illegal interface. Transport actors can equally walk on a thin line between legal and illegal by facilitating illegal transports of e-waste. Legal and illegal transports were even more difficult to distinguish in countries of destination. Although profit or lure play a very important role, this study shows how push, pull and facilitating factors on individual, organizational and societal levels together provide the motivations and opportunities for illegal transports of e-waste. This demonstrates how the social organization and emergence of transnational environmental crime is on a thin line between legal and illegal that needs to be contextualized within the global reality of origin, transit and destination locations.

Summary of Findings about the Illegal Trade in Tropical Timber

The findings reveal legal-illegal interfaces in each step of the tropical timber flow, with both symbiotic and antithetical interactions. In countries of origin, informal loggers competed with legal and illegal actors in forest harvesting, constituting an antithetical interface. At the same time, their harvest feeds into the illegal production, which equals a symbiotic interface between illegal and informal actors. Legal concessionaries are known to work illegally, either by accepting timber from illegal loggers (symbiotic interface) or by harvesting illegally themselves. Illegal forestry in countries of origin is then in an antithetical interface with legal actors. Governments can, moreover, be in an antithetical interface with legal actors in case they tolerate or facilitate the illegal timber trade and are in a symbiotic interface with them because they support them. In the transit phase of the timber flow, it is very difficult to know whether the legal actors, such as shipping lines and agents, terminal operators, banks and insurance firms, knowingly participate in the illegal timber trade. Some participate deliberately and actively and are therefore in a symbiotic relationship with illegal actors. This implies that activities facilitate the illegal timber trade and therefore constitutes an antithetical relationship with the legal market. Others can at least be perceived as lacking due diligence. At the end of the flows, consumers have a symbiotic relationship with illegal actors since they profit from the cheaper prices. Similarly, some timber importers have symbiotic interfaces with illegal timber traders. Consequently, they compete with the legal market (antithetical interface). The social organization of illegal transports of tropical timber consists of different kinds of legal-illegal interfaces, both antithetical and symbiotic. This implies that legal actors are not necessarily knowingly involved in transnational environmental crime or deliberately acting illegally. There is, however, at least a lack of due diligence for some actors who deny the problem or deny responsibility for it. The social organization of the flows of timber is therefore on a thin line between legality and illegality throughout the entire supply chain (Chen 2006). Actors throughout the flows were found to have an ambiguous legal or illegal status since the flows are a result of a multitude of legal-illegal interfaces.

Illegal logging and trade have been recognized as problems of significance, but despite their ecological, social and economic arguments, illegal logging and illegal transports of timber have generally not been criminalized and an institutionalized social reaction to it is lacking. For timber species protected under CITES, the line between legal and illegal is rather clear and this instrument allows for the prosecution of those who trade in these species. Most of the tropical species of timber are, however, not covered by this international convention nor is there adequate national legislation for the prosecution of wrongdoing involving the timber trade. For most timber, once the illegally harvested logs are in transit, there are only limited possibilities for importing countries to act, despite the important steps in tackling illegal timber trade taken by the US Lacey Act and the EU Timber Regulation. This might be because the threat to public safety is much lower than, for instance, for drugs or arms trafficking (Magrath, Younger and Phan 2009). One of the government respondents (G13) put it as follows:

> Timber is not truly criminal yet because forestry has a low priority in terms of national safety and because politicians themselves are very much involved in deforestation. More importantly, forestry is not about the crime concept as such, it is about both legal and illegal, with a long chain from harvest to consumer. It is difficult for the consumer to see the true impact.

Similarly, two corporate respondents stressed that illegal timber causes harm to humans and the environment, but that even legal trade in timber does not necessarily guarantee no harm was imposed in its extraction. Therefore, it is crucial to focus not only on the breaches of international and national legislation, but also on those activities that are on a thin line between legal and illegal and might be equally harmful. Taking environmental harm as a frame of reference for the legal and illegal flows of timber – and, by extension, other transnational environmental crimes – could overcome the challenge of the thin line. Especially for the topic of timber, this is important because legality and illegality does not necessarily coincide with the absence of harm (Roerhorst 2006). A government respondent (G26) added: 'As long as this is not acknowledged, the long term survival of tropical forests is not 'out of the woods' yet'.

This is where an eco-global or green criminology perspective is crucial. A green approach looks beyond what is readily considered as criminal and pays attention to harmful activities on a thin line between legal and illegal. Criminology can contribute to the acknowledgement of this thin line throughout the flows of tropical timber and can help raise awareness in countries of origin, transit and destination. In this, it is crucial to critically assess both demand and supply, because there are in fact various moments along the supply chain when legal and illegal interfaces occur. Each of these interfaces is inextricably linked to a particular social, economic and political context, necessarily shaped by both local and global influences. This needs to be taken into account when drafting policies about how to govern forest activities and trade in timber. Future studies should therefore increasingly focus on the topic of natural resources such as timber, and gain insights into the governance of this phenomenon on a thin line between legitimate forest practices, informal forest activities and corporate or state crime.

Legal-Illegal Interfaces

The social organization of illegal transports of e-waste and tropical timber involves legal, illegal and informal actors and for both cases it proved difficult to distinguish which role they play. By looking at the supply chain from countries of origin over transit to destination, the multiple interconnections between the actors became evident. Despite the manifold interfaces, both competitive (antithetical) and cooperative (symbiotic), that exist for e-waste and tropical timber, similar actors and interfaces were detected. This wide variety of legal-illegal interfaces is similar to other cases of transnational crime such as antiquities smuggling (Tijhuis 2006), food crime (Croall 2009; Croall 2007) and illegal logging (Setiono 2007), which involve small businesses, multinational corporations, opportunistic entrepreneurs and organized criminals.

Although environmental crime has been labelled as a crime of the powerful (Lynch and Stretesky 2003; Pearce and Tombs 1998), the findings of this study show that the social organization is more diverse and more complex than the mere involvement of organized and corporate criminals. It is a crime of the powerful in the sense that corporate actors from the timber and waste sector are involved in setting up the illegal timber trade. There is, therefore, undoubtedly a link with white-collar crime and corporate crime. For e-waste, the respondents in this study referred to organized crime involvement. For the researched timber flow (Africa), the respondents did not mention organized crime, contrary to findings in South American studies (Boekhout van Solinge 2008). Furthermore, the analysis showed the involvement of many informal actors in illegal logging or WEEE 'recycling', often as a sole source of a secure livelihood. Because the trade flow is approachable, individual shippers can get involved in collection and transport of UEEE/WEEE towards for instance Ghana. The trade flow for timber is less easy to organize and, as a consequence, the informal actors reside mostly in the logging rather than in later stages of the supply chain. Therefore, the social organization of this illegal trade is not only shaped by the involvement of corporate actors, but also by informal actors.

Moreover, throughout the flows of these environmental goods, there are several actors that unknowingly feed into illegal trade and in this way facilitate them. Labelling them as criminals might then be a bridge too far. Through inadequate use of appropriate recycling methods, for instance, consumers can facilitate the leakage of electronic waste into the illegal transport network. Much in the same way, unaware consumers of tropical timber can be part of the illegal trade. Especially corporate and government consumers can have an impact on the system and the outcomes. Admittedly, the impact of individual consumers of wood products or electronics is limited, but raising awareness can have an impact of the illegal trade, however small. Awareness-raising campaigns in Belgium have for instance resulted in a high success rate for take back of discarded electronics, even though not all loopholes into illegal trade are closed. The impact of consumers on the timber trade is much smaller.

Particularly for illegal timber is that there are also other sectors (for example gold mining or agriculture) that play a more indirect role in illegal logging and trade. Clear-cutting for farm land can supply timber and gold mining often provides access to formerly inaccessible forests.

In the case of both e-waste and timber, transport actors such as shipping lines and agents play a central role. In both cases, the shipping industry itself does not have a strict legal responsibility for shipping the illegal goods, and will tend to ship the goods others contract to ship. As a consequence, many shipping actors are not concerned about what they ship, thereby facilitating the illegal trade. Only a few shipping actors feel they have a moral responsibility to prevent the shipment of illegal goods, which occurred more frequently for e-waste (and waste in general) than for tropical timber.

The analysis showed the social organization of both cases to be complex, shaped by diverse legal-illegal interfaces. Despite differences in the involvement of informal actors and the role played by transport actors, many dynamics in these transnational environmental crime flows applied to both cases. The implications for the theory on legal-illegal interfaces are discussed in the concluding chapter.

Push, Pull and Facilitating Factors

Characteristics of individuals as well as corporations shape the flows of illegal trade in e-waste and timber. This behaviour is partially motivated by profit seeking. In discussing the criminogenic characteristics of the waste sector, it is often said that the inverse incentive structure is an important factor (van Daele, Vander Beken and Dorn 2007). This applies to e-waste, but the empirical reality proved even more diverse because it is composed of components with two different kinds of values that must be considered: treatments costs (for example CFC fridges or CRT television sets) and treatment profits (for example motherboards, copper wires). For the former, illegal exports save the costs of treatment. For the latter, illegal exports and dismantling save the high labour and recycling costs in the countries of origin. For timber, profit seeking is more straightforward. Illegal logging and trade exempts it from the costs of concession purchase and management, fair wages and so on. This is particularly lucrative given that tropical timber is a high-value product.

In addition, both e-waste and tropical timber have a low product integrity, meaning that the illegal character can be disguised. Illegal transports of e-waste can easily be labelled as second-hand goods or mixed up with other items in transport. The illegal nature of tropical timber is often concealed in processed goods or mixed with legitimate distribution to avoid it from being detected.

Containerization facilitates this kind of fraud by allowing illegal goods to be concealed from easy inspection (Griffiths and Jenks 2012).

The transnational direction of illegal transports of e-waste and tropical timber was different from the outset, but the global characteristics of that trade nevertheless proved to be quite similar. Countries of origin, transit and destination each shape the flows. Timber flows are characterized by an increasingly globalized supply chain with timber logged in Africa, processed in Asia and sold in the EU. Because more actors play a role in the flow from forest until consumer, the (il)legality of the timber becomes obscured. Some transit countries or harbours have a reputation for illegal timber transports and are known not to exercise the necessary due diligence of their raw wood supply chain. Similarly, UEEE and WEEE are part of a global market with complex trade flows from producers over consumers and collectors to dismantlers and recyclers, who then feed their secondary raw materials back to producers. These global trade flows create the opportunity of ‘using the space between the laws’, referred to as legal asymmetries (Passas 1999). Asymmetries in environmental regulation contributed to both cases, but were more prominent for tropical timber than for e-waste. In addressing the illegal timber trade everything falls back on the legislation of countries of origin, since the few existing international agreements depend on them. For e-waste, the international conventions and regulations are relatively solid, although shippers do go in search of the loopholes in the laws (for example shipping as second-hand products).

Transnational environmental crime is also shaped by the asymmetries in knowledge and awareness about the harm inflicted by illegal trade (Andreas 2002; Herbig 2010). Individual push and pull factors to get involved in the illegal trade flows of e-waste and tropical timber also relate to the need for a secure source of livelihood, another asymmetry between countries of origin and destination. These asymmetries apply to both cases, resulting in the dumping of WEEE and the plundering of timber resources. Examining the etiology of transnational environmental crime thus requires looking at push, pull and facilitating factors in the broader socio-economic context of trade.

Criminalization

Illegal trade in endangered species and e-waste can be related to legality and illegality definitions in legislation. However, the harm of both the illegal trade in tropical timber and e-waste transcends this legal-illegal divide. The difficulty of defining the cases as crimes ran as a thread through both the flows. Their criminalization is contentious because definitions are inherently flexible when they are social constructions. What is e-waste today can be a resource tomorrow; what is new EEE today can be WEEE tomorrow; and what is waste for one person, can be a commodity for another. Timber is a less dynamic product, but the degeneration of tropical forests, in general, or of protected species, in particular, can require installing a trade ban or quota, thereby changing the (il)legality of the trade.

The (il)legality of tropical timber trade moreover seems more difficult to define than that of e-waste because it requires the tracking of the timber to its origin.

Both cases have harmful impacts beyond the mere environmental context and also cause social and economic harm. To complicate this even further, legal trade in both products can be equally harmful to the environment as the illegal trade. A look at the broader impact (harm) is therefore necessary to understand the complexity of its constituents and consequences. The awareness and willingness to recognize the cases as harmful plays a role as well. For both, the harm is not immediately visible within the research setting in Belgium. This might explain the lack of priority in policy-making, but disregards the fact that the flows of water and air that are impacted by these harms have global reach (White 2011). What makes it additionally complex is that when looking at the broader context of these illegal flows, these shipments also bring benefits to some who rely on them as a sole secure source of livelihood. Both phenomena illustrated that transnational environmental crime is not easily determined by criminality in the narrow sense. This implies the need to continue thinking critically about the harms that occur and to be dynamic in the definitions of crime. Similarly, this requires criminologists to be critical about the boundaries of criminology (Loader and Sparks 2002).

Comparative Analysis of the Governance of Transnational Environmental Crime

The above comparative analysis demonstrated that the social organization of these transnational environmental crime phenomena is very complex. A diversity of actors and push, pull and facilitating factors shape these global flows. Within the flows, the line between legal, illegal and criminal is narrow and the potential legal-illegal-informal interfaces are multiple. This complexity also holds consequences for governance. To illustrate this, this chapter continues by comparatively examining the governance reality of e-waste and tropical timber.

A summary of the findings of the separate case studies is presented before relating the findings of the individual cases to the responsive regulatory pyramid and networked governance. These two models provided ideal-typical criteria for (environmental) governance. Both models stress the importance of not limiting governance to government involvement. The responsive regulatory pyramid mainly focuses on the type of regulatory activities, whereas networked governance mainly focuses on the structural dimensions of governance interactions. The following is not an exhaustive list of the governance characteristics, but focuses on a number of core themes. This nevertheless demonstrates the richness of the governance reality.

Summary of Findings about the Governance of the Illegal E-Waste Trade

This study examined the governance reality of the illegal trade in e-waste in a European trade hub. Throughout the flows, different actors have a governance responsibility. The analysis of the governance reality illustrated how the control and prevention of illegal e-waste flows is primarily taken up by government actors, which is not surprising given the criminalization of it. Similar to what Holley, Gunningham and Shearing (2012) found, the state is crucial for definitional guidance, for inducing corporate actors to participate through both positive and negative incentives and for using their enforcement capacity. An important challenge, however, is the underfunding of these government actors, with consequences for training, resources and effective follow-up throughout the flows (see also: Brack and Hayman 2002). Despite the good intentions of many, the actual governance of illegal transports of e-waste remains limited. Governments are perceived to be too slow to respond. An important characteristic of responsive regulation is the escalation towards more punitive measures in case of (continued) non-compliance (Braithwaite 2008; Nielsen and Parker 2009). As it has been illustrated here, that is not at all certain for illegal trade in e-waste, not in countries of origin and even less likely in countries of destination.

This analysis of the governance reality in the Port of Antwerp inevitably opened up the scope to a larger-scale approach, because it cannot be analysed without relating it to the global trade flows and to the dynamics of export, transit and import. The sheer scale of global trade makes it very challenging to base the governance framework only on a governmental basis, let alone narrow it down to a penal law perspective (Sassen 1996). Governance actions by one country are necessarily limited in their effectiveness. Due to the global interdependencies of the flows, governance activities on one end are vulnerable to governance activities on the other end (Urry 2003; Yar 2011). Illegal e-waste flows and their governance are inherently transnational, but much of the implementation remains local and fragmented. As a consequence, corporate actors perceive the level playing field to be absent.

To engage corporate actors in the governance of these flows, carefully designed incentives – both positive and negative – are needed, because economic and environmental interests do not necessarily coincide (Gunningham, Graboski and Sinclair 1998). A part of the governance reality is the supply chain of electronics where producers, recyclers and consumers play a role (van Erp and Huisman 2010). Corporate actors already contribute to the governance of illegal e-waste flows, although not all producers, recyclers as well as transport actors play an equally proactive role. For producers and recyclers, the governance involvement largely depends on the profitability they see in it, but they are equally concerned with their corporate image. The economic importance of the subject for these corporate actors, however, can be used to the benefit of the environment. The raw material discussion is a good way to make facilities for recycling more efficient and encourage the eco-design of products. Transport actors could also be encouraged to be more diligent and transparent.

Reducing demand is very complicated because e-waste and second-hand electronics provide a bridge for the digital divide. Moreover, dismantling the goods in search of precious metals is a sole source of secure livelihood for many. In face of this complex governance reality, it is useful to consider governance actors that are not primary stakeholders (cf. so-called missing nodes, Wood 2006). Capacity building in developing countries – addressing the structural causes – is partially present in the current governance reality, but a lot of these initiatives are still small scale and *ad hoc*. The strength of these capacity-building projects is their potential to engage local actors, for instance the informal workers in countries of destination, who are currently not always involved in the governance framework. NGOs seem to be the most suitable actors to engage them in this process. NGOs already play a role in raising consumer awareness and in keeping both corporations and governments attentive. Corporations are increasingly involving informal actors as well, since they see the economic advantages. This risks becoming unbalanced and requires monitoring (Holley, Gunningham and Shearing 2012; Wood and Shearing 2007).

Given the enormous amount of goods and the complexity of this transnational crime flow, a mere reactive approach will always be lagging behind, one step short of the newest route or technique used by the transporters of e-waste. This is evident from this case study of the Port of Antwerp and its illegal e-waste flows towards Ghana. The governance reality of illegal transports of e-waste is about much more than this reactive approach. The analysis showed how actors earlier in the flow and throughout the supply chain – producers, consumers, collectors, informal dismantlers – can be involved. The leading role is taken up by government actors – and law enforcement more in particular – but in looking to address the contextual characteristics that shape this environmental flow, a diversity of actors becomes relevant.

Summary of Findings about the Governance of the Illegal Tropical Timber Trade

This study has analysed what is occurring in governance for the illegal trade in tropical timber in a European trade hub. While case studies cannot provide definitive answers, the analysis does allow the making of a number of observations. It has illustrated how the control and prevention of the illegal timber trade is primarily taken up by corporate and third-party initiatives. Government initiatives to combat illegal timber trade are often perceived to be mere political rhetoric, are limited to endangered species and lack actual implementation.

A core characteristic of the responsive regulatory pyramid is for the approach to escalate to more punitive sanctions when necessary (Braithwaite 2008). Even when self-regulation or multi-stakeholder initiatives exist and governance is more networked or polycentric in nature, there is still a need for punitive interventions when standards are not adhered to (Jänicke 2006). This escalation is hardly ever part of the governance for the illegal trade in tropical timber.

Achieving good governance means multiple challenges for government and corporate actors, as well as civil society actors. In general, the government approach to illegal timber trade in Belgium seems inadequate. There is insufficient legislation that addresses the issue of illegal timber. Moreover, awareness about the importance of the issue is limited. Controls in the ports, the main entry locations, are few. Law enforcement authorities referred to others as being primarily responsible and each stressed the difficulty of determining the type of wood and its legal or illegal nature. The police as well as the judiciary are not treating illegal timber as a priority and such instances have never resulted in convictions – unsurprising given the lack of controls and criminalization. Even environmentally aware administrations do not focus on illegal timber in particular and mainly have CITES as a priority. Internationally, there is also a clear lack of commitment to address the problems, as a government respondent (G12) explained: 'Many of the authorities are simply powerless, have no means to check the data NGOs provide them, have a limited budget and cannot follow-up on it because timber is not high on the priority list'. Insufficient funding hampers the effectiveness of governance networks (Holley, Gunningham and Sinclair 2012).

The analysis of the governance framework for the illegal trade in tropical timber is largely focused on the activities of government actors. The multi-stakeholder initiative that exists for timber however illustrates how private actors – independent of state actors – can shape a governance framework (Bartley 2007). The governance of the timber trade is not the single prerogative of the nation state and state laws are only likely to be effective when linked to other (social) control processes (Scott 2004). Governance is therefore not limited to government actors; to the contrary, the tropical timber trade has seen the emergence of multi-stakeholder initiatives to govern the sector. The strength of this polycentric governance is that it goes beyond command and control and mere market-based incentives. It involves a network of stakeholders as governance actors. Both corporate and civil society actors play a role. A lot currently depends on the self-regulation of the timber sector and the multi-stakeholder initiatives for sustainability certification, but that only accounts for a small share of the timber flows.

Moreover, the incentives for sustainable timber are less remunerative than those in the illegal timber trade. For tropical countries of origin, the costs are very high for legal and sustainable timber. In countries of processing and destination, the profits to be made from illegal timber are high and penalties practically non-inexistent. This will therefore require the careful drafting of positive and negative incentives tailored to the relevant contexts. Producing and consuming countries require a different approach. It is crucial to critically assess both demand and supply, because there are various moments along the supply chain when legal and illegal interfaces occur. Each of these interfaces is inextricably linked to a particular social, economic and political context, inevitably shaped by both local and global influences. These need to be taken into account when drafting policies since they should be attuned to the motivations and characteristics of the sector (Ayres and Braithwaite 1992). This is the intention of the VPA/FLEGT initiatives, but has not yet achieved the desired effect.

This analysis of the governance system in the Port of Antwerp inevitably has opened up the scope for a larger-scale approach, because it cannot be analysed without relating it to the global trade flows and to the dynamics of producers, processing and consumer countries. Governance actions by one country are necessarily limited in their effectiveness. Even if the EU for example closes its market to illegal timber, as the EUTR envisages, it can only have an effect if other major consuming regions do so as well (Contreras-Hermosilla, Doornbosch and Lodge 2007; Center for International Economics 2010). A level playing field needs to be guaranteed to do away with possibilities of circumventing the system. National and even bilateral initiatives are drops on a hot plate in reducing illegal and unsustainable forest practices (Seneca Creek and International Wood Resources 2004). Governance structures to tackle environmental issues therefore need to look at multiple levels to understand governance mechanisms: firm-level, sector-level and macro-level as well as the local, national and global levels (Marx and Cuypers 2010).

In face of this complexity, it might be useful to consider governance actors that might not be primary stakeholders (missing nodes, Wood 2006). In countries of origin, there is for instance potential to encourage small-scale timber producers to become engaged in forest governance. Next, corporate actors that work in sectors that impact forest management (for example mining) could be involved. Besides corporate actors in the timber industry, transport actors might be valuable partners to monitor timber trade flows. Although many NGOs are currently already on the cutting edge of the governance of the timber trade, they have difficulties being participants in the networks as well as continuing environmental advocacy (Holley, Gunningham and Shearing 2012).

Finally, throughout the entire system, there is room for improvement in the involvement of government actors. Despite the (apparent) lack of interest, government actors seem to be best equipped – at least in countries of destination – to undertake enforcement and thus to provide deterrent incentives. A government respondent (G6) argues that '[d]espite this multi-stakeholder governance policy, the government involvement stays crucial. A market initiative such as certification can only truly work when there is pressure by government'. Most importantly, the implementation of governance initiatives is crucial for its success and it is particularly on that issue that the governance of illegal tropical timber trade seems to be lagging. On the one hand, awareness about the environmental severity of the phenomenon is lacking, as is illustrated by the lack of an international convention. Maybe the (environmental) impact is too far removed from the consumers of the products to raise concern (Lynch and Stretesky 2001). On the other hand, drafting a governance framework to address a topic involving (il)legality, (un)sustainability and (in)formality that reaches across the globe is necessarily complex. Such a framework does not necessarily need to be state dominated, especially in light of the inherent challenges to current government action (or lack of action). No matter which governance actor or network of actors is involved, the governance framework will need to bridge the inherent imbalance between producing and consuming countries, because it is exactly this global character that determines this environmental crime flow.

Legal Definitions and Technical Competence

The legal principles at the basis of the environmental governance framework need to be understandable for untrained people (Braithwaite 2008). As this study illustrated, the EU legislation for waste (for example WSR) is very complex. Even prosecutors noted that it is challenging for them to use. This is also illustrated by the dependence of Antwerp customs and HMO on the environmental inspectorates to judge the suspicious shipments and the lack of training on these topics for enforcement officials. Unfortunately, this confirms the finding that waste is a topic with a lot of rules and regulations which are not always practical (Huisman 2001, p. 363).

The legal framework for timber is much less extensive, since there is only limited criminalization of tropical timber transports (for example CITES). The existing legal and governance framework is difficult to use and falls back on the national legislation of the countries of origin. This does not fit the global characteristics of the flows, which are determined by actors that are located in countries of origin, transit and destination. The entry into force of the *European Timber Regulation* could potentially change this, if not in its implementation, then maybe for its symbolic value for the criminalization of illegal timber.

Both topics also require governance actors to have technical expertise. In the studied cases, many actors that are on the crossroads of these trade flows (in harbours) do not have enough time or expertise to deal with the issue. Furthermore, there is a lack of reliable statistics on these phenomena. Despite initiatives to track (illegal) waste flows, many data challenges exist. For timber, official data are even scarcer, a logical consequence of the lack of criminalization, and, therefore, estimates rely on non-governmental sources (research reports, NGO estimates and so on). The low priority and limited resources invested in preventing and controlling the illegal trade in e-waste and tropical timber go against one of the requirements of effective environmental governance as identified by Holley, Gunningham and Shearing (2012). On a global level, the (inter)governmental initiatives have not addressed the emerging transnational environmental problems or are at least characterized by doubtful enforceability (Meidinger 2002).

Restorative Justice or Local Governance at the Basis

The responsive regulatory pyramid requires an array of tools to be available to choose from instead of using a standard toolkit (Braithwaite 2008). This allows regulators to experiment with restorative justice tools to stimulate social responsibility rather than to simply punish offenders. For e-waste, inspectorates have several ways to respond. In import and export cases, environmental inspectorates will usually address corporate licensing regulations and by following the e-waste flow back to its source. The restorative element happens through the inspectorates in their negotiations about licensing of facilities. This, however, does not apply easily to the multitude of small-scale (often individual) shippers of UEEE/WEEE because they are difficult to trace. When addressing transit cases, even though it may deal with large quantities of trade (for example, 80 per cent of the e-waste shipments in Antwerp) – the options are limited because inspectorates rely on other EU states to trace the transports back to the origin. The restorative approach applies to them as well and even to the individual shippers. I witnessed how they allowed the WEEE to be taken out of the unit (container or vehicle) in order to have it recycled and have the remaining UEEE shipped.

Braithwaite (2008) writes that the local governance level has become weaker in the regulatory state. In examining the governance reality of e-waste, the primary actors to control and prevent illegal transports were the regional and federal inspectorates. Also *Recupel* as the official take back agency plays an important role. Belgium has the advantage of having an environmental administration (*OVAM*) that takes up a role that other countries reserve for local administrations. The risk is that local authorities in Belgium are not fully engaged in the process. However, local government actors might be better aware of waste collection that is happening in their municipality. Small-scale collectors are not always known to the environmental inspectorates. Of course, the important share of transit shipments has the consequence that the local authorities could be far removed from the location where the illegal transport is stopped. It is then very difficult to track and monitor the activities of the multitude of actors. This could result in governments focusing primarily on the recyclers rather than on actors earlier in the supply chain (Huisman 2001). For the 20 per cent that is exported, there is follow-up through the supply chain, but the 80 per cent transit shipments are difficult to trace. The judicial aspects seem to be quite well developed (cf. role of the prosecutor in Antwerp) although the implementation – especially the EU wide harmonization of it – definitely has room for improvement.

It is difficult to assess the restorative element or local government involvement in the governance of illegal timber transports. For the Belgian timber importers this primarily goes back to monitoring by certification organizations (for example FSC supply chain). The administrative governance framework, outside the judicial arena, seems to be well developed but this is linked to corporations or NGOs taking the initiative and not to government controls or prevention. This might be a consequence of the lack of prioritization of the topic and the lack of international policy-making and decision-taking.

The local level governance is important for the success of environmental governance despite the inherently transnational nature of those flows (Gille 2006). In developing countries, promising local initiatives are those of collection and dismantling of e-waste (in Ghana), but they are currently very few, often fuelled by NGOs and not by local administrations. Similarly, there are initiatives to foster sustainable and/or legal forest management, fuelled by NGOs as well as by governance initiatives such as FLEGT. In these instances, it is very difficult to apply one model to all regions or countries because local characteristics need to be taken into account. Insights are thus needed about how and why governance initiatives work and what conditions there are for it to function (Ayling 2013). Only after this first step is taken, can we evaluate whether it could apply elsewhere. This also implies the need to avoid imposing a Western frame of reference without considering the local differences.

(Regulated) Self-Regulation

Several corporate actors shape the (il)legal transports of e-waste and tropical timber and can play a role in the control and prevention of these flows. Self-regulation is said to be carried out mainly by multinationals whereas the major threat is with smaller actors (Haines 1997). In the present study, the major corporations such as EEE producers, WEEE recyclers, timber importers and processors and shipping lines indeed appeared to take initiatives to self-regulate. This conclusion, however, should not be broadly generalized since random sampling techniques could not be employed in examining large and small shipping lines.

Why might larger companies have a greater interest in self-regulation? Gunningham, Kagan and Thornton (2003) list several reasons for firms to set standards that go beyond the legal requirements: to increase profit; to ward off more intrusive regulation; to anticipate future tightening of rules (and avoid costs of that); and to protect the company's reputation and social legitimacy (avoid adverse publicity). The motivation for self-regulation lies both in market-based dynamics and in the broader political and social context (Bartley 2007). At the same time, economic pressure on smaller shipping companies may increase the incentive to accept illegal shipments and to avoid self-regulation to enhance profit making.

As for the cases under study, e-waste was related to the importance of keeping the secondary raw materials within the EU, with high standards of environmental effectiveness in recycling. The raw materials issue is therefore an economic incentive to develop self-regulation. Refurbishers and recyclers were thus keen to adhere to high environmental standards because this was profitable for their business or because they hoped to influence legislation. Some firms even set more stringent standards for their UEEE exports than what the law requires. These are usually the firms that made this their niche market. As long as it is win-win, investments seem to be made, but, beyond that, it reaches certain practical limitations related to profit making (Gunningham, Kagan and Thornton 2003). Producers were for instance found to be cherry picking in terms of their responsibility to take back WEEE. There is thus room to take this a step further and to truly integrate the environmental costs throughout the entire life cycle (van Erp and Huisman 2010). To address this, extended producer responsibility policies have emerged such as the RoHS and WEEE directives (Pellow 2007), but their implementation can be improved. Also the timber sector has taken initiatives to regulate its business. The incentive is the long-term sustainability of the sector. Timber importers also fear shaming by NGOs or in the media. Not all timber loggers, processors or importers are, however, equally concerned with their reputation or with long-term consequences. Transport firms are also sensitive to a bad reputation, which explains their concern with illegal transports of e-waste and timber on their vessels. Once again, not all shipping lines or agents were concerned with this pressure by local governments, NGOs or the media, and future research should more explicitly explore the factors that promote or undermine self-regulation. Regulatory elements also influenced the compliance of these corporate actors, because firms do not want to go lower than the regulatory standards and thereby avoid constant checks by distrusting regulators (Gunningham, Kagan and Thornton 2003). The case studies showed how the EUTR and WEEE seem to have this effect on firms. However, there is a big risk of regulation becoming a mere paper tiger, especially when standards and definitions are not always clear. The compliance with regulation and the extent of self-regulation is thus influenced by a combination of economic, social and regulatory elements.

Although there are self-regulatory initiatives installed in the case studies – mainly by bigger actors – this does not address all actors. Smaller actors can, however, be connected to these multinationals through supply chain management and due diligence. This is happening with the timber trade by means of the 'due diligence' in the FSC certification and the EUTR. Labels like FSC engage both producers and consumers in the biodiversity debate and thus manage to bridge the gap between corporate, government and civil society actors in the global trade flow. Criteria for these labels vary but they manage to merge social, economic and ecological concerns into regulation and global trade, allowing for new governance mechanisms to occur. These labels fit the hybrid governance logic of today and tomorrow (van Koppen 2006). The certification they require, however, is very expensive. As a consequence, the certification (for example FSC) risks staying limited to a small part of the timber market. For e-waste, some big corporations in collection and recycling choose which influx of WEEE/UEEE to accept, depending on whether they deem the source trustworthy. Shipping agents address their shipper-clients through information campaigns. Self-regulation might be more flexible in addressing the dynamic reality of preventing illegal transports of e-waste (for example perceiving CRT television sets as WEEE), but self-regulation cannot address the entire market. The multitude of small-scale actors makes it difficult to install self-regulation sector-wide, for instance through certification schemes or extended responsibility, especially when private and public interest do not coincide (Holley, Gunningham and Shearing 2012). In comparing this governance reality with the ideal-typical models of the responsive regulatory pyramid and networked governance, the governance approach could look to better involve corporate actors. First, by raising awareness since many are unaware of what they are shipping and do not know what to look out for. Secondly, increased information exchange about the flows might provide better grounds to address illegal transports. Setting this up through (regulated) self-regulation of course implies that all parties need to agree on the purpose and benefits.

Given the enormous volume of actors and containers that need to be controlled, inspectors or customs cannot rely on command and control. Environmental inspectorates often simply cannot keep up with the increased environmental regulation (Gunningham, Kagan and Thornton 2003). A solution for this is found in regulated self-regulation or meta-regulation. This means that controls happen on a higher level either by third-party actors or by government, and are based on the management system of the corporation. System-based controls have the advantage of being able to impact the underlying processes of a corporation rather than the shallow effects when only the outcomes are controlled (de Bree 2011). The governance of illegal transports of e-waste and tropical timber was to a certain extent addressed through regulated self-governance. This, for instance, happens in the AEO system of customs which bases its controls on the management systems of the corporations. Earlier on, the reasons why this system is not airtight were addressed. Similarly, the inspectorates work through meta-regulation to control waste corporations. Meta-regulation exists for timber as well, but this relies on auditing controls or through certificating companies rather than other forms of government control. The conditions necessary for meta-governance are not always practically possible. For instance, should the criteria meet those of big or small corporations in the sector? In both of the case studies, corporate actors have an interest in the success of these governance frameworks: European e-waste recyclers want to guarantee the inflow of metals and European timber importers need the responsible management of forests to guarantee the sustainability of their business. However, some actors involved in the flows of WEEE/UEEE and tropical timber have to win and others to lose with more stringent laws or self-regulation. Another issue is the question of who has the expertise to evaluate the criteria. Often only few people have that knowledge and experience.

Yielding a Big Stick

The high complexity and dynamism of the cases hold an intrinsic problem of compliance for environmental regulation (Huisman 2001). A crucial characteristic of the responsive regulatory pyramid is for it to escalate to more punitive sanctions when necessary. The pyramid persuades compliance when the 'slippery slope will inexorably lead to a sticky end' (Braithwaite 2008, pp. 93–4). In the studied cases, the escalation is very uncertain as the following examples demonstrate. Waste fraud is a priority in policy-making and different actors focus on it. All of them, however, have very few staff and resources to accomplish their goals. There is prosecution of waste cases, but this is hardly ever successful in court because laws are very complex. Fines that are imposed for illegal e-waste transports are perceived as too low to be effective and become part of shippers' business plans. Environmental inspectorates and HMO recently saw their possibilities to fine shippers (also for transit) increased, but it is too soon to tell what the result will be. A major flaw in enforcement is that the implementation of the EU conventions in view of determining sanctions is lacking which leaves member states a great margin of interpretation (Billiet et al. 2010; Billiet and Meeus 2010). The harmonization of policy implementation throughout the EU is often minimal. There is, for instance, a risk analysis on the import and export of transports, but for transit shipments the customs in the Port of Antwerp need to trust the risk analysis of the EU port of origin. As a consequence, there is no level playing field for controls in the EU, so there are definite weaknesses due to the EU-wide system. One way to come across any of these actors transporting e-waste illegally is through the controls of shipments in harbours. The governance analysis illustrated why this is like looking for a needle in a haystack and seldom results in judicial follow-up despite the good intentions.

Controls on tropical timber in countries of origin and transit are generally limited due to the unwillingness (cf. corruption) or the inability to act upon this. Countries of origin also have limited information about the natural resources they have available. Moreover, adequate national legislation and enforcement to address this is missing. Governments in countries of destination, such as Belgium, do not see illegal tropical timber transports as a priority. Although the EUTR now addresses the placing on the EU market of illegally harvested timber, it is unclear how that will be implemented. Currently there is no stick to yield when the self-regulation and third-party verification fails. There are no resources to deal with illegal timber trade and neither is there sufficient knowledge to check the transports on their legality. Despite the good intentions of several actors, the current governance framework for illegal trade in tropical timber does not address the complexity of its social organization. This means that the pyramid of increased sanctions for serious violations has yet to be well established.

The criminal justice system has been labelled as light-handed and inadequate in dealing with environmental crime (White 2009). For the cases examined in this study, governmental control was generally in the hands of passionate, but very few, individuals. This corresponds to the findings of Fyfe and Reeves (2010) about environmental law enforcement being under-resourced and marginalized. Although this applies to the studied cases, there are more actors than those of the criminal justice system that prevent and control illegal transports of e-waste and tropical timber. The governance framework seems to be government dominated for e-waste, whereas the corporate and civil society actors are more passive. For timber the active governance actors are the corporations and NGOs and the multi-stakeholder initiatives, whereas the government actors seem to be mostly passive. Even when self-regulation or multi-stakeholder initiatives exist, there is still a need for more punitive intervention in case standards are not adhered to (Jänicke 2006). Non-state actors can take these more punitive measures (for example consumer boycotts, naming and shaming, loss of certification). The cases illustrated that this does not encompass all actors with a motivation or opportunity to get involved in illegal transports of e-waste and tropical timber. Therefore, the local, national and international government agencies remain crucial, willing to invoke command and control, when the rest fails (Holley, Gunningham and Shearing 2012; Keohane and Nye 2000). Actual enforcement is then the best stimulus for compliance, but that cannot be guaranteed.

Pyramid becomes Network

Holley, Gunningham and Shearing (2012) prompted that complex problems such as environmental issues are not easily governed by a single actor and that a networked governance model might fare better. Haines (1997) suggested that the pyramid is incomplete and should become a pluralist pyramid, adding corporations and NGOs to the governance actors. Ayling (2013, p. 3) wrote that 'the state cannot effectively act alone [but] is positioned in a central and crucial position in relation to these other actors'. Braithwaite (2008), inspired by networked governance, suggested combining the responsive regulatory pyramid with a network metaphor, where a broader range of stakeholders cooperate. In making the pyramid into a network model, there are a number of prerequisites to fulfil. Networked governance for the environment requires the nurturing of governance capacities through sufficient funding, expertise, transparency and knowledge about the strengths and responsibilities of each stakeholder (Holley, Gunningham and Shearing 2012). As mentioned earlier, both of the studied cases indicate that there is a lack of control resources. Given the high priority for e-waste fraud, resources for controlling and preventing illegal transports are higher than those for timber or endangered species. As for expertise, the controls for e-waste and timber fall back on the knowledge and experience of few individuals. Training of other actors (for example customs) has been organized *ad hoc*. There is a starting cooperation between government, corporate and civil society actors to prevent illegal e-waste transports. For timber this cooperation is more established within the FSC system, but it has a limited market share. Transparency and information exchange – both horizontal and vertical – is needed between the nodes in the network to encourage peer review (Holley, Gunningham and Shearing 2012). This study found a hindrance to this in the commercial secrets about the timber and waste trade and in the lack of reliable statistics.

The diversity of actors and push, pull and facilitating factors in illegal e-waste and tropical timber transports inevitably means a networked governance approach would have to take many actors into account in countries of origin, transit and destination and on local, national and international level. This of course renders the networked governance set-up complex, going against Holley, Gunningham and Shearing's (2012) idea that networked governance for the environment is easiest in a small-scale setting with limited complexity. There is potential to work on a small scale on the governance of illegal trade in e-waste and tropical timber, but the transnational element is so inherent that it inevitably needs to be addressed. In having actors be part of a governance network, the weaker actors can enrol stronger ones as a way of escalating up the pyramid, even across transnational borders

(Braithwaite 2008). In West Africa, states have, for instance, forced shipping lines to take up responsibility for the waste shipments by chaining their vessels. Local Ghanaian NGOs also combine forces with international organizations to develop capacity building. Similarly, they cooperate with (European) corporations for the take back of equipment (for example motherboards). Although a number of these initiatives in the prevention and control of illegal e-waste transports are still in their infancy, some evidence of this broader network thus exists for the e-waste case. As discussed earlier, the network of actors in governing timber transports has an ideal-typical example in the FSC system. In the absence of governmental legislation, other actors stepped in to govern the timber trade. The control and prevention beyond this voluntary framework is, however, still rather limited.

The governance reality of illegal transports of e-waste and tropical timber is shaped by the global trade flows and by the interconnections between different actors across borders. This does not imply that state actors are necessarily weaker, especially if they are able to govern through and with global institutions (Braithwaite 2008). Within this governance framework, the state needs to act strategically, because it is dependent on a broader network of actors (Holley, Gunningham and Shearing 2012). To an extent, this corresponds to the empirical reality of the studied cases, because both the EU and international level set a lot of environmental standards and agreements. The many gaps and challenges remaining show that this is not yet used to its full potential and might even be an extra incentive for illegal transports. The EU's lacking harmonization of implementation of WEEE/WSR is an example of that. The uncertainty about the implementation of the EUTR points to similar problems despite the strong moral message it sends.

Perceiving governance as a network rather than a pyramid seems to make governance even more complex. It does provide the potential to deal with the complexity that is transnational environmental crime. By focusing on the structural characteristics of governance, networked governance allows exploring potential cooperation even when the objectives or starting points of potential partners are not identical. Note that an inherent challenge for joined governance efforts – be it within a pyramid or a networked governance approach – is that some actors start from initial trust and others from initial distrust of the actors whose behaviour they try to prevent and control. The nodal analysis allowed getting a grip on the objectives and realities of each separate governance actor. This proved crucial to understanding basic assumptions of actors that might be influencing their cooperation. The success of either of these hybrids arrangements, then, inevitably depends on trying to overcome these differences and working towards the same end, despite different objectives and means. Through a networked governance approach you can take those different interests into account, negotiate about what the approach should entail and address this based on each actor's capacity. This allows taking into account not only what is strictly defined as illegal but also discusses the broader dimensions, allowing a more complete account of social phenomena. For either choice of governance model – whether networked or pyramidal – it is then crucial to evaluate the end goal against the objectives, allowing for government or third-party scrutiny.

Capacity Building and Strength-based Governance

The current governance system partially addresses the legal criminogenic asymmetries, but fails to sufficiently address other asymmetries (Passas 1999). Getting the necessary legislation and enforcement in place remains a clear concern. However, this cannot be a solution unless underlying structural causes such as the need for a source of livelihood, the desire to bridge the digital divide, the demand for raw materials and the lack of recycling facilities are addressed. This closely relates to the cultural and knowledge asymmetry where countries of destination or origin are less aware of the environmental harm of illegal timber or e-waste trade, or simply see more benefits in continuing the trade. Only small steps have been taken to address these asymmetries, mostly by NGOs or *ad hoc* capacity-building projects. These initiatives involve informal recyclers, refurbishers, shipping agents and UEEE shop owners, raise awareness about the issue and look for solutions to deal with the immediate harm (for example, avoiding the burning of waste). Similarly, awareness raising with local port authorities and terminal operators could be useful. These initiatives could be inspired by the capacity building which timber governance initiatives such as FSC and FLEGT are setting up. Informal production is an important share of the illegal exports of tropical timber. These informal actors rely on this timber for income and therefore capacity-building initiatives address structural causes. NGOs as well as corporate actors are, for instance, helping small-size timber concessions to achieve certification and help them overcome the financial barriers for this. Inspired by the tropical timber case, multi-stakeholder initiatives could be a welcome addition to this governance framework. These initiatives provide resources for stakeholders to self-regulate. Braithwaite (2008) referred to this as the strength-building pyramid as a complement to the responsive regulatory pyramid. This requires the consultation of all stakeholders and their agreement about how the monitoring will occur. As this study showed, for both the cases there is a difficulty of balancing economic and environmental concerns. Local governments in Belgium are afraid corporations will go bankrupt (loss of jobs) if controls on e-waste transports are too severe. The same applies in Ghana where the economic pressure of major corporations puts these countries in a weak negotiation position. These economic concerns also play out in the Port of Antwerp. Economic relations are inherent to both flows since they involve commodities. These flows are shaped by apparent and less visible roles or economic actors throughout the flows. The global trade and power relations also relate to the economic asymmetries between north and south. This might make it difficult to reach consensus about whether there is a problem and whether and how it should be addressed. When controlling and preventing illegal transports of e-waste and tropical timber through the collaboration between different actors, this requires the nodes in the network or the stakeholders in the pyramid to agree on the severity of the problem that is addressed (Holley, Gunningham and Shearing 2012). In examining the governance reality of both e-waste and tropical timber, this study found a lack of agreement about the problem. This might explain why both the regulatory pyramid and the networked metaphor sound good in theory but are not actual governance practice. The comparative analysis of the cases reveals that although the governance practice answers to some of the criteria of these two ideal-typical models, the governance reality of illegal transports of e-waste and tropical timber lacks complying with essential prerequisites of them.

Chapter 8
Conclusion

Introduction

The goal of this study was to provide insights into the empirical reality of governing transnational environmental crime flows. By analysing the case of illegal transports of e-waste and tropical timber in a European trade hub, this research responded to the call for more empirical knowledge about transnational environmental crime. This final chapter first discusses the implications of this study for green and critical criminology. Second, the implications for environmental governance studies are addressed. This provides inspiration for the third section examining the avenues for future research. In a fourth part of this chapter, the policy implications of this research are discussed. A brief summary draws this book to a close.

Implications for (Green/Critical) Criminology

Green and critical criminology was an inspiration and a frame of reference for this research. It inspired to look at crime beyond a strict legalistic approach. Critical criminology argued the importance of going beyond a strict definition of crime and looking at the role of the powerful in defining it (for example Box 1983; Hillyard et al. 2004). In green criminology one of the basic premises is to consider a broad notion of crime, thinking about the environmental harm while taking into account effects across time and space (Lynch 1990; White 2011). This social and environmental harm approach also allowed paying attention to the externalization of harm and the dynamics between the Global North and South. The strength of this broad approach is that it accounts for more aspects of the social phenomenon under study. It enables researchers to think differently about social problems. It inspires to think about harm in the broad sense, while still thinking about very real circumstances. It makes it easier to realize how something local can have a global impact, but also how it is impossible to understand the local without taking the broader social, economic and political context into account. Therefore also the role of the powerful such as states and corporations in defining, facilitating and governing crime needs to be considered. However, using a social harm approach proved to be an empirical challenge, because definitional problems arose, especially when studying governance issues. This study therefore tried to stay in the near of the law by using definitions of transnational environmental crime in international law. Thinking based on environmental and global harmfulness avoids a limited picture of contemporary crime. However, even by focusing on social harm, the risk remains of missing a part of the complex social phenomenon. Think for instance of the benefits related to some of these illegal transports. So it is important to stay mindful about the positive elements as well, to understand the emergence of a phenomenon. This was illustrated in both the case of e-waste and tropical timber.

Although based in this green and critical approach, this study has simultaneously demonstrated the relevance of applying other criminological theories to transnational environmental crime. More in particular, this refers to the theory on legal-illegal interfaces and criminogenic asymmetries (Passas 1999, 2002). The model of legal-illegal interfaces has been used to assess interactions between actors that lie at the basis of crimes. Passas (2003) conceptually applied it to money laundering, fraud and the mafia. Tijhuis (2006) made it into a more concrete case study of the trade in antiquities. In this study on e-waste and tropical timber trade, quite similar interfaces between legal and illegal actors were found. Overall, by using the model of legal-illegal interfaces as a basis, this study gained insights about the phenomenon, necessary to inform us on why governance works or might not work. Think for instance of the risk of regulatory capture. The legal-illegal interfaces theory proved very useful to understand the dynamics of transnational crime flows. Overall these interfaces stand for instances in which crime and society meet. The interfaces for timber and e-waste reach the entire spectrum from antithetical to symbiotic, but some nuances apply. First, the funding interface did not necessarily have a financial character but rather one of supporting an actor through the drafting of laws. Differences were also observed in the extent to which legal actors were aware of the illegality by involved actors and the extent to which illegal actors aimed to extort or harm the legal ones. What is particularly relevant in the cases studies here is the observation of informal actors next to the legal and the illegal. Informal actors in fact proved to be inherent to the social organization of both the illegal trade in e-waste and tropical timber. A strict focus on the illegal, in reference to that which has been criminalized, misses part of the picture of transnational environmental crime.

The findings were thus connected to theories despite the somewhat a-theoretical characteristics of green criminology. Indeed, green criminology is not a theory nor does it claim to be, but in this way it maybe risks being neglected or misunderstood. At the end of this book, I want to highlight the importance of not losing track of theoretical developments. It might prove valuable to relate green criminological publications more to existing frameworks in criminology or other disciplines and demonstrate the added value of a green criminology or social harm approach. By applying existing theories to transnational environmental crime, they can be taken outside of a focus on more traditional crimes. This requires methodological creativity to deal with the challenges and inherently comes with some limitations, as discussed in the methodological chapter.

This study intended to contribute to green criminology by empirically analysing transnational environmental crime cases. As a rather new field of study, green criminology publications often lack an empirical focus. This study does not claim to have filled this gap, but did take up the challenge to think about this 'blind spot' in criminology. The contribution of this study is the original data it brings to the discipline.

Implications for Environmental Governance Studies

The above implications relate to defining and understanding the emergence of transnational environmental crime. Another element central to criminology is the question of the social reaction to crime and harm. The complex social organization and criminalization inevitably render the governance complicated as well. Reflecting on this theoretically, it is useful for criminology in general and green criminology in particular to focus on issues of governance and the social reaction to crime. In this, they could fare well by including insights from other disciplines such as public administration, ecology or business ethics.

This research provided insights into the end stages of governance, which, in the research setting of this study, basically comes down to yielding a relatively small stick. Interestingly, this study also provided insights into the stages that come before that. Exactly because it concerns a phenomenon about which empirical criminological study is limited and exactly because it is a phenomenon on the outskirts of crime, it allowed us to learn something about governance. It allowed thinking differently about security and social problems by looking through a broad governance lens and being critical about definitions of crime, linking those to social harm. In thinking about the role of non-state actors, operating at different levels, a hybrid model of governance also devises new roles for the state in the globalized context. By focusing on the interactions and the changing role of the state, this study highlighted the relevance of the state actors while at the same time illustrating the necessity of a broader framework for the governance of transnational environmental crime. A traditional focus on what government can do is only part of the picture.

It proved vital to stay critical about the functioning of hybrid governance models, of interactions between governance actors and the changing role of the state. The findings about governance teach us about the responsive regulatory pyramid and the interactions between governance actors. Models are often not as realistic in practice as they claim to be in theory. Within a networked governance model the focus is on horizontal rather than vertical relationships. The idea is promising because it involves several relevant stakeholders, leaves room for creativity and for social control. Prerequisites are transparency, knowledge about the strengths and weaknesses of all governance actors and of course the necessary funding and expertise. It also requires trust and transparency amongst the governance actors. Establishing networked governance for the complex transnational environmental crime flows would require the network to embrace both the local and the global (origin-transit-destination) and engage governments, corporations as well as civil society actors.

Within the responsive regulatory pyramid, a focus on a strengths-based dimension allows addressing issues outside of those strictly legal or law enforcement, extending the picture to asymmetries in knowledge, awareness and economy that lie at the origin of crime and harm. Think for instance of addressing the lack of recycling facilities through setting up take-back systems (Williams et al., 2013). For this, a major role to play is there for NGOs. In some sectors also corporate actors are stepping up. This implies (environmental) governance studies can benefit from thinking outside of traditional nation state frameworks. In this, the state could be a strategic partner who intervenes only when it is necessary, implying that the issue could not be dealt with through the network. This requires the actors within the network to overcome differences in goals and work realities. There is an inherent difficulty in engaging a broad range of governance actors. Even within international networks of government agencies there are difficulties to cooperate when the intentions or the goals are different or when there is no agreement about the seriousness of the problem. Unsurprisingly, the objectives, means and strategies of governments, corporations and NGOs are not necessarily aligned. Nevertheless, there is some common ground even if economic and ecological interests need to be combined and compromises need to be looked for. It is therefore without a doubt difficult to design a governance framework for complex flows like transnational environmental crime but it is not impossible. The instances in which this is possible would be something for empirical research into (environmental) governance to address.

Avenues for Future Research

This book dealt with a topic that is difficult to approach and that required creativity in grasping it empirically. Despite these challenges, this study can serve as a call to continue research on this topic, both comparatively and interdisciplinary.

Of course, there is a need to test these findings in other contexts. Future research could analyse other types of transnational environmental crime or apply them to other regions in the world. The two cases that were studied in this research had an opposite transnational dimension and are differently positioned on the line between legal and illegal. Nevertheless, the analysis found many similarities in the way these transnational environmental crime flows are organized. In their governance, they are essentially different, the one relying mostly on government actions and the other on governance initiatives by corporate and civil society actors. Even in face of those differences, several similar observations about their governance reality could be made. It would be interesting to see how these findings compare to other transnational environmental crime cases such as for instance (illegal) trade in traditional Chinese medicines, (il)legal fishing or the trade in other types of hazardous waste. It could also be interesting to apply it to other cases at the crossroad of trade facilitation and harm prevention such as, for instance, the clothing industry or the oil industry. Similarly, it would be interesting to see how the findings apply to other research settings: a comparative analysis could be made with other European ports (for example Rotterdam, Hamburg, Le Havre) or with other regions of the world (for example North America, South East Asia).

Besides these comparative designs it seems interesting to approach the topic from a different perspective, such as by looking at the victimology of transnational environmental crimes. Within the field of green criminology there is attention for environmental crime, but not necessarily for environmental victimization by particular cases of it (Hall 2011). The power and rights of victims were not explicitly part of this study, except for those local actors in Ghana that were involved in the e-waste case. It could be interesting to reach out to them for future research, also in thinking about conflict resolution. Identifying the victims is not straightforward, because it requires thinking about both geographical and temporal dimensions to victimization, evoking a more abstract and hidden victim (Goodey 2005). The analysis of the cases revealed asymmetries between regions of the world and also inequalities in both harm and access to governance. Future research could focus on this more in detail and develop ideas about restorative regulatory solutions or ways to improve local governance of these transnational environmental crimes. Action research could be particularly relevant here. Both local communities and NGOs could be engaged in evaluating multi-stakeholder initiatives or locally embedded networked governance initiatives, especially since this opens up possibilities for restorative justice. Even though they remain contested concepts, scholars agree that environmental harm and victimization deserve more attention than has been the case (White 2011). Also learning about environmental governance is ongoing, requiring continued refinement (Gunningham, Grabosky and Sinclair, 1998). A more comprehensive understanding of environmental harm can shed light on the theoretical, normative and practical value of environmental governance and help explain whether and how environmental governance can contribute to preventing and managing environmental harm.

Further understanding about the role of corporations is also a challenge for future (environmental) governance research. It would be interesting to further explore where the economic incentive – the business case – lies to get involved in governance. Researchers could study the role of corporations on how their social responsibility can be addressed (for example factorial surveys on particular smuggling situations).

Finally, it would be interesting to corroborate these findings by designing quantitative research. It might be interesting to test whether the assumption is correct that people in developed countries are less concerned about environmental crime and its impact because the most devastating harm is not happening in their backyard. Survey designs could proof useful for this. Quantitative studies could also provide insights on the perceptions of corporate actors (shipping lines, timber importers, WEEE collectors) and government actors (customs) about their responsibilities in controlling and preventing illegal trade in e-waste and/or tropical timber.

Policy Recommendations

This study shows the complexity inherent to the social organization of transnational environmental crime, and illegal transports of e-waste and tropical timber in particular, and illustrates the diversity inherent to their governance reality. This requires the governance framework to be able to deal with the dynamic context. Theoretically we can design the most beautiful answers to account for the complexity of a phenomenon, but policy practice can paint a different picture. On the definitional aspect, it is a matter of choosing to be flexible about the definition to account for a dynamic phenomenon. This implies assessing the social organization as well as possible to understand gaps in the approach taken. Addressing structural issues is then needed and this requires a broader view than mere illegality. This requires taking into account the local level in both understanding the social organization and thinking about a governance framework. As illustrated in this study, the existing framework of enforcement is not always adjusted to that.

The research setting of the Port of Antwerp adds an extra challenge to that because it is a typical transit port. This means that governance of the trade flows largely relies on the control and prevention in other ports. Within the EU, the lack of harmonized enforcement of environmental legislation is currently hampering the control and prevention of transnational environmental crime. In face of the sheer quantity of commodities that are traded each day, a risk analysis system is logical. It is, however, necessary to try and account for transit shipments as well. Bottlenecks in the follow-up of environmental enforcement should also be reduced to a minimum.

By comparing the case of e-waste, which has an extensive legislative framework, with the case of tropical timber, which largely relies on non-governmental actors to govern the flows, this study illustrated that governance initiatives can also arise in the absence of a clear legislative framework. The e-waste case could learn from the timber case by involving a broader array of actors in the governance framework. Local communities or NGOs can for instance influence the informal actors in Ghana as a country of destination, but also in Belgium as a country of origin. This can happen through capacity building, thereby addressing the structural causes in the broader socio-economic context that shape illegal trade. Similarly, corporate actors could be more involved in controlling and preventing illegal transports of e-waste by establishing links between governments and shipping lines. An important step is raising awareness about the topic and interacting with these corporate actors about what their role could be. The supply chain management and certification of FSC could be an inspiration for this. It might also be good to nurture the connections between NGOs and government agencies.

Controlling and preventing the illegal trade in timber can also be inspired by the e-waste case. Despite the remaining weaknesses, there is a much clearer legal framework for e-waste and there is a rather close-knit network of government actors that deal with this topic. The possibility of yielding a stick is crucial as the ultimate step in both a government dominated and a broader governance framework. That escalation to more punitive reactions is missing in the governance reality of both cases. Despite the importance of judicial coordination and follow-up, this should be balanced with initiatives on administrative level.

This study did not intend nor succeed in providing an answer to all governance challenges of transnational environmental crime. The insights can nevertheless be used for the further development, implementation and enforcement of governance initiatives on transnational environmental crime.

Concluding Summary

The goal of this study was to provide insights into the empirical reality of governing transnational environmental crime flows. By analysing the case of illegal transports of e-waste and tropical timber in a European trade hub, this research responded to the call for more empirical knowledge about transnational environmental crime. It addressed the question what the governance consequences are of controlling and preventing transnational environmental crime flows. This research was based on a qualitative multi-method research design combining a document analysis of various primary and secondary sources, 81 interviews with key informants and field visits.

A first step in studying the governance of the transnational environmental crime flows was to understand the etiology of the phenomenon. The social organization and emergence of the two cases was examined. The data analysis revealed various legal-illegal interfaces throughout the flows. The analysis showed how push, pull and facilitating factors on individual, organizational and societal levels together shape the illegal transports of e-waste and tropical timber. It demonstrated how the transnational environmental crime cases are on a thin line between legal and illegal and need to be contextualized within the global reality of origin, transit and destination locations.

The core focus of this study was the governance reality of dealing with these cases on a fine line between legal and illegal and, in particular, the governance reality of illegal transports of e-waste and tropical timber. Relating back to the responsive regulatory pyramid and networked governance, this study made several observations about the cases. Some findings are in line with earlier publications, but this study further substantiated those claims with empirical data. The findings reveal that although the governance reality of illegal transports of e-waste and tropical timber answers to some of the criteria of these models, it lacks complying with essential prerequisites of them. These models might theoretically or normatively provide good foundations for addressing the cases, but the governance reality paints a different picture. This can of course be due to the fact that illegal transports of e-waste and tropical timber involve so many types of actors: corporate actors in the waste or timber sector, but equally in the transport sector, individual shippers, informal recyclers or loggers, fraudulent or unaware governments and consumers. The governance framework to control and prevent these transports then needs to take into account each of these actors and push, pull and facilitating factors across the global flows. The governance approach faces the complex reality of balancing environmental and economic concerns, policy dynamism and judicial clout, capacity building and crime fighting.

Appendix 1: Checklist

What elements characterize the social organization and emergence of illegal transports of e-waste and tropical timber?

Sub-question 1.1: What elements of harmfulness or scope are taken into account in the criminalization of illegal transports of e-waste and tropical timber?

- Harmfulness for humans, ecology, economy and so on? (arguments behind the criminalization)
- What is the estimated frequency/scope of the transports?

Sub-question 1.2: How are illegal transports of e-waste and tropical timber socially organized?

- What are the origin, intermediary and destination locations? *Orientation of the flows (South-North)*
- What sorts of products (metals vs. timber) are transported?
- How are goods transported, distributed or made transportable? What is the method of exchange?
- Illegal/legal nature of the transport and the goods (for example false documents, black market and so on).
- Are the involved actors legal or illegal?
- Are the involved actors individuals or organizations (corporations/state actors)?
- What kind of interactions are there between the involved actors?

Sub-question 1.3: Which push and pull factors explain the emergence of illegal transports of e-waste and tropical timber?

- Push factors in countries of origin (supply)?
- Pull factors in countries of destination (demand)?
- What legal, economic and cultural asymmetries play a role?

What elements characterize the governance of illegal transports of e-waste and tropical timber?

Sub-question 2.1: Who are the actors that participate in the governance of illegal transports of e-waste and tropical timber?

- Government actors? (police, inspectorate, customs, port authority, judiciary and so on)
- Corporate actors? (producers, transporters, recyclers and so on)
- Civil society actors? (NGOs, journalists, labour unions, consumers and so on).

Sub-question 2.2: What knowledge, capabilities and resources do each of these actors make use of for the governance of illegal transports of e-waste and tropical timber?

- Knowledge
- Capabilities
- Resources
- Institutional structures.

Sub-question 2.3: What is the mentality of these actors towards illegal transports of e-waste and tropical timber in particular?

- What do these actors see as the causes?
- What does transnational environmental security mean to them?
- What strategies to influence human/corporate behaviour in transnational environmental matters do they adhere to?
- What are the finalities of these actors? (environmental, economic, judicial or administrative nature) What outcomes to they put forward and how do they measure success?

Sub-question 2.4: How do these different actors interact?

- Cooperative? Competitive? Non-existent?
- Government directs? Use other actor for own goals?

Sub-question 2.5: What are the strengths and weaknesses in the governance of illegal transports of e-waste and timber?

- What weaknesses in technologies, mentalities and resources of existing nodes exist (for each actor, local/national and global/transnational and for entire governance spectrum)?

- What opportunities for change exist in the internal characteristics of nodes whose governance behaviors are important but are not currently addressing security issues?
- Are there nodal gaps or missing nodes? (Individuals or groups who are currently not mobilized in these governance processes and this in despite of their relevant knowledge, capacities and resources in view of desired governance outcomes.)
- Are there missing links in the governance network? (Places in the network where new connections could be advantageous.)

References

Aas, K.F., 2007. Analysing a world in motion. *Theoretical Criminology*, 11(2), pp. 283–303.

Aas, K.F., 2011. 'Crimmigrant' bodies and bona fide travelers: Surveillance, citizenship and global governance. *Theoretical Criminology*, 15(3), pp. 331–46.

Alvazzi del Frate, A., Benjamin, A., Heine, G., Norberry, J. and Prabhu, M., 1999. Environmental protection at national and international levels: Potentials and limits of criminal justice. An overview of the empirical study. In G. Heine, M. Prabhu and A. Alvazzi del Frate, eds, *Environmental Protection – Potentials and Limits of Criminal Justice. Evaluation of legal structures*. Freiburg im Breisgau: United Nations Interregional Crime and Justice Research Institute (UNICRI), pp. 19–57.

Amoyaw-Osei, Y. Opoku Agyekum, O., Pwamang, J., Mueller, E., Fasko, R. and Schluep, 2011. *Ghana e-Waste Country Assessment. SBC e-Waste Africa Project*. Green Advocacy Ghana (Green Ad), Environmental Protection Agency (EPA), Secretariat of the Basel Convention (SBC), United Nations Environment Programme (UNEP), Eidgenössische Materialprüfungs- und Forschungsanstalt (EMPA).

Anon, 2009. Flemish Parliament – Interpellation by Mr. Rudi Daems of Mr. Kris Peeters, minister-president of the Flemish Government, Flemish Minister of Institutional Reform, Governance, Foreign Affairs, Media, Tourism and Ports.

Anton, W.R.Q., Deltas, G. and Khanna, M., 2004. Incentives for environmental self-regulation and implications for environmental performance. *Journal of Environmental Economics and Management*, 48(1), pp. 632–54.

Antonopoulos, G.A. and Winterdyk, J., 2006. The Smuggling of Migrants in Greece. *European Journal of Criminology*, 3(4), pp. 439–61.

Applied Research Institute – Jerusalem (ARIJ), 2012. *The Impacts of Electronic Waste Disposal on the Environment and Public Health in the Occupied Palestinian Territory: A case study from Idhna, Hebron Governorate*, Water and Environment Research Department in Cooperation with Sunflower Association for Human & Environment Protection.

Auld, G., Cashore, B., Balboa, C., Bozzi, L. and Renckens, S., 2010. Can Technological Innovations Improve Private Regulation in the Global Economy? *Business and Politics*, 12(3), Article 9.

Ayling, J., 2013. What Sustains Wildlife Crime? Rhino Horn Trading and the Resilience of Criminal Networks. *Journal of International Wildlife Law and Policy*, 16(1), pp. 57–80.

Ayres, I. and Braithwaite, J., 1992. *Responsive Regulation: Transcending the deregulation debate*. New York: Oxford University Press.

Babbie, E., 2007. *The Practice of Social Research*. 11th ed. Belmont, CA: Thomson Higher Education.

Babbitt, C., Williams, E. and Kahbat, R., 2011. Institutional Disposition and Management of End-of-Life Electronics. *Environmental Science & Technology*, 45(2), pp. 5366–72.

Baker, E., Bournay, E., Harayama, A. and Rekacewicz, P. 2004. *Vital Waste Graphics*. Nairobi: United Nations Environment Programme, Basel Convention, GRID Arendal, DEWA Europe.

Baldwin, R. and Black, J., 2008. Really responsive regulation. *The Modern Law Review*, 71(1), pp. 59–94.

Banks, D., Davies, C., Gosling, J., Newman, J., Rice, M., Wadley, J. and Walravens, F. 2008. *Environmental Crime. A threat to our future*. London: Environment Investigation Agency.

Bannon, I. and Collier, P., 2003a. Natural Resources and Conflict: What We Can Do. In I. Bannon and P. Collier, eds, *Natural Resources and Violent Conflict*. Washington, DC: International Bank for Reconstruction and Development/The World Bank, pp. 1–16.

Bannon, I. and Collier, P., 2003b. Natural Resources and Violent Conflict : What We Can Do. In I. Bannon and P. Collier, eds, *Natural Resources and Violent Conflict*. Washington, DC: International Bank for Reconstruction and Development/The World Bank, p. 409.

Bartley, T., 2007. Institutional Emergence in an Era of Globalization: The Rise of Transnational Private Regulation of Labor and Environmental Conditions. *American Journal of Sociology*, 113(2), pp. 297–351.

Basel Convention Secretariat, 2011. *Partnership on Computing Equipment (PACE)* [online]. Available at: http://archive.basel.int/industry/compartnership/ [Accessed 13 February 2012].

Beirne, P. and South, N., 2007. *Issues in Green Criminology. Confronting harms against environments, humanity and other animals*. Portland: Willan Publishing, p. 317.

Bernstein, S. and Cashore, B., 2007. Can non-state global governance be legitimate? An analytical framework. *Regulation & Governance*, 1(4), pp. 347–71.

Beyens, K. and Tournel, H., 2009. Mijnwerkers of ontdekkingsreizigers? Het kwalitatieve interview. In T. Decorte and D. Zaitch, eds, *Kwalitatieve methoden en technieken in de criminologie*. Leuven: Acco, pp. 195–228.

Bhrem, J. and Hamilton, J., 1996. Noncompliance in Environmental Reporting: Are Violators Ignorant, or Evasive, of the Law? *American Journal of Political Science*, 40(2), pp. 444–77.

Billiet, C., 2009. *Bestuurlijke sanctionering van milieurecht. Wetgeving en praktijk*. Antwerpen/Oxford: Intersentia.

Billiet, C., Rousseau, S., Meeus, R. and Balcaen, A. 2010. Minnelijke Schikkingen Voor Milieumisdrijven in Vlaanderen. *Panopticon*, 31(4), pp. 78–84.

Billiet, C. and Meeus, R. 2010. Europese Verordeningen En de Handhaver. De Sanctieregelingen van Milieuverordeningen in Het Licht van de Handhavingspraktijk. *Tijdschrift voor Milieurecht*, 19(2), pp. 164–202.

Bisschop, L., 2012a. Is it all going to waste? Illegal transports of e-waste in a European trade hub. *Crime, Law and Social Change*, 58(3), pp. 221–49.

Bisschop, L., 2012b. Out of the woods: the illegal trade in tropical timber and a European trade hub. *Global Crime*, 13(3), pp. 191–212.

Bisschop, L., 2013a. Go with the e-waste flows. The governance reality of illegal transports of e-waste in a European trade hub. In P. van Duyne, J. Harvey, G. Antonopoulos, K. von Lampe, A. Maljević and J. Spencer, eds, *Human Dimensions in Organised Crime, Money Laundering and Corruption*. Nijmegen: Wolf Legal Publishers, pp. 393–424.

Bisschop, L., 2013b. Governance throughout the flows. Case study research on the illegal tropical timber trade. In P. Saitta, J. Shapland and A. Verhage, eds, *Getting By Or Getting Rich? The formal, informal and illegal economy in a globalized world*. The Hague: Eleven, pp. 167–99.

Bisschop, L. and Vande Walle, G., 2013. Environmental victimization and conflict resolution. A case study of e-waste. In T. Wyatt, R. Walters and D. Westerhuis, eds, *Debates in Green Criminology: Power, justice and environmental harm*. Basingstoke: Palgrave Macmillan, pp. 34–54.

Black, J., 2008. Constructing and contesting legitimacy and accountability in polycentric regulatory regimes. *Regulation & Governance*, 2(2), pp. 137–64.

Blokland, H., 2010. Afvallozers glippen te vaak door de mazen van het net [Waste dumpers too often slip through meshes of the net]. *De Morgen*, 27 June.

Blondé, B. and Deceulaer, H., 2002. The port of Antwerp and its Hinterland: Port Traffic, Urban Economies and Government Policies in the 17th and 18th Centuries. In R. Ertesvag, D. Starkey and A. Anne, eds, *Maritime Industries and Public Intervention – The Fourth North Sea History Conference*. Stavanger: Maritime Museum, pp. 21–44.

Bloor, M. and Wood, F., 2006. Keywords in qualitative methods. *Sage Research Methods* [online]. Available at: http://www.srmo.sagepub.com/view/keywords-in-qualitative-methods/n54.xml# [Accessed 6 April 2011].

Boekhout van Solinge, T., 2008. Eco-Crime: the Tropical Timber Trade. In D. Siegel and H. Nelen, eds, *Organized Crime: Culture, markets and policies*. New York: Springer, pp. 97–111.

Box, S. 1983. *Power, Crime and Demystification*. London: Tavistock.

Braat, L. and ten Brinks, P., 2008. *The Cost of Policy Inaction: The Case of Not Meeting the 2010 Biodiversity Target*. Wageningen: Alterra.

Brack, D., 2002. Combating transnational environmental crime. *Global Environmental Change*, 12, pp. 143–7.

Brack, D., 2004. Illegal logging and the illegal trade in forest and timber products. In F. Comte and L. Krämer, eds, *Environmental Crime in Europe. Rules of sanctions*. Groningen: Europe Law Publishing, pp. 37–47.

Brack, D. and Hayman, G., 2002. International Environmental Crime: The Nature and Control of Environmental Black Markets. *International Affairs,* May issue, pp. 27–8.

Braithwaite, J., 2000. The New Regulatory State and the Transformation of Criminology. *British Journal of Criminology*, 40, pp. 222–38.

Braithwaite, J., 2002. *Restorative Justice and Responsive Regulation.* New York: Oxford University Press.

Braithwaite, J., 2008. *Regulatory Capitalism: How it works, ideas for making it work better*. Cheltenham: Edward Elgar.

Braithwaite, J. and Fisse, B., 1987. Self-regulation and the control of corporate crime. In C. Shearing and P. Stenning, eds, *Private Policing*. Newbury Park: Sage, pp. 221–46.

Brigden, K., Labunska, I., Santillo, D. and Johnston, P. 2008. *Chemical Contamination at E-Waste Recycling and Disposal sites in Accra and Korforida, Ghana. Greenpeace Research Laboratories*. Greenpeace Research Laboratories, Technical Note 10/2008, Greenpeace International, Amsterdam.

Brook, B., Ellis, E., Perring, M., Mackay, A. and Blomqvist, L., 2013. Does the terrestrial biosphere have planetary tipping points? *Trends in Ecology & Evolution*, 28(7), pp. 396–401.

Brown, W., 2010. *Walled States, Waning Sovereignty*. New York: Zone Books.

Bruinsma, G., 1996. De afvalverwerkingsbranche. In G. Bruinsma and F. Bovenkerk, eds, *Inzake opsporing: enquêtecommissie opsporingsmethoden, Deel II onderzoeksgroep Fijnaut: branches*. Den Haag: SDU, pp. 261–310.

Campbell, J., 2007. Why would corporations behave in socially responsible ways? An institutional theory of corporate social responsibility. *Academy of Management Review*, 32(3), pp. 946–67.

Cardinale, B. Duffy, J., Gonzalez, A., Hooper, D., Perrings, C. and Venail, P., 2012. Biodiversity loss and its impact on humanity. *Nature*, 486, pp. 59–67.

Carrabine, E., Cox, P., Lee, M., Plummer, K. and South, N., 2009. *Criminology. A sociological introduction.* 2nd ed. London/New York: Routledge.

Cashore, B., van Kooten, G., Vertinsky, I., Auld, G. and Affolderbach, J., 2005. Private or self-regulation? A comparative study of forest certification choices in Canada, the United States and Germany. *Forest Policy and Economics*, 7(1), pp. 53–69.

Casson, A. and Obidzinski, K. 2007. From New Order to Regional Autonomy: Shifting Dynamics of Illegal Logging in Kalimantan, Indonesia. In L.Tacconi, ed., *Illegal Logging: Law Enforcement, Livelihoods and the Timber Trade.* London & Sterling, VA: Earthscan & *Center for International Forestry Research*, pp. 43–68.

Castells, M., 2000. *The Rise of the Network Society, The Information Age: Economy, society and culture Vol. I.* 2nd ed. Cambridge, MA/Oxford, UK: Blackwell Publishers.

Celik, H.E., 2008. Forests and Natural Disasters. In H.G. Coskun, H.K. Cigizoglu and M.D. Maktav, eds, *Integration of Information for Environmental Security*. Dordrecht: Springer, pp. 327–35.

Cerutti, P., Assembe-Mvondo, S., German, L. and Putzel, L., 2011. Is China unique? Exploring the behavior of Chinese and European firms in the Cameroonian logging sector. *International Forestry Review*, 13(1), pp. 23–34.

Chen, H.K., 2006. *The Role of CITES in Combating Illegal Logging–Current and Potential*. Cambridge: TRAFFIC International.

Clinard, M. and Yeager, P., 1980. *Corporate Crime*. New York: Free Press.

Coleman, J., 1987. Towards an Integrated Theory of White-Collar Crime. *American Journal of Sociology*, 93(2), pp. 406–39.

Contreras-Hermosilla, A., Doornbosch, R. and Lodge, M., 2007. *The Economics of Illegal Logging and Associated Trade*. Paris: Organisation for Economic Co-operation and Development.

Coosemans, D., 2009. Antwerpse haven draaischijf illegaal afvaltransport [Port of Antwerp hub for illegal waste transports]. *Het Laatste Nieuws*, 7 February, p. 11.

Crawford, A., 2006. Networked governance and the post-regulatory state?: Steering, rowing and anchoring the provision of policing and security. *Theoretical Criminology*, 10(4), pp. 449–79.

Crem, 2008. *Een analyse van stromen electronica-afval in Nederland [Analysis of e-waste flows in the Netherlands]*, Amsterdam: CREM Milieu Onderzoeks- en Adviesbureau.

Croall, H., 2005. Transnational white collar crime. In J. Sheptycki and A. Wardak, eds, *Transnational and Comparative Criminology*. London: Greenhouse Press, pp. 227–45.

Croall, H. 2007a. Food Crime. In P. Beirne and N. South, eds, *Issues in Green Criminology. Confronting Harms against Environments, Humanity and Other Animals*. Devon Collumpton: Willan Publishing, pp. 206–29.

Croall, H. 2007b. Victims of White Collar and Corporate Crime. In P. Davies, P. Francis and C. Greer Victims, eds, *Crime and Society*. London: Sage Publications, pp. 78–108.

Croall, H., 2009. White collar crime, consumers and victimization. *Crime, Law and Social Change*, 51(1), pp. 127–46.

Crossin, C., Hayman, G. and Taylor, S., 2003. Where did it come from? Commodity tracking systems. In I. Bannon and P. Collier, eds, *Natural Resources and Violent Conflict*. Washington, DC: International Bank for Reconstruction and Development/The World Bank, pp. 97–159.

Darnall, N. and Sides, S., 2008. Assessing the Performance of Voluntary Environmental Programs: Does Certification Matter? *Policy Studies Journal*, 36(1), pp. 95–117.

de Bree, M. 2011. Ontwikkelingen in Systeemtoezicht. In M. de Bree, ed., Managementsystemen En Toezicht. Erasmus Universiteit Rotterdam: Erasmus Instituut Toezicht & Compliance, pp. 51–60.

Decorte, T. and Zaitch, D., 2009. *Kwalitatieve methoden en technieken in de criminologie*. Leuven: Acco.

Dellepiane, S., 2009. *Case Study Methods*. Essex: University of Essex.

Delmas, M. and Young, O., 2009. *Governance for the Environment: New Perspectives*. Cambridge: Cambridge University Press.

Denoiseux, D., 2010. L'exportation de déchets dangereux vers l'Afrique: de las du Probo Koala. *Courrier hebdomadaire*, 2071, p. 47.

Duan, H., Miller, T., Gregory, J. and Kirchain, R., 2013. *Quantitative Characterization of Domestic and Transboundary Flows of Used Electronics. Analysis of generation, collection, and export in the United States*. Massachussetts Institute of Technology, Material Systems Laboratory, National Center for Electronics Recycling, Solving the E-Waste Problem and US Environmental Protection Agency.

Ducenne, Q. 2008. *Etude Des FLux Transfrontaliers de Bois Entre Les Pays de La COMIFAC Actuellement Impliqués Dans Le Processus FLEGT*. Brussels: COMIFAC & Union Européenne.

Duffy, R., 2007. Global Governance, Criminalisation and Environmental Change. *Global Crime*, 7(1), pp. 25–42.

van Duyne, P., 1993. Organized crime and business crime enterprises in the Netherlands. *Crime, Law and Social Change*, 19(2), pp. 103–42.

Edwards, S., Edwards, T. and Fields, C., 1996. *Environmental Crime and Criminality: Theoretical and practical issues*. London: Garland Publishing.

Eidgenössische Materialprüfungs- und Forschungsanstalt (EMPA), 2009. *Ewaste-guide.info: Hazardous Substances in e-Waste ewasteguide.info*' [online]. Available at: http://ewasteguide.info/node/219 [Accessed 23 August 2011].

Elliot, L., 2009. Combating transnational environmental crime : 'joined up' thinking about transnational networks. In K. Kangaspunta and I. Haen Marshall, eds, *Eco-Crime and Justice : Essays on environmental crime*. Turin: United Nations Interregional Crime and Justice Research Institute, pp. 55–77.

Elliot, L., 2011. *Transnational Environmental Crime: Applying network theory to an investigation of illegal trade, criminal activity and law enforcement responses*. Transnational Environmental Crime Project – Working Paper 1/2011.

Environmental Investigation Agency, 2011. *System Failure. The UK's harmful trade in electronic waste*. London: Environmental Investigation Agency.

Environmental Protection Agency, 2011. *Statistics on the Management of Used and End-of-Life Electronics* U.S.E.P. Agency [online]. Available at: http://www.epa.gov/osw/conserve/materials/ecycling/manage.htm [Accessed 12 December 2011].

Eski, Y. 2011. 'Port of Call': Towards a Criminology of Port Security. *Criminology and Criminal Justice* 11(5), pp. 415–31.

Espejo, 2010. *Assessment of the Flow and Driving Forces of Used Electrical and Electronic Equipment from Germany to Nigeria*. Cottbus: Brandenburg University of Technology – United Nations University, Institute for Sustainability and Peace.

Euromettaux, 2012. Recycling for a Resource Efficient EU Economy. European Recycling Industries' Position on the challenges of secondary Raw Materials Markets and policies needed to enable resource efficiency EuPC CEPI, CIRFS, Euromettaux, EuPR [online]. Available at: http://www.eurometaux.org/DesktopModules/Bring2mind/DMX/Download.aspx?TabID=57&Command=Core_Download&EntryId=2126&PortalId=0&TabId=57 [Accessed 2 February 2013].

European Commission, 2008. *Assessment of the Impact of Potential Further Measures to Prevent the Importation or Placing on the Market of Illegally Harvested Timber or Products Derived from Such Timber*. Helsinki: European Commission – DG Environment, Indufor, European Forest Institute, Nepcon, Markku Kiikeri Ky.

European Commission, 2011a. *Recast of the WEEE Directive* [online]. Available at: http://ec.europa.eu/environment/waste/weee/index_en.htm [Accessed 12 December 2011].

European Commission, 2011b. *Timber Regulation* [online]. Available at: http://ec.europa.eu/environment/forests/timber_regulation.htm [Accessed 7 June 2011].

European Commission – *Taxation and Customs Union, 2012. Implementing risk management in the EU* [online]. Available at: http://ec.europa.eu/taxation_customs/customs/customs_controls/risk_management/implementing/index_en.htm#rif [Accessed 13 February 2012].

European Environment Agency, 2009. *Waste Without Border in the EU? Transboundary shipments of waste*. Copenhagen: European Environment Agency.

FAO, 2010. *Global Forest Resources Assessment 2010*. Rome: Food and Agriculture Organization of the United Nations.

Fattah, E., 2010. The Evolution of a Young, Promising Discipline: Sixty Years of Victimology, a Retrospective and Prospective Look. In S.G. Shoham, P. Knepper and M. Kett, eds, *International Handbook of Victimology*. Boca Raton (FL): CRC Press, pp. 43–94.

Faure, M., 1991. De gevolgen van de 'administratieve afhankelijkheid' van het milieustrafrecht: een inventarisatie van knelpunten. In M. Faure, J. Oudijk and D. Schaffmeister, eds, *Zorgen van heden. Opstellen over het milieustrafrecht in theorie en praktijk*. Arnhem: Gouda Quint, pp. 91–150.

Faure, M., 2012. Instruments for environmental governance: What works? In P. Martin, Z. Li, T. Qin, A. Du Plessis and Y. Le Bouthillier, eds, *Environmental Governance and Sustainability*. Cheltenham: Edward Elgar, pp. 3–23.

Faure, M. and Heine, G., 2005. *Criminal Enforcement of Environmental Law in the European Union*. The Hague: Kluwer Law International.

Fischer, C., Hedal, N., Carlsen, R., Doujak, K., Legg, D., Oliva, J., Lüdeking Sparvath, S., Viisimaa, M., Weissenbach, T. and Werge, M., 2008. *Transboundary Shipments of Waste in the EU. Developments 1995–2005 and possible drivers*. Copenhagen: European Environment Agency – European Topic Centre on Resource and Waste Management.

Flejzor, L., 2005. Reforming the International Tropical Timber Agreement. *Review of European Community & International Environmental Law*, 14(1), pp. 19–27.

Friedman, M., 1970. The Social Responsibility of Business Is to Increase Its Profits 1. *The New York Times*.

Fyfe, N. and Reeves, A. 2010. The Thin Green Line? Police Perceptions of the Challenges of Tackling Wildlife Crime in Scotland. In R. Yarwood and R. Mawby,eds, *Policing, Rurality and Governance*. London: Ashgate.

Garland, D., 2001. *The Culture of Control: Crime and social order in contemporary society*. Oxford: Oxford University Press.

Geddes, B., 2003. *Paradigms and Sand Castles: Theory building and research design in comparative politics*. Ann Arbor, MI: University of Michigan Press.

George, A. and Bennet, A., 2005. *Case Studies and Theory Development in the Social Sciences*. Cambridge (MA-USA) – London (UK): MIT Press.

Gerring, J., 2007. *Case Study Research: Principles and practices*. Cambridge University Press.

Gibbs, C., Gore, M., McGarrell, E. and Rivers, L., 2010. Introducing Conservation Criminology: Towards Interdisciplinary Scholarship on Environmental Crimes and Risks. *British Journal of Criminology*, 50(1), pp. 124–44.

Gibbs, C., McGarrell, E.F. and Axelrod, M., 2010. Transnational white-collar crime and risk. Lessons from the global trade in electronic waste. *Criminology & Public Policy*, 9(3), pp. 543–60.

Gibbs, C. and Simpson, S.S., 2009. Measuring corporate environmental crime rates: progress and problems. *Crime, Law and Social Change*, 51(1), pp. 87–107.

Gilbert, M.J. and Russell, S., 2002. Globalization of criminal justice in the corporate context. *Crime, Law and Social Change*, 38(3), pp. 211–38.

Gille, Z., 2006. Detached flows or grounded place-making projects? In G. Spaargaren, A. Mol and F. Buttel, eds, *Governing Environmental Flows. Global challenges to social theory*. London/Cambridge (MA): MIT Press, pp. 137–56.

Goetzl, A., 2005. Why don't trade numbers add up? *ITTO Tropical Forest Update*, 15(1), pp. 8–10.

Gonzales, A., Schofield, R. and Hagy, D., 2007. *Asian Transnational Organized Crime and Its Impact on the United States*. Washington, DC: National Institute of Justice – US Department of Justice Office of Justice Programs.

Goodey, J., 2005. *Victims and Victimology: Research, policy and practice*. Harrow, England: Pearson Longman.

Grabosky, P. and Gant, F., 2000. *Improving Environmental Performance, Preventing Environmental Crime*. Canberra: Australian Institute of Criminology Research and Public Policy Series.

Grant, J.A. and Taylor, I.A.N., 2004. Global governance and conflict diamonds: the Kimberley Process and the quest for clean gems. *The Round Table*, 93(375), pp. 385–401.

Green, P., Ward, T. and McConnachie, K., 2007. Logging and Legality : Environmental Crime, Civil Society, and the State. *Sociology The Journal Of The British Sociological Association*, 34(2), pp 94–110.

Griffiths, H. and Jenks, M., 2012. *Maritime Transport and Destabilizing Commodity Flows*. Solna: Stockholm International Peace Research Institute.

Gunningham, N., 2004. Beyond compliance: next generation environmental regulation. In R. Johnstone and R. Sarre, eds, *Regulation: Enforcement and Compliance*. Canberra: Australian Institute of Criminology, pp. 49–60.

Gunningham, N., Grabosky, P. and Sinclair, D., 1998. *Smart Regulation : Designing environmental policy*. Oxford: Clarendon Press.

Gunningham, N., Kagan, R. and Thornton, D., 2003. *Shades of Green: Business, regulation and environment*. Stanford, CA: Stanford University Press.

Gunningham, N., Norberry, J. and McKillop, S., 1995. *Environmental crime. Proceedings of a conference held 1–3 September in Hobart*. Australian Institute of Criminology. Canberra.

Haines, F., 1997. *Corporate Regulation: Beyond 'punish or persuade'*. Oxford: Clarendon Press.

Haken, J., 2011. *Transnational Crime In The Developing World* [online]. Global Financial Integrity, A Program from the Center for International Policy, Washington. Available at: http://www.gfintegrity.org/storage/gfip/documents/reports/transcrime/gfi_transnational_crime_web.pdf [Accessed 30 August 2012].

Hall, M., 2011. Environmental victims: challenges for criminology and victimology in the 21st century. *Varstvoslovje/Journal of Criminal Justice and Security*, 13(4), pp. 371–91.

Hall, M., 2013. *Victims of Environmental Harm: Rights, recognition and redress under national and international law*. London: Routledge.

Halsey, M., 2004. Against 'green' criminology. *British Journal of Criminology*, 44(4), pp. 833–53.

Hatcher, A., Jaffry, S. and Bennett, E., 2000. Normative and Social Influences Affecting Compliance with Fishery Regulations. *Land Economics*, 76, pp. 61–448.

Heckenberg, D., 2008. Studying environmental crime: key words, acronyms and sources of information. In R. White, ed., *Environmental Crime: A reader*. Cullompton: Willan Publishing.

Heckenberg, D., 2010. The global transference of toxic harms. In R. White, ed., *Global Environmental Harm: Criminological perspectives*. Collumpton: Willan Publishing, pp. 37–61.

Heine, G., 2006. Marine (oil) pollution: Prevention and protection by criminal law – International perspectives, corporate and/or individual criminal liability. In M. Faure and J. Hu, eds, *Prevention and Compensation of Marine Pollution Damage: Recent Developments in Europe, China And the Us (Comparative and Environmental Law and Policy)*. Alphen aan de Rijn: Kluwer Law International, pp. 41–60.

Heiss, R., Ruessink, H., Isarin, N., Koparova, M. and Grabiel, D., 2011. International hazardous waste inspection project at seaports: results and recommendations. *INECE 9th International Conference.*

Helm, D., 2006. Regulatory Reform, Capture, and the Regulatory Burden. *Oxford Review of Economic Policy*, 22(2), pp. 169–85.

Herbig, F. and Joubert, S., 2006. Criminological semantics: conservation criminology: vision or vagary? *Acta Criminologica*, 19(3), pp. 88–103.

Hewitt, J., 2005. *Failing the Forests. Europe's illegal timber trade.* Godalming: WWF.

Hillyard, P., Pantazis, C., Tombs, S. en Gordon, D. 2004. Beyond criminology: Taking harm seriously. Manitoba: Fernwood Publishing, p. 332.

Hirschberger, P., 2008. *Illegal Wood for the European Market. An analysis of the EU import and export of illegal wood and related products.* Frankfurt am Main: World Wide Fund for Nature.

Hogg, R., 2002. Criminology beyond the nation-state: global conflict, human rights and the 'new world disorder'. In K. Carington and R. Hogg, eds, *Critical Criminology: Issues, debates and challenges.* Culompton: Willan Publisher, pp. 185–217.

Holderbeke, J., 2009. *Ons vuil in Afrika* [TV Programme: Our dirt in Africa]. Vranckx – Canvas.

Holley, C. and Gunningham, N., 2011. Natural resources, new governance and legal regulation: When does collaboration work? *New Zealand Universities Law Review*, 24, pp. 309–36.

Holley, C., Gunningham, N. and Shearing, C., 2012. *The New Environmental Governance.* Abingdon: Routledge.

Houghton, R.A., 2003. *Emissions (and Sinks) of Carbon from Land-Use Change (Estimates of National Sources and Sinks of Carbon Resulting from Changes in Land Use, 1950 to 2000).* Falmouth, MA: World Resource Institute – Woods Hole Resource Center.

Huisman, W., 2001. *Tussen winst en moraal: Achtergronden van regelnaleving en regelovertreding door ondernemingen.* Den Haag: Boom Juridische Uitgevers.

Huisman, W. and Vande Walle, G. 2010. 'The Criminology of Corruption'. In G. de Graaf, P. von Maravic and P. Wagenaar, eds, *The Good Cause. Theoretical Perspectives on Corruption.* Leverkusen: Burdich Publishing, pp. 115–45.

Huisman, W. and van Erp, J., 2013. Opportunities for Environmental Crime: A Test of Situational Crime Prevention Theory. *British Journal of Criminology*, 53(6), pp. 1178–200.

Huisman, W., van Erp, J. and van Wingerde, K., 2009. Hoe stevig is de pyramide van Braithwaite. *Tijdschrift voor Criminologie*, 49(4), pp. 386–99.

Humphreys, D., 2013. *Forest Politics. The evolution of international cooperation.* Abingdon: Routledge.

IMPEL-TFS, 2006. *IMPEL-TFS Seaport Project II: International Cooperation in Enforcement Hitting Illegal Waste Shipments. Project report septemer*

2004–May 2006. European Union Network for the Implementation and Enforcement of Environmental Law (IMPEL).

IMPEL-TFS, 2012. *IMPEL – TFS Enforcement Actions III Project Report Enforcement of the European Waste Shipment Regulation Document Control Sheet Project: Client: Document title: IMPEL Enforcement Actions III IMPEL / SEPA Project No: Originated Document status*. Brussels.

INECE, 2010. *International Hazardous Waste Inspection Project at Seaports: Results and recommendations*. INECE Seaport Environmental Security Network.

Interpol, 2009. *Electronic Waste and Organized Crime. Assessing the links. Phase II report for the Interpol Pollution Crime Working Group*. Interpol.

Interpol, 2014. *The Environmental Crime Crisis. Threats to sustainable development from illegal exploitation and trade in wildlife and forest resources*. Interpol.

Jänicke, M., 2006. The environmental state and environmental flows: the need to reinvent the nation-state. In G. Spaargaren, A. Mol and F. Buttel, eds, *Governing Environmental Flows. Global challenges to social theory*. London/ Cambridge (MA): MIT Press, pp. 83–105.

Johnston, L. and Shearing, C., 2003. *Governing Security : Explorations in policing and justice*. London/New York: Routledge.

Karanth, K. and Nepal, S., 2012. Local Residents Perception of Benefits and Losses From Protected Areas in India and Nepal. *Environmental Management*, 49(2), pp. 372–86.

Keohane, R. and Nye, J., 2000. Introduction. In J. Nye and J. Donahue, eds, *Governance in a Globalizing World*. Washington, DC: Brookings Institution, pp. 1–27.

King, G., Keohane, R. and Verba, S., 1994. *Designing Social Inquiry: Scientific inference in qualitative research*. Princeton, NJ: Princeton University Press.

Kleemans, E. and van de Bunt, H. 2008. Organised Crime, Occupations and Opportunity. *Global Crime* 9(3), pp. 185–97.

Klima, N., 2011. The Goods Transport Network's Vulnerability to Crime: Opportunities and Control Weaknesses. *European Journal on Criminal Policy and Research*, 17(3), pp. 203–19.

Kraan, I., Nijssen, C., Dols, N. and Huijbregts, C., 2006. *Is What you See What You Get?*, IMPEL-TFS, 2006b. *IMPEL-TFS verification – 2 Project Report*. December 2004–May 2006. IMPEL – European Union Network for the Implementation of Environmental Law, Brussels.

Kramer, R., Michalowski, R. and Kauzlarich, D., 2002. The Origins and Development of the Concept and Theory of State-Corporate Crime. *Crime and Delinquency*, 48(2), pp. 263–82.

Kummer Peiry, K. 2010. Basel Convention on the Control and Transboundary Movements of Hazardous Wastes and Their Disposal. *United Nations Audiovisual Library of International Law*, 10.

Kuper, Jo, and Martin Hojsik. *Poisoning the Poor. Electronic waste in Ghana*. Amsterdam: Greenpeace International.

Landro, J. and Lo, A., 2007. *Study on the International Transportation of Tropical Timber Products*. Port Moresby, Papua New Guinea: International Tropical Timber Organization.

Lawson, S. and MacFaul, L., 2010. *Illegal Logging and Related Trade : Indicators of the global response*. London: Chatham House.

Lazarus, R., 1995. Meeting the demands of integration of the evolution of environmental law: reforming environmental criminal law. *Georgetown Law Journal*, 83, pp. 2407–529.

Le Billon, P., 2001. The political ecology of war: natural resources and armed conflicts. *Political Geography*, 20, pp. 561–84.

Lefevere, F., 1999. In beslag genomen tropenhout 'het topje van de ijsberg' [Confiscated tropical timber is tip of the iceberg]. *De Morgen,* 9 June.

Levinson, M., 2006. *The Box: How the Shipping Container Made the World Smaller and the World Economy Bigger*. Princeton, NJ: Princeton University Press.

Leys, M., 2009. De gevalstudie. In T. Decorte and D. Zaitch, eds, *Kwalitatieve methoden en technieken in de criminologie*. Leuven: Acco, pp. 174–94.

LNE, 2010. *Afvalstromen in Vlaanderen: risicoprofiel*. Brussel: Leefmilieu, natuur en energie (LNE).

LNE, 2011. *Milieu-inspectieplan 2011*. Brussel: Departement Leefmilieu, Natuur en Energie. Afdeling Milieu-inspectie.

LNE and Haskoning, 2010. *Onderzoek van de mogelijkheden van ketentoezicht op. afvalstromen*. Mechelen: Haskoning Belgium NV – LNE Afdeling milieu-inspectie.

Loader, I., 2002. Policing, securitization and democratization in Europe. *Criminology and Criminal Justice*, 2(2), pp. 125–53.

Loader, I. and Sparks, R., 2002. Contemporary Landscapes of Crime, Order and Control: Governance, Risk and Globalization. In M. Maguire, M. Morgan and R. Reiner, eds, *The Oxford Handbook of Criminology*. Oxford: Oxford University Press.

Long, M., Stretesky, P., Lynch, M. and Fenwisk, E. 2012. Crime in the Coal Industry: Implications for Green Criminology and Treadmill of Production. *Organization & Environment*, 25(3), pp. 328–46.

Loosveldt, G., Swyngedouw, M. and Cambre, B., 2007. *Measuring Meaningful Data in Social Research*. Leuven/Voorburg: Acco.

Lynch, M., 1990. The Greening of Criminology: A Perspective for the 1990s. *The Critical Criminologist*, 2–3(3–4), pp. 11–12.

Lynch, M., 2013. Reflection on Green Criminology and its Boundaries: Comparing Environmental and Criminal Victimization and Considering Crime from an Eco-city Perspective. In N. South and A. Brisman, eds, *The Routledge International Handbook of Green Criminology*. London: Routledge, pp. 43–57.

Lynch, M., Long, M., Barrett, K. and Stretesky, P., 2013. Is it a Crime to Produce Ecological Disorganization? Why Green Criminology and Political Economy Matter in the Analysis of Global Ecological Harms. *British Journal of Criminology*, 53(6), pp. 997–1016.

Lynch, M. and Stretesky, P., 2003. The meaning of green: contrasting criminological perspectives. *Theoretical Criminology*, 7(2), pp. 217–38.

Lynch, M. and Stretesky, P., 2007. Green criminology in the United States. In P. Beirne and N. South, eds, *Issues in Green Criminology. Confronting harms against environments, humanity and other animals*. Portland: Willan Publishing, pp. 248–69.

Lynch, M. and Stretesky, P., 2011. Similarities between green criminology and green science: Toward a typology of green criminology. *International Journal of Comparative and Applied Criminal Justice*, 35(4), pp. 293–306.

Maesschalck, J., 2009. Methodologische kwaliteit in het kwalitatief criminologisch onderzoek. In T. Decorte and D. Zaitch, eds, *Kwalitatieve methoden en technieken in de criminologie*. Leuven: Acco, pp. 120–145.

Magrath, W., Younger, P. and Phan, H., 2009. *Chainsaw Project: An Interpol perspective on law enforcement in illegal logging*. Lyon: Interpol and Washington, DC: World Bank.

Marx, A. and Cuypers, D., 2010. Forest certification as a global environmental governance tool: What is the macro-effectiveness of the Forest Stewardship Council? *Regulation & Governance*, 4(4), pp. 408–34.

Mazerolle, L. and Ransley, J., 2006. *Third Party Policing*, Cambridge: Cambridge University Press.

McBarnet, D., 2006. After Enron will "Whiter than White Collar Crime" Still Wash? *British Journal of Criminology*, 46 (6), pp. 1091–109.

McLaughlin, E. and Muncie, J., 2006. *The Sage Dictionary of Criminology*. Thousand Oaks, CA and London: Sage, p. 485.

Meidinger, E., 2002. Forest certification as environmental law making by global civil society. In E. Meidinger, C. Elliot and G. Oesten, eds, *Social and Political Dimensions of Forest Certification*. Remagen-Oberwinter: Forstbuch, pp. 293–329.

Michalowski, R. 2009. Power, Crime and Criminology in the New Imperial Age. *Crime, Law and Social Change*, 51(3–4), pp. 303–25.

Miller, F., Taylor, R. and White, G., 2006. *Keep it Legal: Best Practices for keeping Illegally Harvested Timber out of your Supply Chain*. Gland: WWF International and Global Forest & Trade Network.

Miller, R., Gregory, J., Duan, H., Kirchain, R. and Linnel, J., 2012. *Characterizing Transboundary Flows of Used Electronics: Summary Report*. Boston, MA: Massachusetts Institute of Technology, Parkersburg, VW: Materials Systems Laboratory, Bonn: National Center for Electronic Recycling, Solving the E-waste Problem (StEP) and Washington, DC: US EPA.

Mohai, P. and Saha, R., 2007. Racial inequalities in the distribution of hazardous waste: a national-level assessment. *Social Problems*, 54, pp. 343–70.

Mol, A. and Spaargaren, G., 2006. Toward a sociology of environmental flows: a new agenda for twenty-first century environmental sociology. In G. Spaargaren, A. Mol and F. Buttel, eds, *Governing Environmental Flows. Global challenges to social theory*. London/Cambridge (MA): MIT Press, pp. 39–82.

Morselli, C., Turcotte, M. and Tenti, V., 2011. The mobility of criminal groups. *Global Crime*, 12(3), pp. 165–88.

Mortelmans, D., Decorte, T. and Zaitch, D., 2009. Observaties. In T. Decorte and D. Zaitch, eds, *Kwalitatieve methoden en technieken in de criminologie*. Leuven: Acco, pp. 261–86.

Naylor, R., 2004. The underworld of ivory. *Crime, Law & Social Change*, 42, pp. 261–95.

Nelken, D., 2002. White Collar Crime. In M. Maguire, M. Morgan and R. Reiner, eds, *The Oxford Handbook of Criminology*. Oxford: Oxford University Press.

Nordbrand, S., 2009. *Out of Control. E-waste trade flows from the EU to developing countries*. Stockholm: SwedWatch.

Odeyingbo, O.A., Deubzer, O. and Schluep, M., 2011. *Assessment of the Flow and Driving Forces of Used Electrical and Electronic Equipment Into and Within Nigeria*. Cottbus: Brandenburgische Technische Universität – United Nations University.

Oliver, R., 2012. *2011 Statistics – Belgium Timber Trade Monitoring in Support of Effective, Efficient and Equitable Operation of the EU Timber Regulation (EUTR)* [online]. Department of International Development, European Timber Trade Federation & Forest Industries Intelligence Limited, Settle. Available at: http://www.ettf.info/sites/default/files/ettf_2011-statistics_france.pdf [Accessed 2 November 2013].

Oosterveer, P., 2006. Environmental governance of global food flows: the case of labelling practices. In G. Spaargaren, A. Mol and F. Buttel, eds, *Governing Environmental Flows*. London/Cambridge (MA): MIT Press, pp. 267–301.

Otterson, K. and Meiser, U., 2009. *UNODC – WCO. Container Control Programme*. Vienna: UNODC – WCO.

Ottisch, A., Moiseyev, A, Burdin, N. and Kazusa, L. 2005. *Impacts of Reduction of Illegal Logging in European Russia on the EU and European Russia Forest Sector and Trade*. Joensuu: European Forest Institute.

Parker, C. and Braithwaite, J., 2003. Regulation. In P. Cane and M. Tushnet, eds, *The Oxford Handbook of Legal Studies*. Oxford: Oxford University Press, pp. 119–45.

Passas, N., 1999. Globalization, criminogenic asymmetries and economic crime. *European Journal of Law Reform*, 1(4), pp. 399–423.

Passas, N., 2000. Global Anomie, Dysnomie, and Economic Crime: Hidden Consequences of Neoliberalism and Globalization in Russia and Around the World. *Social Justice*, 27(2), pp. 16–44.

Passas, N., 2002. Cross-border crime and the interface between legal and illegal actors. In P. van Duyne, K. von Lampe and N. Passas, eds, *Upperworld and Underworld in Cross-Border Crime*. Nijmegen: Wolf Legal Publishers, pp. 11–41.

Passas, N., 2003. Cross-border crime and the interface between legal and illegal actors. *Security Journal*, 16(1), pp. 19–38.

Passas, N. and Goodwin, N., 2004. It's legal but it ain't right: harmful social consequences of legal industries. Ann Arbour, MI: University of Michigan Press.

Pearce, F. and Tombs, S. 1998. *Toxic Capitalism: Corporate Crime and the Chemical Industry*. Aldershot: Dartmouth Publishing Company.

Pellow, D., 2007. *Resisting Global Toxics: Transnational movements for environmental justice*. Cambridge, MA: MIT Press.

Peloza, J. and Falkenberg, L., 2009. The role of collaboration in achieving corporate social responsibility objectives. *California Management Review*, 51(3), pp. 95–113.

Pensaert, J., 2011. Waste controls in Belgian ports … a matter of cooperation. Presented at the International workshop on counteracting illegal waste shipments. Rotterdam.

Peskett, L., Brown, D. and Luttrell, C., 2006. *Can Payments for Avoided Deforestation to Tackle Climate Change also Benefit the Poor?* London: Overseas Development Institute.

van der Pijl, Y., Oude Breuil, B.C. and Siegel, D., 2011. Is there such a thing as 'global sex trafficking'? A patchwork tale on useful (mis)understandings. *Crime, Law and Social Change*, 56(5), pp. 567–82.

Pink, G., 2013. *Law Enforcement Responses to Transnational Environmental Crime: Choices, challenges and culture*. Canberra: Transnational Environmental Crime Project – Working Paper 4/2013.

Ponsaers, P., Easton, M., Cools, M. and Gilleir, F., 2008. *Nodale politie in de Antwerpse haven [Nodal Policing in the Port of Antwerp]* [Unpublished research report]. Subcontracting for Nyenrode University and commissioned by Programma Politie en Wetenschap [Program for Police and Science, the Netherlands].

Ponsaers, P. and Hoogenboom, B., 2004. Het moeilijke spel van wortel en stok – Organisatiecriminaliteit en handhaving-strategieën van bijzondere inspectie- en opsporingsdiensten. *Tijdschrift voor Criminologie*, 46(2), pp. 165–81.

Ponsaers, P. and De Keulenaer, S., 2003. Met strafrecht tegen milieudelicten? Rol en functie van bijzondere inspectiediensten in de strijd tegen milieucriminaliteit. *Panopticon*, 24(3), pp. 250–265.

Prakash, A. and Potoski, M., 2006. *The Voluntary Environmentalists: Green Clubs, ISO 14001, and voluntary environmental regulations*. Cambridge: Cambridge University Press.

Prakash, S. and Manhart, A., 2010. *Socio-Economic Assessment and Feasibility Study on Sustainable E-waste Management in Ghana*. Freiburg: Öko-Instutut e.V.; Inspectorate of the Ministry of Housing, Spatial Planning and the Environment of the Netherlands (VROM-Inspectorate) and the Dutch Association for the Disposal of Metal and Electrical Products (NVMP).

Puckett, J. and Smith, T., 2002. *Exporting Harm: The high-tech trashing of Asia*. Seattle–San Jose: The Basel Action Network (BAN) – Silicon Valley Toxics Coalition (SVTC).

Puckett, J., Westervelt, S., Gutierrez, R. and Takamiya, Y., 2005. *The Digital Dump. Exporting re-use and abuse to Africa.* Seattle, WA: The Basel Action Network (BAN).

Punch, M., 1996. *Dirty Business. Exploring corporate misconduct, analysis and cases.* London: Sage.

Quadri, S., 2010. An analysis of the effects and reasons for hazardous waste importation in India and its implementation of the Basel Convention. *Florida Journal of International Law*, 22(3), p. 467.

Reingoud, J., 2010. *Verslag Internationale Conferentie 'Genetic and isotopic fingerprinting methods – practical tools to verify the declared origin of wood'* [Personal Communication].

REM, 2009. *Progress in Tackling Illegal Logging in Cameroon – IM-FLEG Cameroon.* Cambridge: Resource Extraction Monitoring.

De Rijck, R., 2011. A flaw in the criminal approach of international waste transport in Europe. INECE 9th International Conference.

RILO, 2007. *Evaluation Report on Project Sky-Hole-Patching.* WCO Regional Intelligence Liaison Office for Asia and the Pacific.

Rock, P., 2002. Sociological theories of crime. In M. Maguire, M. Morgan and R. Reiner, eds, *The Oxford Handbook of Criminology*. Oxford: Oxford University Press.

Roerhorst, I. 2006. *Legal Forest Destruction. The wide gap between legality and sustainability* [online]. Friends of the Earth, Greenpeace, Interchurch Organization for Development Cooperation, IUCN Netherlands World Conservation Union, Netherlands Center for Indigenous People, World Wide Fund for Nature. Available at: http://www.dogwoodalliance.org/wp-content/uploads/2012/08/Legal_Forest_Destruction_-_February_2006.pdf [Accessed 15 June 2010].

Ross, M., 2003. The Natural Resource Curse: How wealth can make you poor. In I. Bannon and P. Collier, eds, *Natural Resources and Violent Conflict.* Washington, DC: International Bank for Reconstruction and Development/The World Bank, pp. 17–42.

Rothe, D. and Friedrichs, D., 2015. *Crimes of Globalization. New Directions in Critical Criminology*. London and New York: Routledge.

Rufener, S., 2012. *Overview of Existing and Planned Activities in the Field of Formal E-waste Recycling in Accra, Ghana.* Zurich: NADEL – Centre for Development and Cooperation.

Ruggiero, V., 1996. *Organized and Corporate Crime in Europe: Offers that can't be refused.* Aldershot, Brookfield, Singapore, Sydney: Dartmouth Publishing Company.

Ruggiero, V., 2000. Crime and Markets: Essays in Anti-Criminology. Oxford: Oxford University Press.

Ruggiero, V., 2009. Transnational Crime and Global Illicit Economies. In E. Wilson and T. Lindsey, eds, *Government of the Shadows. Parapolitics and criminal sovereignty*. New York: Pluto Books, pp. 117–29.

Ruggiero, V. and South, N., 2013. Green Criminology and Crimes of the Economy: Theory, Research and Praxis. *Critical Criminology*, 21, pp. 359–73.
Sanax, A., 1996. Corporations, organized crime and the disposal of hazardous waste: an examination of the making of a criminological regulatory structure. *Criminology*, 24(1), pp. 1–27.
Sander, K. and Schilling, S., 2010. *Transboundary Shipment of Waste Electrical and Electronic Equipment/Electronic Scrap – Optimization of material flows and control*. Hamburg: The Federal Environment Agency (Germany) – Ökopol GmbH.
Sassen, S., 1996. *Losing Control? Sovereignty in an age of globalization*. New York: Colombia University Press.
Saunders, J. and Reeve, R., 2014. *The EU Timber Regulation and CITES. Programme Paper*, London: Chatham House & Center for International Forestry Research.
Schluep, M., Rochat, D., Wanjira Munyua, A., Eddine Laissaoui, S., Wone, S., Kane, C., Hieronymi, K. 2008. Assessing the e-waste situation in Africa. *Electronics Goes Green 2008+* Presented at the Electronics Goes Green 2008+ Conference, 8–10 September 2008, Berlin/Germany.
Schluep, M., Manhart, A., Osibanjo, O., Rochat, D., Isarin, N. and Mueller, E., 2011. *Where are WEEE in Africa. Findings from the Basel Convention E-waste Africa Programme*. Berlin: Secretariat of the Basel Convention, UNEP, EU, EMPA, Öko-Institut, IMPEL.
Schmidt, C., 2004. Environmental Crimes: Profiting at the Earth's Expens. *Environmental Health Perspectives*, 112(2), pp. 96–103.
Scott, C. 2004. Regulation in the Age of Governance: The Rise of the Post-Regulatory State. In J. Jordana and D. Levi-Faur, eds, *The Politics of Regulation*. Cheltenham: Edward Elgar, pp. 145–74.
Seale, C., 1999. *The Quality of Qualitative Research*. London: Sage.
Seneca Creek and International Wood Resources, 2004. *'Illegal' Logging and Global Wood Markets: The competitive impacts on the US wood products industry*. Poolesville, MD: American Forest & Paper Association.
Sepúlveda, A., Schluep, M., Renaud, F., Streicher, M., Kuehr, R., Hagelüken, C. and Gerecke, A., 2010. A review of the environmental fate and effects of hazardous substances released from electrical and electronic equipments during recycling: Examples from China and India, *Environmental Impact Assessment Review*, 30(1), pp. 28–41.
Setiono, B. 2007. Fighting Illegal Logging and Forest-Related Financial Crime: The Anti-Money Laundering Approach. In L. Elliot, ed., *Transnational Environmental Crime in the Asia-Pacific: A workshop report*. Canberra: Australia National University.
Sharp, Z. and Zaidman, N., 2010. Strategization of CSR. *Journal of Business Ethics*, 93(1), pp. 51–72.
Shearing, C. and Johnston, L., 2010. Nodal wars and network fallacies: A genealogical analysis of global insecurities. *Theoretical Criminology*, 14(4), pp. 495–514.

Shearing, C. and Wood, F., 2003. Nodal governance, democracy and the new denizens: Challenging the Westphalian ideal. *Journal of Law and Society*, 30(6), pp. 400–419.

Sheptycki, J., 2005. Relativism, transnationalisation and comparative criminology. In J. Sheptycki and A. Wardak, eds, *Transnational and Comparative Criminology*. London: Glasshouse Press, pp. 69–88.

Sheptycki, J., 2007. Criminology and the Transnational Condition: A Contribution to International Political Sociology. *International Political Sociology*, 1(391–406).

Sheptycki, J. and Wardak, A., 2005. *Transnational and Comparative Criminology*. London: Glasshouse Press, p. 375.

Shover, N. & Aaron, S.R., 2005. Environmental Crime. *Crime and Justice*, 32(ArticleType: research-article / Full publication date: 2005 / Copyright © 2005 The University of Chicago Press), pp. 321–71.

Slapper, G. and Tombs, S., 1999. *Corporate Crime*. Essex: Pearson Education Limited.

Smith, J., Obidzinski, K., Subarudi, S.and Suramenggala, I 2007. Illegal logging, collusive corruption and fragmented governments in Kalimantan, Indonesia. *International Forestry Review* 5(3), pp. 293–302.Snider, L., 2008. Corporate Economic Crimes. In J. Minkes and L. Minkes, eds, *Corporate and White-Collar Crime*. London: Sage, pp. 39–60.

South, N., 1998. A green field for criminology: a proposal for a perspective. *Theoretical Criminology*, 2(2), pp. 211–33.

South, N., 2007. The corporate colonisation of nature: bio-prospecting, bio-piracy and the development of green criminology. In P. Beirne and N. South, eds, *Issues in Green Criminology. Confronting harms against environments, humanity and other animals*. Portland: Willan Publishing, pp. 230–247.

Spaargaren, G., Mol, A. and Bruyninckx, H., 2006. Introduction: Governing Environmental Flows in Global Modernity. In G. Spaargarten, A. Mol and F. Buttel, eds, *Governing Environmental Flows. Global challenges to social theory*. London/Cambridge (MA): MIT Press, pp. 1–36.

Spaargaren, G., Mol, A. and Buttel, F., 2006. *Governing Environmental Flows. Global challenges to social theory*. London/Cambridge (MA): MIT Press.

Stretesky, P.B., 2006. Corporate Self-Policing and the Environment. *Criminology*, 44(3), pp. 671–708.

Stretesky, P. and Lynch, M., 1998. Corporate environmental violence and racism. *Crime, Law and Social Change*, 30(2), pp. 163–84.

Stretesky, P. and Lynch, M., 2009. Does self-policing reduce chemical emissions? *The Social Science Journal*, 46(3), pp. 459–73.

Stretesky, P. and Lynch, M., 2011. Coal Strip Mining, Mountaintop Removal, and the Distribution of Environmental Violations across the United States, 2002–2008. *Landscape Research*, 36(2), pp. 209–30.

Struiksma, N., de Ridder, J. and Winter, H., 2007. *De effectiviteit van bestuurlijke en strafrechtelijke milieuhandhaving*. Boom Jurid: Den Haag.

Swanborn, P., 2008. *Case Studies: Wat wanneer en hoe?* Amsterdam: Boom.

Szasz, A., 1986. Corporations, Organized Crime, and the Disposal of Hazardous Waste: an Examination of the Making of a Criminogenic Regulatory Structure. *Criminology*, 24(1), pp. 1–27.

Tacconi, L., 2007a. Illegal Logging: Law Enforcement, Livelihoods and the Timber Trade, *Earthscan & Center for International Forestry Research*, London – Sterling (VA).

Tacconi, L., 2007b. The Problem of Illegal Logging. In L. Tacconi, ed., *Illegal Logging: Law enforcement, livelihoods and the timber trade*. London – Sterling, VA: Earthscan & *Center for International Forestry Research*, pp. 1–16.

Talley, W., 2009. *Port Economics*. Florence: Routledge.

Tarasofsky, R., 1999. *Assessing the International Forest Regime*. IUCN Envir., Gland, Switserland.

Tijhuis, A., 2006. *Transnational Crime and the Interface between Legal and Illegal Actors. The case of the illicit art and antiquities trade*. Leiden: NCSR.

Tombs, S., 2008. Corporations and health and safety. In J. Minkes and L. Minkes, eds, *Corporate and White-Collar Crime*. London: Sage, pp. 18–38.

Toyne, P., O'Brien, C. and Nelson, R. 2002. *The Timber Footprint of the G8 and China*. Gland: WWF International.

TRACER, 2011. The Rough Guide to Traceable Certified Forest Products. Viborg: Special-Trykkeriet.

Trochim, W., 2006. Nonprobability sampling [online]. Available at: http://www.socialresearchmethods.net/kb/sampnon.php [Accessed 10 September 2010].

UNEP, 2011a. *Forests in a Green Economy: A Synthesis*. Nairobi: United Nations Environment Programme.

UNEP, 2011b. Forests: Investing in Natural Capital. In UNEP, ed., *Towards a Green Economy: Pathways to sustainable development and poverty eradication*. United Nations Environment Programme, pp. 152–92.

UNODC, 2009. *Transnational Trafficking and the Rule of Law in West-Africa: A threat assessment*. Vienna: United Nations Office on Drugs and Crime.

UNODC, 2011. Countering the world of smuggling through container control [online]. Available at: http://www.unodc.org/unodc/en/frontpage/2011/May/countering-the-world-of-smuggling-through-container-control.html [Accessed 7 February 2012].

Urrunaga, J.M., Johnson, A., Dhaynee Orbegozo, I. and Mulligan, F. 2012. *The Laundering Machine. How fraud and corruption in Peru's concession system are destroying the future of its forests*. Washington, DC and London: Environmental Investigation Agency

Urry, J., 2003. *Global Complexity*. Cambridge: Polity Press, p. 172.

Vanacker, B., 2010. Verdacht hout in Antwerpen [Suspicious timber in Antwerp] [online]. *MO* Mondiaal Nieuws*. Available at: http://www.mo.be/artikel/verdacht-hout-antwerpen [Accessed 2 February 2011].

van Daele, S., Vander Beken, T. and Dorn, N., 2007. Waste management and crime: regulatory, business and product vulnerabilities. *Environmental Policy and Law*, 37(1), pp. 34–8.

van de Bunt, H. and Huisman, W., 1999. Het kan ook anders: overwegingen bij de keuze tussen klassiek of alternatief reguleren op milieuterrein. *Justitiële Verkenningen*, 28(2), pp. 29–43.

Vander Beken, T., 2007. *The European Waste Industry and Crime Vulnerabilities*. Antwerp: Maklu.

Vander Beken, T. and van Daele, S., 2008. Legitimate business and crime vulnerabilities. *International Journal of Social Economics*, 35(10), pp. 739–50.

Vande Walle, G. and Bisschop, L., 2012. Conflict resolution and environmental harm: case-study of e-waste dumping. 12th Annual Conference of European Society of Criminology.

Vande Walle, G. and Ponsaers, P., 2006. Formal and informal pharmaceutical economies in Third World countries: Synergetic, symbiotic or parasitical? *Crime Law and Social Change*, 45(4–5), pp. 361–72.

van Dijk, J., Sagel-Grande, H. and Toornvliet, L., 1996. *Actuele criminologie*. Lelystad: Koninkljke Vermande.

van Erp, J., 2008. Lessen voor toezicht in de 21e eeuw. Actuele inzichten van Braithwaite en Sparrow. *Justitiële Verkenningen*, 34(6), pp. 9–21.

van Erp, J. and Huisman, W., 2010. Smart regulation and enforcement of illegal disposal of electronic waste. *Criminology & Public Policy*, 9(3), pp. 579–90.

van Koppen, K., 2006. Governing Nature? On the Global Complexity of Biodiversity Conservation. In G. Spaargaren, A. Mol and F. Buttel, eds, *Governing Environmental Flows. Global challenges to social theory*. London/ Cambridge (MA): MIT Press, pp. 187–219.

van Sluis, A., Marks, P, Gilleir, F. and Easton, M., 2012. Nodal Security in the Ports of Rotterdam and Antwerp. In V. Bekkers and H. Fenger, eds, *Beyond Fragmentation and Interconnectivity: Public governance and the search for connective capacity*. Amsterdam: IOC Press, pp. 73–94.

Veenstra, A., Wang, C., Fan, W. and Ru, Y., 2010. An analysis of E-waste flows in China. *International Journal of Advanced Manufacturing Technology*, 47, pp. 449–59.

Verschuren, P. and Doorewaard, H., 2010. *Designing a Research Project*. 2nd ed. The Hague: Eleven International Publishing.

Verstraeten, R., 2007. *Handboek Strafvordering*. Antwerpen-Apeldoorn: Maklu.

Vig, N.J. and Faure, M.G., 2004. Green giants? Environmental policies of the United States and the European Union. Boston, MA: Massachussetts Institute of Technology.

VROM-inspectie, 2011. *Evaluatie en vooruitblik ketenproject elektrische en elektronische apparaten 2010*. Den Haag: Volkshuisvesting, Ruimtelijke Ordening en Milieubeheer (VROM) Inspectie – Directie Uitvoering.

Walters, R., 2010. *Eco-Crime and Genetically Modified Food*. London: Routledge-Cavendish.

WEEE-forum, 2008. *WEEE Forum Guidance Document on Compliance with Directive 2002/96/EC on Waste Electrical and Electronic Equipment (WEEE)* [online]. European Association of Electrical and Electronic Waste Take-

Back Systems. Available at: http://www.weee-forum.org/ [Accessed 10 February 2010].

Wells, A., del Gatto, F., Richars, M., Pommier, D. and Contreras-Hermosilla, A., 2007. Rural livelihoods, forest law and the illegal timber trade in Honduras and Nicaragua. In L. Tacconi, ed., *Illegal logging: Law enforcement, livelihoods and the timber trade*. London–Sterling, VA: Earthscan & Center for International Forestry Research, pp. 138–66.

Westra, L., 2004. *Ecoviolence and the Law – Supranational Normative Foundations of Ecocrime*. Ardsley, NY: Transnational Publishers Inc.

White, R., 2003. Environmental issues and the criminological imagination. *Theoretical Criminology*, 7(4), pp. 483–506.

White, R., 2008. *Crimes Against Nature: Environmental criminology and ecological justice*. Cullompton: Willan Publishing.

White, R., 2010. Prosecution and sentencing in relation to environmental crime: recent socio-legal developments. *Crime Law and Social Change*, 53(4), pp. 365–81.

White, R., 2011. *Transnational Environmental Crime. Towards an eco-global criminology*. New York: Routledge.

White, R., 2013. *Environmental Harm: An eco-justice perspective*. Bristol: Policy Press.

Wielenga, K., 2010. *Waste Without Frontiers. Global trends in generation and transboundary movements of hazardous wastes and other wastes. Analysis of the data from national reporting to the secretariat of the Basel convention for the years 2004–2006*. Châteleine: Secretariat of the Basel Convention.

Wijnstekers, W., 2004. Protection of endangered species of fauna and flora. In F. Comte and L. Krämer, eds, *Environmental Crime in Europe. Rules of sanctions*. Groningen: Europe Law Publishing, pp. 17–23.

Williams, E., Yu, J., Yu, M. and Yang, Y., 2010. Forecasting Global Generation of Obsolete Personal Computers. *Environmental Science & Technology*, 44(9), pp. 3232–7.

Williams, E., Kahhat, K., Bengtsson, M., Hayashi, S., Hotta, Y. and Totoki, Y. 2013. Linking Informal and Formal Electronics Recycling via an Interface Organization. *Challenges*, 4(2), pp. 136–53.

Wood, J., 2006. Research and innovation in the field of security. In J. Wood and B. Dupont, eds, *Democracy, Society and the Governance of Security*. Cambridge/New York: Cambridge University Press, pp. 217–40.

Wood, J. and Dupont, B., 2006. *Democracy, Society and the Governance of Security*. Cambridge/New York: Cambridge University Press.

Wood, J. and Shearing, C., 2007. *Imagining Security*. Cullompton: Willan Publishing.

World Customs Organization, 2009. *Operation Demeter Yields Tons of Illegal Shipments of Hazardous Waste* [online]. World Customs Organization. Available at: http://www.wcoomd.org/en/media/newsroom/2009/july/operation-demeter-yields-tons-of-illegal-shipments-of-hazardous-waste.aspx [Accessed 25 March 2011].

Wright, J. and Head, B., 2009. Reconsidering Regulation and Governance Theory: A Learning Approach. *Law & Policy*, 31(2), pp. 192–216.

WWF, Greenpeace and Friends of the Earth, 2009. *Tackling the EU's Role in Illegal Logging. NGO recommendations for the proposed regulation concering the placing of timber and timber products on the EU market* [online]. Available at: http://awsassets.panda.org/downloads/tackling_the_eus_role_in_illegal_logging.pdf [Accessed November 10 2014].

Xiufang, S. and Canby, K., 2011. *Baseline Study 1 China: Overview of forest governance, markets and trade*. Kuala Lumpur: European Forest Institute – FLEGT Asia Regional Offic.

Yin, R., 2003. *Applications of Case-Study Research.* 2nd ed. Thousand Oaks, CA: Sage Publications.

Yin, R., 2009. *Case Study Research: Design and Methods*. 4th ed. Thousand Oaks, CA: Sage.

Young, O., 2009. Governance for sustainable development in a world or rising interdependencies. In M. Delmas and O. Young, eds, *Governance for the Environment: New perspectives*. Cambridge: Cambridge University Press.

Zartman, I.W., 2005. Comparative Case Studies. *International Negotiation*, 10(1), pp. 3–16.

Zinn, M., 2002. Policing Environmental Regulatory Enforcement: Cooperation, Capture, and Citizen Suits. *Stanford Environmental Law Journal*, 21, pp. 81–174.

Index

Bold page numbers indicate figures.

For Product Safety Concerns and Information please contact our EU representative GPSR@taylorandfrancis.com Taylor & Francis Verlag GmbH, Kaufingerstraße 24, 80331 München, Germany

Batch number: 08165901

Printed by Printforce, the Netherlands